Tracing Your
Irish
Family History

Tracing Your
Irish
Family History

Anthony Adolph

A Firefly Book

Published by Firefly Books Ltd. 2009

First printing

Publisher Cataloging-in-Publication Data (U.S.)

Adolph, Anthony.
   Tracing your Irish family history / Anthony Adolph.
[224] p. : photos. (some col.) ; cm.
Includes bibliographical references and index.
Summary: A book that demonstrates how the reader may trace his or her Irish family history using family trees, the internet, contact information and other resources.
ISBN-13: 978-1-55407-458-7 (pbk.)
ISBN-10: 1-55407-458-4 (pbk.)
1. Ireland -- Genealogy -- Handbooks, manuals, etc. 2. Irish Americans - Genealogy - Handbooks, manuals, etc. I. Title.
929.1/0720415 dc22   CS483.A465 2009

Library and Archives Canada Cataloguing in Publication

Adolph, Anthony
   Tracing your Irish family history / Anthony Adolph.
Includes bibliographical references and index.
ISBN-13: 978-1-55407-458-7
ISBN-10: 1-55407-458-4
   1. Ireland--Genealogy--Handbooks, manuals, etc. I. Title.
CS483.A36 2009   929'.10720415   C2008-906437-2

Published in the United States by
Firefly Books (U.S.) Inc.
P.O. Box 1338, Ellicott Station
Buffalo, New York 14205

Published in Canada by
Firefly Books Ltd.
66 Leek Crescent
Richmond Hill, Ontario L4B 1H1

Printed in China

To Ann Lavelle, for *Extraordinary Ancestors* and everything else that followed as a consequence — and whose surname, incidentally, speaks eloquently of her family roots in Co. Mayo.

Illustration p. 2: Ireland's troubled story depicted as a great tree, with the Irish nationalist politician Daniel O'Connell (1775–1847) and Erin, the personification of Ireland herself, at its base. Under an Act of Parliament of 1848, publication of this image was deemed seditious. But Catholic or Protestant, native Gael or immigrant, all Irish family histories are irrevocably entwined with the great narrative of Irish history portrayed here.

Contents

Foreword

Recently, I interviewed an Irish economist who was explaining the phenomenal impact of the Irish in Britain. From Lennon/McCartney to Wayne Rooney and even Tony Blair, the Irish strain has always produced second and third generation performers. In London, some of the major landmark buildings are being snapped up by men who started life making tea on building sites off Regent Street. So, is this reverse-colonization or just the natural upshot of an emigration-prone nation?

In America, President John Fitzgerald Kennedy helped not only to put the emigrant Irish on the map but also to take them out of the "no dogs, no blacks, no Irish" generation. Ever since, nearly every American president has found some class of connection to this small but beautiful island. As I write, Senator Hillary Clinton continues to parade her Irish roots and Barack Obama has claimed a bloodline to Co. Offaly.

How times have changed in Ireland. There have always been Irish sons and daughters on the move in search of better times, but the great "brain drain" that characterized generation after generation of migrants from the Famine to the dark economic days of the 1980s has now halted, thanks to the welcome appearance of peace in the 1990s. A new prosperity has stopped Irishmen and women leaving and brought many of them home to an emotional reunion with families who had expected empty places at the dinner table forever.

With over 70 million people across the globe claiming Irish ancestry, the arrival of Anthony Adolph's book couldn't be more apt. A hotel in Dublin recently hired an archivist to help tourists trace their roots as part of the service provided. Such is the demand for and interest in the past that people feel the desire to investigate further. For those who can't make it to Ireland or wish to research before they travel, this genealogical manual will do the trick. It's accessible and helpful as it guides you through the potentially fraught route to your past. The importance of history and the respect that the author has for the past is evident on every page.

Each of us has a story, first generation Irish and beyond, and here is an opportunity to shine a torch into the past and discover what lies beneath. Whatever you find, be it skeletons or gold dust, it promises to be a fascinating and enjoyable journey. *Ce astra per ardua.*

Ryan Tubridy
Dublin, 2007

How to use this book

This book is designed to help you trace your Irish roots back as far as they can go.

- **If you are living outside Ireland, the first task is to trace back to your Irish immigrant ancestor. Most people alive now with Irish roots live outside Ireland — mainly due to the mass migration of the 19th century, and in particular the Great Famine of the 1840s.**
- **If you are using this book in Ireland or already know your Irish place of origin, after reading part 1 of the book you may want to turn directly to part 3 (p. 72), where you'll find resources for tracing ancestry within Ireland.**
- **This book will be useful, too, for anyone wanting to trace relatives, because all Irish families, without exception, have cousins all over the world, from Britain to Argentina and Canada to New Zealand, often within only a handful of generations.**

For many people, the most difficult step is finding where in Ireland your ancestors came from. If records in the country of migration don't tell you, there are various techniques you can employ to ascertain the most likely areas — mainly by localizing the surname and, now, seeking DNA matches. In most cases you will succeed. Then, you can explore your family using Irish records, seeking cousins, learning about your family's social history, and tracing back as far as records allow. You may get back many centuries but, sadly, due to lack of records, many lines don't go back much further than the early 19th century.

The world, seen from the perspective of Irish emigrants, helping to explain the extraordinary journeys of the Irish in the last couple of centuries.

If so, you'll still have the immense pleasure of being able to visit an obscure corner of Ireland, and say (or just think, if you're more modest) "my people came from here!" But having done so, please don't let the limitations of the sources blind you into thinking you've reached the end of the trail. For within Ireland, families have tended to remain fairly stationary for long periods of time. Where any earlier records for your ancestral area survive, you may pick up members of earlier generations — serving in local militias, employed as officials on landed estates or in an Elizabethan pardon for taking part in a local rising.

The same applies to going back yet further. Because Ireland was not invaded by Rome, yet was converted to Christianity early on, it has one of the richest storehouses of traditional genealogy in the world. Most surnames fit into old family trees showing when and how they originated. Early pedigrees in many cases trace back to the younger sons of the Irish kings, to within a few centuries of the start of the Christian era. Before then, pedigrees based perhaps more in myth than reality stretch right back into the mists of time, to the heroic days when the Sons of Mil, the Milesian ancestors of the modern Irish, wrested green Erin (old Ireland) from the ancient gods, the *Tuatha de Danann*. Such old pedigrees tell of legendary ancestors, and we simply don't know how many grains of truth they may contain.

When I was writing this book, the Chief Herald of Ireland himself was kind enough to talk to me about our Milesian ancestors. "Ultimately," he said, "the myth is what sustains you. It doesn't matter if it is true: for what is unquestionably true is the belief our ancestors had in the myth." Neither he nor I would ever advocate imagining that ancient Irish ancestors were definite historical characters. But to research your Irish ancestry and not thoroughly enjoy finding personal connections, albeit just through your surname, to the grand, heroic traditions of this beautiful island, would be as daft as flying all the way from New York to Dublin and then not leaving your hotel room.

There's never been a better time to research your Irish ancestors either. With the great advances in the way records are cataloged, indexed, archived and even made available on the Internet, it's vastly cheaper and easier to trace your Irish roots than ever before. But these positive developments are nothing compared to what comes next. At each stage of your journey, from finding your Irish kin, your ancestral home and testing out the ancient cousinships suggested by Medieval and even legendary pedigrees, the spanking-new science of genetics has completely revolutionized this revered old subject of ours. Having your DNA examined is incredibly easy and now relatively cheap. The more people who add their test results to databases, the more extraordinary the emerging results become. Some long-established genealogical "truths" have already been crushed. And amazingly, some ancient family trees that most serious scholars thought couldn't possibly be true have been tested by this cutting-edge scientific approach — and been found to be correct after all.

If you're already well ahead on your journey, I hope this book will assist you to make wonderful new discoveries. If you've just started — behold the world of possibilities that awaits you!

Abbreviations		
CHC	County Heritage Centre (Irish)
CoE	Church of England (Anglican)
CoI	Church of Ireland
FHC	Mormon Family History Centre
FRC	Family Records Centre (London)
GPC	Genealogical Publishing Company
Grenham	John Grenham, *Tracing your Irish Ancestors: The Complete Guide* (Gill & Macmillan, 3rd edn., 2006)
GO	Genealogical Office
GRO	General Register Office
GRONI	General Register Office of Ireland
MMF	Mormon microfilm
NAI	National Archives of Ireland
NARA	National Archives and Records Administration
NAS	National Archives of Scotland
NLI	National Library of Ireland
NLS	National Library of Scotland
NSW	New South Wales
NZNA	New Zealand National Archives
NZNL	New Zealand National Library
PRONI	Public Record Office of Northern Ireland
RCBL	Representative Church Body Library
RGNI	Registrar General of Northern Ireland
Ryan	James G. Ryan, *Irish Records, Sources for Family and Local History* (Ancestry Incorporated [USA] and Flyleaf Press [Ireland], 1997, revised edn., n.d.)
TNA	The National Archives (Great Britain)

PART 1

Tracing back to Ireland: first steps

Unless your family has never left Ireland, the very first step in researching your Irish family history is to trace back to your migrant ancestor. Although there are many reasons why the Irish have spread so widely across the world, the Great Famine of the 1840s accounts for over 2 million people alone — and you may very well find that one of these migrants was your ancestor. For those who already know where their Irish ancestors lived, this section will be useful for tracing down other branches to find relatives living all around the world.

Mrs. Bridget Casey, of Co. Cork, Ireland, with nine of her children, having arrived in New York on the *S.S. Berlin*, 2 December 1929.

First, find your immigrant

The first task in tracing your Irish roots is to trace back to your migrant ancestor.

Clues to Irish roots

Most people start with a hunch or a story. The most obvious clue is a surname in your family that sounds Irish. While having an Irish surname yourself may make you feel more Irish than otherwise, it doesn't actually matter which lines you investigate — whether they come through your father or mother or any grandparent or great-grandparent, Irish roots are Irish roots.

"O" and "Mac" surnames often indicate Irish (or Scottish) ancestry, but in past centuries many such prefixes were dropped. Some, like Murphy

A cartoon in the May 15, 1878 edition of *Puck* entitled "The Difference Between Them" depicts Irish and Chinese immigrants entering the U.S. The Chinese were there temporarily, but the Irish had come to stay!

and Kelly, are still obviously Irish: others, like Crowley and Denning, may be Irish but don't sound it, while some Irish surnames, like Comiskey and Costello, sound anything but. The chapter on Irish names (p. 146) will help you determine what are likely to be genuine Irish surnames, and which might be red herrings.

First names tend to pass down through generations, so distinctively Irish ones might still be in use even in families that no longer realize their original significance. Theresa, Bernadette, Ellen, Timothy, Laurence and indeed my own name, Anthony, are good clues.

Often, stories will survive. Some can arise because of a recent relative's incorrect research or just their imaginings, and be thoroughly unreliable. But most are genuinely inherited from people who knew what had happened, and contain at least a grain of truth. The Crowleys in Glasgow, for example, believe their family left Ireland because an ancestor couldn't pay his rent and shot the man who came to collect it. I don't know if the last bit is true, but they were absolutely right about having Irish roots and that's what matters. Always record the stories you hear faithfully, for you never know when they may give you a vital clue for your research.

Sometimes, family traditions survive through less obvious routes. In my maternal grandmother's case, it turned out that the name of her family home in Ruislip, "Knockatane," was that of her father's native townland (see p. 78) in Ireland.

Further clues may be so obscure that you will only recognize them after you have found your Irish roots. Pet names used within families, ways of preparing food or superstitions handed down through generations may turn out to have originated in Ireland. In fact, most of us never realize how much of "us" has been inherited from earlier generations until we start tracing our family history.

Ask the family

The first resource for tracing your Irish family is — your family! Telephone, email or meet your immediate relatives and ask for their stories and copies of any old family photographs and papers, especially family bibles, old birth, marriage and death certificates or memorial cards, which were especially popular among Catholics. When I traced my Irish roots, my late grandmother's old address book led me to relatives in England, Ireland and America, all of whom gave me more information to extend my family tree.

It's best to structure your questions by asking the person about themselves, then:

- their siblings (brothers and sisters)
- their parents and their siblings
- their grandparents and their siblings ... and so on. Then, ask about any known descendants of the siblings in each generation. The key questions to ask about each relative are:
- full name
- date and place of birth
- date and place of marriage (if applicable)
- occupation(s)
- place(s) of residence
- religious denomination — for Irish ancestry, this is of course of key importance
- any interesting stories and pictures

Next, ask for addresses of any relatives, contact them and repeat the process (which will result in some repeated information and some contradictory details: write it all down and check it in original sources later). And don't neglect the Irish in Ireland. Once you have traced Irish ancestors, it is worth tracing down other branches of the family who remained there to find cousins who may know much about your earlier ancestors. Sometimes, they'll even have tales about relatives who emigrated.

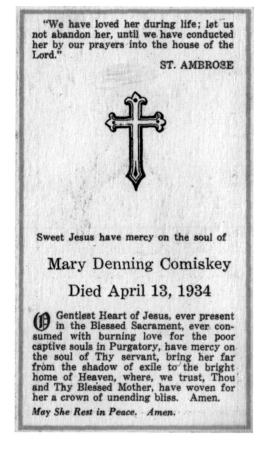

"We have loved her during life; let us not abandon her, until we have conducted her by our prayers into the house of the Lord."

ST. AMBROSE

Sweet Jesus have mercy on the soul of

Mary Denning Comiskey

Died April 13, 1934

Gentlest Heart of Jesus, ever present in the Blessed Sacrament, ever consumed with burning love for the poor captive souls in Purgatory, have mercy on the soul of Thy servant, bring her far from the shadow of exile to the bright home of Heaven, where, we trust, Thou and Thy Blessed Mother, have woven for her a crown of unending bliss. Amen.

May She Rest in Peace. Amen.

LEFT: **A Catholic memorial card. Despite the way they sound (English and Polish respectively), both Denning and Comiskey are in fact Irish names. Comiskey is *Mac Cumascaigh* in Gaelic. Both are found in Co. Cavan, where the Dennings lived, though Mary actually died in New York.**

BELOW: **The Scottish birth certificate of Sarah Frances Gaw shows that her parents John Gaw and Rose Tingle married in Co. Down, but it was a scrap of paper among the old family documents that gave the actual place where the family originated — Ballycastle.**

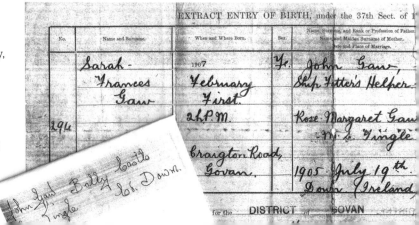

The consequences of famine

Whether potatoes reached Ireland with Sir Walter Raleigh, or from Spain (as their early Irish name, *an spáinneach*, suggests) is open to question. They first appear in a lease in Co. Down of 1606. They were grown initially to break up soil in fields used for cereals. By the late 18th century, most grain was grown for landlords to export, and the potato had become the peasants' staple crop. Potatoes were boiled and eaten and mixed where possible with milk or fish.

Peasants tied to the land tended to marry young, thus producing large families. Nourished by potatoes, the population grew from 2 million in 1700 to 2.3 million in 1754, 5 million in 1800 and 8 million in 1841. There were scarcely any industrial towns to soak up this excess population, so peasant landholdings had to be subdivided, making families dependent on increasingly tiny plots.

The potato harvest had failed occasionally, but from 1821, when the crop failed in Munster and many people in Cork and Clare starved, a series of calamities took place. In Irish folklore, the famine-bringing fairy was the *Fear-Gorta*, the "man of hunger," who stalked the land as an emaciated beggar. He reappeared again with fresh crop failures in 1825-30, followed by "stark famine" in Munster and south Leinster in 1832. From then on, the crop failed periodically.

Despite their terrible living conditions, relatively few Catholics had left Ireland. Besides legal restrictions on their movement — not lifted until 1827 — both poverty and an emotional tie to their ancestral land kept most in Ireland. Between 1827 and 1837, 400,000 souls had scrambled aboard ships leaving Belfast, Dublin, Sligo, Waterford and Youghal. Those who could afford it headed for America: the less costly option was Canada; once there, many planned to walk south. The cheapest option was the ferry fare to mainland Britain. Most Irish Catholics, however, were still in Ireland when disaster struck.

In 1845, an American disease, *phytophthora infestans*, "potato blight," swept Ireland. Exacerbated by three weeks' heavy rain at harvest time, it destroyed 30-40 percent of the crop. The *Fear-Gorta* stalked the land again, and people were forced to eat the parts of the crop they would otherwise have sold to pay their rent. Connacht, west Munster and rural Ulster were the worst affected, but nowhere was unaffected and starvation even spread to the towns. If the blight had lessened in 1846, conditions might have eased, but instead it struck even harder, reducing 95 percent of the year's crop to rotten slime. The cruellest irony is that people knew that every surviving potato they ate meant one less to plant next year: although the blight eased in 1847, the potato yield was a mere 10 percent of what it had been in 1844.

Failure of the potato crop, 1846 (courtesy of National Library of Ireland).

The Internet

Computers are readily available in libraries or internet cafés (or friends' houses!). If you don't use the Internet already, I would strongly recommend learning from a friend or joining a class, as it will make tracing your Irish roots vastly easier. If you absolutely can't bear the idea, ask an Internet-savvy friend or relative to do your look-ups for you.

The Internet is a vast, random whirlpool of information. Besides the research sites recommended later on, there are several excellent ones that put like-minded genealogists in touch with each other, such as the British **www.genesreunited.com**, American **www.onegreatfamily.com** and **www.ancestry.com/uk** which is American and British — though there's much overlap, especially for Ireland. You enter names, dates and places for your family and the sites tell you if anyone else has entered the same ancestors. Equally, when new ancestors join and enter the same relatives, they'll easily find you. It's a new method that really works.

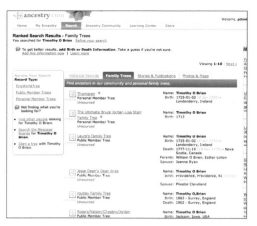

Pages from www.ancestry.com's OneWorldTree and www.genesreunited.com. By clicking on the names here you can learn more about them and contact whoever submitted the information, who is likely to be a relative.

The online route to Wogan's roots

One Irish trait you'll encounter often is a love of storytelling. To trace the family tree of Irish broadcaster and disc-jockey Terry Wogan for *Family History Monthly* I keyed "Wogan" and "genealogy" into an Internet search engine — **www.google.com** and **www.altavista.com** are two good ones. I quickly came up with *The Wogan Genealogy Site*, **www.wogan.info**, whose webmaster, Ken Wogan, put me in touch with Joanne Hartung, whose sister Nancy Dreicer had traced a link with Terry. Two days after starting, I had an email from Nancy, telling me about her grandfather Thomas Joseph Wogan, who was Terry's great-uncle. Thomas had migrated from Enniskerry, Co. Wexford, to New York's Ellis Island on the *Lusitania* in 1908. "He was a charmer," Nancy wrote, "with a Shakespeare quote for any occasion." Thomas became the sommelier at the Statler Hilton Hotel, Philadelphia, until one day he vanished. An astonishing two weeks later, Thomas was finally found — in the furthest reaches of the hotel's wine cellar! It transpired that he had gone down two weeks earlier for a drink, but had so many that he'd lost track of time. He left the hotel with no job and, one assumes, a very sore head. That's typical of the family stories you'll hear when you ask around — and maybe it betrays my own Irish genes that I've retold you the same tale now.

BBC radio presenter Terry Wogan.

Terry's family tree, as published in *Family History Monthly*.

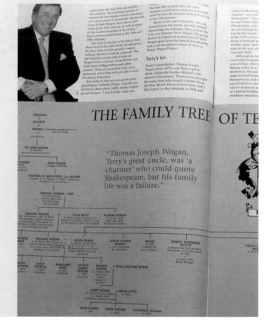

THE FAMILY TREE OF TE

"Thomas Joseph Wogan, Terry's great uncle, was 'a charmer' who could quote Shakespeare, but his family life was a failure."

Workhouses

Ireland's 163 Poor Law Unions, each with its own workhouse, were established to distribute relief to the poor in 1838, uncannily anticipating the Great Famine. Before then, relief had been "outdoor" — handed out to people in their own homes — but from 1838, if you wanted help you had to submit to the appalling conditions of the workhouses.

Workhouses were supposed to be unpleasant enough to discourage all but the genuinely needy. Life for most, however, was so bad that, as one of the Poor Law Commissioners wrote, "it must be obvious to anyone conversant with the habits and mode of living of the Irish people that to establish a dietary [system] in the workhouse inferior to the ordinary diet of the poor classes would be difficult, if not, in many cases, impossible." Instead, the authorities enforced draconian working regimes lasting 7 am to 8 pm, with card-playing and alcohol banned and most misdemeanors punishable by flogging.

Thanks to the Great Famine, the workhouses were overflowing by autumn 1845. Disease became rife, and the way to the workhouse became known as *Cosan na Marbh* — "the pathway of the dead." Up to 25 percent of those admitted died, along with many staff: even Lord Lurgan, chairman of the Lurgan Board of Guardians of the Poor, succumbed to fever in 1847. In 1848, outdoor relief was adopted again, but for many it was far too late.

A soup depot in Cork, 1847 (courtesy of National Library of Ireland).

Workhouse records

The few workhouse records that survive are available on MMF, as cataloged in Ryan (see p. 9) and detailed in D. Lindsay and D. Fitzpatrick, *Records of the Irish Famine, a Guide to Local Archives, 1840-55* (Dublin Irish Famine Network, 1993). See also J. O'Connor, *The Workhouses of Ireland* (Anvil Books, 1995). PRONI has records from 27 Unions, 1838-48; those for Eire are in local archives, with Co. Mayo's at NLI. Records include birth and death registers, punishment and admission records — the latter stating name, gender, age, marital condition, family relationships, denomination, townland and date of departure (often the date of death). See also **http://www.askaboutireland .ie/search.do?search_string=workhouses**.

Starving peasants at the gates of a workhouse, September 1847 (courtesy of National Library of Ireland).

For a key to abbreviations used, see p. 9.

The Irish diaspora

Emaciated, rag-clad and tinged green by starvation, with an average life-expectancy of 19 years, the stark choice faced by many Irish people during the Great Famine in 1845 was migrate or die. Some 1.5 million people left for America, 340,000 for Canada, 300,000 for mainland Britain and 70,000 for Australia. Large numbers sailed west in "coffin ships," unseaworthy vessels pressed into service by necessity and the owners' venality. Some ships sank as soon as they had left port and others far out at sea. Passengers typically were unable to afford enough supplies or had no idea the voyage could take 4–6 weeks, so many starved and disease was rife.

They left behind a debilitated population, most of whom yearned to escape. Though the exodus slowed after 1855, migration had become a normal expectation. Many left due to terrible weather and crop failures between 1879 and 1888. Uniquely in Europe, Ireland's population shrunk, from 8 million in 1841 to only 4 million in 1921. By 1891, 43 percent of living Irish-born people were resident abroad. It is only in the last couple of decades that Ireland's "Tiger" economy has improved and immigration has started to reverse the trend.

The famine migrants belong to a much broader trend of emigration, due mainly to English interference and economic depression, starting with the Wild Geese (see p. 207) in the 17th century and only effectively ending a few decades ago. The legacy of 400 years' emigration is that an estimated 70 million people living outside Ireland have Irish roots. Because the famine drove both genders to migrate in equal numbers, fully-Irish communities were established all over the world. Equally, many of the estimated 70 million have some Irish ancestry mixed in with much other blood.

Irish immigrants arriving in New York by Samuel B. Waugh, 1847.

Much depends on perception: descents from downtrodden groups, such as Jews or black slaves, have become marks of proud distinction, to be sought after in otherwise dull family trees. And, far from being synonymous with terrorism, as it was 20 years ago, Irishness has resumed its gorgeous ancient mantle, velvet green shot through with gold, of Gaelic myth and folk music, topped up by the music of The Pogues and the successful marketing campaigns of Guinness. Its best synonym now is the *craic* of St. Patrick's night, so no wonder people with only the slenderest strand of Gaelic blood today proudly call themselves "Irish." Consequently, when the English 2001 census allowed, for the first time, people to choose "Irish" as the best description of their ethnicity, the figure for people in England with Irish origins leapt from 10 percent (1991) to 25 percent!

The true number of people with Irish roots is still unknown. But I know one thing for sure: the more people dig into their family past, the more Irish roots will be uncovered.

further reading

■ A. Bielenberg (ed.), *The Irish Diaspora* (Longman, 2000), contains fascinating articles on many of the countries where the Irish settled.

■ Irish Diaspora website: **www.irishdiaspora.net**.

Using and storing records

Once you've found out all you can from the family, it's time to start using original records in public archives.

First, you need to trace back to identify your migrant ancestor. Then, you must seek as many clues as possible to help find where in Ireland they originated. Finally, you can use Irish records to prove the place of origin and trace further back. Each country's records are different, so later we'll look in detail at Argentina, Australia, Canada, England and Wales, New Zealand, Scotland and the United States, and finally Ireland itself. First, however, we will look at the main categories of records you'll encounter in all these countries, and how they can be used.

The "Irish" royal family?

The British Royal family has its fair share of Irish blood. Henry II's maternal grandmother was the daughter of Malcolm III of Scotland, descended from Fergus Mor Mac Erc, the Irish prince who founded the Scottish monarchy (see p. 41). All subsequent English monarchs have had Irish blood, with an important extra dose when Fergus's heirs, the Stuart kings of Scotland, became kings of England as well in 1603. In the 19th century, John O'Hart hoped that by publishing a family tree showing this in his *Irish Pedigrees* he would "conduce a kindly feeling on behalf of Her Gracious Majesty towards *ourself* and our bleeding country." In addition, the late Queen Mother's maternal great-grandmother Anne Wellesley was the niece of the Irish-born Duke of Wellington and a 4 x great-granddaughter of Mary O'Brien, a 19 x great-granddaughter of the Irish king Brian Boru (d. 1014), through the Barons of Inchiquin and the Kings of Thomond. Prince William's mother, the late Princess Diana, was daughter of Frances Burke-Roche, descended from the Barons Fermoy, a family with extensive Anglo-Irish ancestry.

Prince William with the Queen Mother and Princess Diana, 1987.

Archives

Records will usually be held either in the archives of the organization that created them or in public archives, either local or national. Use **www.cyndislist.com** to find the archives you want. Their websites will tell you opening times and what identification you'll need and many have online catalogs. If you are unsure, contact them in advance of your visit to be certain they have what you want.

It is not always practical or sensible to visit an archive, so luckily there are other options:

1. The Church of Jesus Christ of Latter-day Saints (also called the Mormon Church) has the world's largest (and ever-growing) archive of microfilm copies of original records from all over the world, including many for Ireland. Founded in 1830, the Utah-based church has a religious mission to trace all family trees, identifying all humanity in the context of living descendants or relatives. The living hold ceremonies giving the deceased the opportunity of becoming Mormons should their souls so desire. They have Family History Centers in most major towns: find your nearest at **www.familysearch.org**. They are open to all — entirely without any need to convert — and here you can order any Mormon microfilms (MMFs) to be delivered from the Mormon's Family History Library in Utah.

2. Genealogical societies often have substantial libraries. For example, the Society of Genealogists (SoG) in London has a vast collection of printed and manuscript sources covering all Great Britain and Ireland, including much on the Irish in Britain detailed in A. Camp, *Sources for Irish Genealogy in the Library of the Society of Genealogists* (SoG, 1998), which you can buy when you arrive.

A web page from **www.cyndislist.com**, showing a listing of archives in New Zealand.

Part of the website of the British National Archives (TNA), **www.national archives.gov.uk**.

Catholic registers

Many Catholic registers remain with the church where they were created. To see them, telephone or write (enclosing a prepaid envelope or international reply coupon) and ask for a search or for permission to do so yourself. Be extremely clear and courteous — most priests' spiritual duties are more pressing to them than tracing your ancestry — but if you meet real obstacles you can always try enlisting the local bishop's help instead.

3. You can hire genealogists or record agents. Genealogists like myself charge higher fees and organize and implement all aspects of genealogical research. Record agents charge less and work to their clients' specific instructions — "please search the parish registers of X for the period 1730 to 1790 for baptisms of any Fitzgeralds," for example. Most archives have a search service or a list of local researchers. Many advertise in genealogy magazines or at **www.genealogypro.com**, **www.expertgenealogy.com** and **www.cyndislist.org**. Most are trustworthy and many offer excellent services, though ability varies enormously. Generally, the more prompt and professional their response and neater their results, the more likely they are to be any good. Hiring help is not "cheating": if you only want one record examined but are not sure it will contain your ancestor, it makes no sense to undertake a long journey when you can pay someone a small fee for checking for you and a local searcher's expertise may then point you in the right direction anyway.

Civil Registration records

Most countries have a system of civil registration (sometimes called General Registration) of births, marriages and deaths. Some started very recently, but most of the countries that received Irish immigrants have systems that started in the 19th century — often coinciding with the Irish diaspora, making them particularly useful.

Usually, your mining of family knowledge will result in a family tree starting with a name ("John or maybe James O'Brien") followed by their child, with a bit more information (say, "Thomas O'Brien, born in 1922"), and then a third generation down, with much more definite

Storing information

Some people prefer using family tree computer programs. A comparative table of those available is at **www.my-history.co.uk**. Many are based in "Gedcom" format so once you have typed in your data you can transfer it between programs — including the ones used in Genes Reunited and ancestry.com. Others (like me) aren't so excited by these programs: most have limitations or pester you for "vital data" that you don't have. I prefer handwriting family trees and keeping more detailed notes in computer word documents. The following "narrative" method allows much flexibility:

Joseph O'Riley
Write everything you know about Joseph. Then write "his children were" and list them:

1 ***Eustace O'Riley**, the next member of the direct line, so after his name type "see below."*
2 *Thomas O'Riley. Put anything you know about Thomas and his descendants here. If he had children, then write: his children were*
   1 *Anthony O'Reilly.*
   2 *Ignatius O'Reilly. And if he had offspring, then...*
      1 *Connor O'Reilly, and so on.*
3 *Josephine O'Riley*
4 *Aloysius O'Riley. If you have a lot of information about Aloysius and his descendants, you might want to open a separate "chapter" for him and put him at the top of his own narrative document.*

Eustace O'Riley, *son of Joseph.*
Write what you know about Eustace, and so on.

GEMEENTE AMSTERDAM
BURGERLIJKE STAND

UITTREKSEL uit het register van: *Huwelijken en Echtscheidingen*

Op vijftien September achttien honderd eenentachtig is in de gemeente AMSTERDAM gehuwd: Gerhard Dornagen, geboren te Wesen, gemeente Brühl in Duitschland, oud drieendertig jaren, zoon van: Johann Dornagen en Anna Maria Hemmeler, met: Anna Lewis, geboren in het kerspel Fermoy in Ierland, oud zeven twintig jaren, dochter van: John Lewis en Mary Anne Sweeny.

Voor gelijkluidend uittreksel.

Vrij van zegel, op grond van art. 32, N°. 6 der „Zegelwet 1917",
ten dienste eener Vreemde Regeering.
AMSTERDAM, 17 Maart 1938.

De Ambtenaar van den Burgerlijken Stand,

Coll.:

Kosteloos

An unusual reference to Irish origins in a civil marriage record of 1881 from Amsterdam. It shows Gerhard Dornagen marrying Anna Lewis, 'born in the parish of Fermoy in Ireland', daughter of John Lewis and Mary Anne Sweeny. Sadly, few countries' records provide such useful details on origins!

information ("Ellen O'Brien, born on 22 February 1951, Lismore, New South Wales"). You may think you'll save money and time if you start with John (or James!), but then what will you look for? Starting with Thomas would be better as you can look for a birth in 1922, but since you don't know where he was born, you've no idea where to look. You're probably not 100 percent sure that the year 1922 was correct — this might be a year calculated from an age at death which seldom take into account when in the year people's birthdays fell — so Thomas could have been born in 1921 (or 1923!). Therefore, start with what you know for sure and seek Ellen's birth certificate. Once you have this, you've established a firm foothold, and can work back with confidence.

Generally, birth records tell you when and where the child was born, the names of both parents and the father's occupation. Some countries' records will give more, such as when the parents married.

The birth certificate is a contemporary source providing the parents' names, probably from their own mouths — not half-remembered hearsay, but fact. Now, work back through the marriage indexes, seeking their wedding.

Marriage certificates usually state names, occupations and places of residence of the couple, as well as their ages and names of their parents (usually just fathers, but sometimes mothers too). Thus, following our example, you'll now have a definite age for Thomas and know his father's name (James, not John), all recorded at the time from the people concerned. Sometimes they lied about ages — if you discover discrepancies, you'll simply have to widen the period of your subsequent search. The next step is to seek Thomas's birth: if his father's name matches the one given on his marriage record, you'll know you have the right document.

A major problem in seeking births is when you have a very common combination of names, leaving a long list of possible entries. This can sometimes be overcome by building up a picture of all families of the surname in the area using civil registration and religious registers, thus eliminating false possibilities. Where possible, gain extra coordinates on ages from census returns.

Try to confirm the names of both parties (i.e. from a birth certificate) before seeking marriage records. You can then work back from when the eldest known child of the couple was born (be aware that a census may list all the children of a father, but won't let on that half of them were by his present wife and the other half by a previous, now deceased spouse: a significant gap in children's ages may alert you to this). Choose the least common surname or combination of names and whenever you find an instance of it, look for the other party's name in the index: if the other details (district, volume and page number) match up, it's yours.

Occupations could change. If the father on a 1950 marriage certificate was a factory manager and on a 1922 birth certificate was a junior clerk, you can see that the clerk could have been promoted to factory manager. If, however, you find an implausible jump from, say, army officer to fishmonger, then you may have the wrong certificate and should widen your search for better possibilities. Only when you're sure you've found the right document should you continue working backwards.

Death certificates vary in use from country to country. Those in Ireland just give the age and place of death. This is useful if you are stuck — it will suggest when the person was born, if you can't find their marriage record. It's good to seek these records to complete your ancestors' stories anyway and it's helpful to confirm that someone who you think was your ancestor died after their child was born, *not* some years before! Countries such as Scotland and New Zealand have much more detailed death certificates including both parents' full names, making them fantastic tools that should be searched for as a matter of course. Just bear in mind that names of the deceased's parents as supplied by their children may not be accurate, for the informants may never have met their grandparents. But only disbelieve what you read if you have firm evidence to the contrary.

Deaths can be hard to find without knowing when the event took place. It's often easier to gain further coordinates: for example, marriage entries sometimes state that a father was deceased. Will indexes provide a short-cut for better-off families. In Ireland, Griffith's Valuation (see p. 84) for any landholder, however small, can give a good idea when someone may have died.

If civil registration reaches back to your migrant ancestor, then the earliest documents will actually name people living in Ireland. For example, if your migrant ancestor married after having already migrated, then the father's/parents' names on the marriage certificate will be those of people back in Ireland. The same applies to parents' names on a migrant's death certificate. Of course, the parents may have migrated too, so you can always seek *their* deaths in the country of arrival just in case!

Censuses

The quality and quantity of censuses vary greatly from country to country. Generally, they list the occupants of a country on a specific day. Compiled by place, listing each household in turn, they give varying degrees of information about each person: at best they state names, ages, interrelationships, occupations and places of birth (and in the United States, for example, the countries of origin of each person's parents). They are best used in tandem with civil registration. Censuses indicate ages and places to seek birth certificates. These in turn supply the names of parents who can be searched for in earlier censuses.

Census returns for migrant ancestors may confirm "Ireland" as their birth place and they may give a county or even an exact place. You will often find other Irish people living nearby with whom your ancestor may have migrated, who could well be close relations. You could actually find several generations born and bred in Ireland living in the same place.

Many countries' censuses, including Ireland's, are now partially online and can be found through **www.censusfinder.com**.

Problems are often lessened simply by being aware of them. Sometimes, places of origin were not given accurately. Famine migrants were so scared of repatriation that they would tell census enumerators that they were born "here!" hen they admitted to being Irish, the enumerators often simply wrote "Ireland," never imagining that we'd want to know more detail. In both cases, seek your ancestor in all available censuses, for some will list more accurate or detailed answers than others.

Migrants sometimes assumed nobody would have heard of their tiny townland of origin, so gave their birthplace as the nearest market town instead. When they did give a precise birthplace such as a farm, you may have quite a time locating it, especially if its name appears on modern maps under a different spelling or a translation into or out of Gaelic. You may need to try your own translation and see if that appears on maps instead.

Much Irish migration was a two-stage process — to Argentina via England, New Zealand via Australia or the United States via Canada. Always bear this in mind and work back patiently, finding out the most common migratory patterns for the period and country concerned.

Directories

Directories started in England in 1677 as lists of prominent merchants but rapidly spread abroad, proliferating in the 19th century and flourishing until the spread of telephone directories after World War II. They generally listed tradesmen, craftsmen, merchants, professionals, farmers, clergy, gentry and

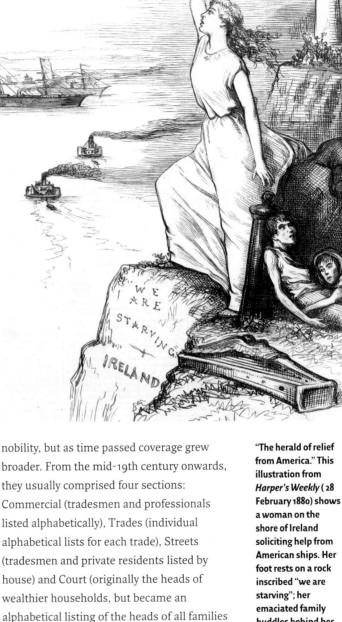

"The herald of relief from America." This illustration from *Harper's Weekly* (28 February 1880) shows a woman on the shore of Ireland soliciting help from American ships. Her foot rests on a rock inscribed "we are starving"; her emaciated family huddles behind her.

nobility, but as time passed coverage grew broader. From the mid-19th century onwards, they usually comprised four sections: Commercial (tradesmen and professionals listed alphabetically), Trades (individual alphabetical lists for each trade), Streets (tradesmen and private residents listed by house) and Court (originally the heads of wealthier households, but became an alphabetical listing of the heads of all families except for the poor). They provide a snap-shot of the communities in which ancestors lived, including useful historical sketches and descriptions of the places concerned. By searching a series of directories, you can work out when ancestors lived and died. Bear in

A typical immigrant wagon train in North America, c. 1866 — a familiar experience for many Irish migrants.

mind, though, that directories were usually printed a year or so after the data had been collected, so were always slightly out of date. Directories also provide addresses for manual census searches.

Religious registers

Religious registers are also called church registers and parish registers. Parishes were fixed geographical units in which priests kept registers. However, registers were also kept by priests on the move — on wagon trains crossing 19th-century America, or moving furtively among scattered communities of persecuted Catholics in 17th-century England.

Some denominations recorded births, but you will generally find baptisms, marriages and burials. The records are often slightly less detailed than Civil Registration, but not always — many Catholic and Quaker registers, for example, can sometimes be even more informative. They can be used in a similar way to Civil Records. Many people start using them for the period before Civil Records. Actually, there are cases where it is

sensible to seek both types of record. An Irish civil marriage, for example, will state the father's name, whereas the corresponding Catholic one may give the mother's too.

Baptism records usually state the child's name, date of baptism, father's name and mother's first name. You may get less (16th-century English baptisms sometimes omit parents' names altogether) or more, such as date of birth, father's occupation and mother's maiden name. It's worth finding out what information registers are likely to contain before searching them to ensure the level of detail matches your needs.

Especially with Catholic records, baptisms will give the names of the godparents (also called "gossips" or "sponsors"). These were people undertaking to look after the child's physical and spiritual needs should the parents die. Sometimes they might be powerful patrons — the family's landlord, employer or a distant, rich relative. Usually, they were close friends, relatives and neighbours. It therefore makes sense to find the baptisms of all the family's children, for the godparents' names will build up a picture of the wider ties of friends and family.

If the baptism record tells you both parents' full names, you can seek their marriage with confidence. If it just states the mother's first name, then you must seek the marriage "blind," looking, for example, for any Thomas O'Briens marrying a Joanna. If you find Thomas O'Brien marrying Joanna O'Flynn, you won't know for sure that this is the right wedding. You therefore need to make fairly broad searches to make sure there are no other possibilities and look for any other pointers that will help decide. If occupations and places of residence are known, you can see if these match up. And you may recognize names from the list of the next generation's godparents. There are no hard and fast rules, and you seldom get

100 percent proof — your aim, though, is to seek as high a percentage of proof as you can.

Some baptism registers state dates of birth, but many don't. Most children were baptized soon after birth: infant mortality was very high, and an unbaptized child could not enter Heaven. However, for many reasons, such as practical difficulties or religious indifference, it could take weeks, months or years for parents to present their children to the font. So *never* record a date of baptism as a birthdate, and when looking for someone born in 1810 you may need to search several years or more further forward before finding a baptism.

Some marriage registers give both parents' full names, while others just name the fathers. The burial registers usually just state the name, date and age — thus indicating when people were born: occupations and places of residence sometimes appear.

A useful seach aid is **www.familysearch.org**. Compiled by the Mormons, it is an index to many baptism and marriage registers. It is by no means complete: not all existing registers are indexed (its coverage of Catholic registers is relatively low) and some of the registers included have only been partially indexed. Therefore, you will not always find your family here and finding someone of the right name in FamilySearch does not automatically mean it's the right person! Nonetheless, it is an impressive tool always worth checking, and if you find what appear to be the right people, always check the original registers from which the index references came.

Associated with burial records are gravestones. These often mention more than one member of the family ("...beloved wife of X," for example) but their great use in Irish genealogy is that migrants' graves sometimes state the place of origin. Many gravestone inscriptions have been transcribed and these are available in archives or on the Internet.

Grave of an Irish-American migrant from Co. Tyrone, laid to rest in Maryland, USA.

Newspapers

Newspapers have been published since the 17th century and proliferated in the 19th century, around the time of the Irish diaspora. They can provide fascinating background material on the causes of migration, the establishment of new colonies and settlements, the departure and arrival of ships carrying migrants and much else.

Newspapers, both secular and those produced by religious denominations (often to be found in denominational archives), frequently

Irish peasants foraging for the potato crop of an evicted tenant.

Pedigree conventions

- '=' indicates a marriage, accompanied by "m-" and the date and place.
- solid lines indicate definite connections; dotted lines indicate probable but unproven ones.
- wiggly lines are for illegitimacy and "x" for a union out of wedlock — important on old pedigrees but I think it's time to move past this distinction and use straight lines, though "x" instead of "=" seems reasonable enough.
- loops are used if two unconnected lines need to cross over, just like electricians' wiring diagrams.
- wives usually go on the right of husbands, though only if that doesn't interfere with the chart's overall layout.
- Common abbreviations are:

b.	born
bpt or c.	baptized or christened (same thing)
bach.	bachelor
spin.	spinster
unm.	unmarried
d.	died
bur.	buried
d.s.p. or o.s.p.	died without children
d.v.p. or o.v.p.	died before father married
lic.	marriage license
w.wr./pr.	will written/proved
m.i.w.	"mentioned in the will of…" followed by f. for father, gf. for grandfather and so on
inft	infant
MI	monumental inscription
wid.	widow or widower (as appropriate)

placed by husbands disclaiming financial responsibility for wives who had eloped.

Newspapers are valuable for tracing ancestry and also for adding color and detail to your ancestors' stories. Many Irish immigrants and their descendants came from poor backgrounds in Ireland yet made great successes of themselves in their places of settlement. The rise to prosperity of families of farmers, businessmen and politicians is often well chronicled in newspapers. Especially useful are obituaries of Irish migrants, or their children or grandchildren. American newspapers are very good for this and may state the Irish place of origin of the parent, grandparent or even earlier ancestor of the deceased. So if you have no American ancestors but know of cousins who settled there, you might discover your Irish roots by seeking their American newspaper obituaries.

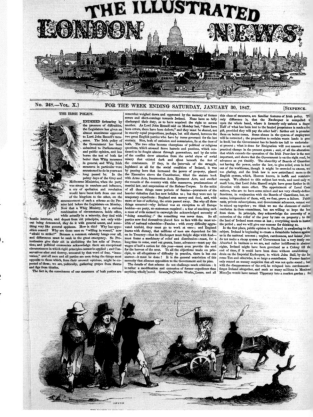

carried announcements of births, baptisms, marriages, deaths, obituaries and burials. Such announcements can be very sparse — "to the lady of Michael O'Brien Esq., of Newgrange, Co. Meath, a son" — but many are far more detailed. They very seldom include the illiterate poor (for obvious reasons) but poor people may be mentioned retrospectively, for example, as parents of people who had risen in the world thanks to migration.

You may also encounter advertisements concerning bankruptcy, business partnerships being made and dissolved and even notices

A page from *The Illustrated London News*, 30 January 1847, showing a funeral at Skibbereen, Co. Cork (courtesy of National Library of Ireland).

M.A. Corpus Christi College, Cambridge, 1597 ; M.D., 1603 ; practised medicine in Northampton, 1603 till death : published 'Discoverie of . . . Ignorant Practisers of Physicke,' 1611, 'The Triall of Witchcraft,' 1616, and 'Cotta contra Antonium,' 1623 (against Francis Anthony [q. v.]) [xii. 288]

COTTAM, THOMAS (1549–1582), jesuit : born in Lancashire ; M.A. Brasenose College, Oxford, 1572 ; schoolmaster in London ; embraced Roman catholicism ; withdrew to Douay ; afterwards lived at Rome and at Rheims ; joined the jesuits ; imprisoned in London, 1580–2 ; executed at Tyburn. [xii. 289]

COTTENHAM, EARL OF (1781–1851). [See PEPYS CHARLES CHRISTOPHER.]

COTTER, GEORGE SACKVILLE (1755–1831), trans- ★ lator ; educated at Westminster School, and, 1771, Peterhouse, Cambridge ; M.A., 1779 ; beneficed in co. Cork, Ireland ; published poems, 1788 ; translated Terence, 1826 and Plautus, 1827. [xii. 289]

COTTER, PATRICK (1761 ?–1806), Irish giant ; born at Kinsale ; a bricklayer ; exhibited himself in Great Britain as O'BRIEN, 1779–1804 ; his height sometimes gave as over eight feet. [xii. 289]

COTTERELL, SIR CHARLES (1612 ?–1702), courtier ; ★ knighted, 1644 ; master of the ceremonies, 1641–9 ; at Antwerp, 1649–52 ; steward at the Hague to Elizabeth, queen of Bohemia, 1652–4 ; secretary to Henry, duke of Gloucester, 1655–60 ; master of the ceremonies, 1660–86 ; master of requests, 1670–86 ; M.P., Cardigan, 1663–78 ; translated French romances and histories, and 'The Spiritual Year,' a Spanish devotional tract. [xii. 290]

COTTERELL, SIR CHARLES LODOWICK (1654– ★ 1710), courtier ; son of Sir Charles Cotterell [q. v.] ; LL.D. Trinity College, Cambridge ; knighted, 1687 ; master of the ceremonies, 1686–1710 ; published memoir of Prince George of Denmark, 1708. [xii. 291]

COTTERELL, SIR CLEMENT (d. 1758), courtier ; son of Sir Charles Lodowick Cotterell [q. v.] ; knighted, 1710 ; master of the ceremonies, 1710–58 ; assumed the name DORMER, 1741 ...

...1770–1800), landscape-painter ; [xii. 234]

1777), painter and architect : ouse and Hampton Court. [xii. 234]

(1631–1660). [See MARY.]

·IARD, WILLIAM (d. 1504), loyed by Waynflete at Magt Eton. [xii. 235]

1822), antiquary ; nephew of resident of Society of Anti-Gough, Nichols, and others ; apressions of brasses and of is Suffolk collections in the [xii. 235]

·IEORGE (1819–1885), colonial ; served with royal engineers st on naval works at Ascenst African questions, 1856–7 ; inica, 1857–60 ; governor of colonial governor of Straits th Australia, 1877–9 ; major- 81. [xii. 236]

4), lawyer and politician, son Trinity College, Cambridge, ister, Lincoln's Inn ; master time chairman of committees ℓ, successively for Midhurst, 74–90). [xii. 237]

(1811–1853), journalist and a Literary Journal' and 'Briund 'History and Antiquities [xii. 237]

·RT (d. 1778), chief baron of [xii. 238]

baronet (1751–1824), admiral ; etion of Philadelphia, 1778 ; eston, 1780 ; created baronet, nor of Dominica (appointed and under St. Vincent made by Nelson and Curtis ; comterre, 1804–5 ; admiral, 1805 ; ght), 1807–24. [xii. 238]

·DE-POWLETT, THOMAS, 1807), chief secretary for Ire- Orde [q. v.] ; while fellow of tched portraits of local celester, Lincoln's Inn ; F.S.A., ·4, Harwich, 1784–96 and in...

O'REILLY, ALEXANDER (1722 ?–1794), Spanish general ; born in Ireland ; served against Austrians in Italy ; in Austrian service against Prussians ; joined French army, 1759, but soon re-entered Spanish service ; served in Portuguese war, 1762 ; became governor of Havana and Louisiana ; governor of Madrid during émeute of 1765 ; commanded disastrous expedition against Algiers, 1775 ; commander-in-chief in Andalusia and Cadiz ; died when about to lead army of Eastern Pyrenees against French. [xii. 244]

O'REILLY, ANDREW (1742–1832), Austrian general of cavalry ; born in Ireland ; served in Bavarian succession war, and against the Turks and in Flanders ; captured by French, 1796 ; distinguished himself in Italy, 1800, and at Coldrerio, 1805 ; as governor of Vienna surrendered to Napoleon, 1809. [xii. 245]

O'REILLY, EDMUND (1606–1669), Roman catholic archbishop of Armagh ; prefect of college of Irish secular ecclesiastics at Louvain ; vicar-general of Dublin, 1642–9 ; governor of Wicklow, 1642 ; deprived of vicar-generalship on suspicion of treachery, 1649, but restored, 1650 ; convicted of murder, 1654, but pardoned ; archbishop of Armagh, c. 1654 ; lived at Lille till 1657 ; ordered to withdraw from Ireland, 1660 ; remained at Rome five years ; attended Dublin synod, 1666 ; again banished, 1666 ; died at Saumur. [xii. 246]

O'REILLY, EDMUND JOSEPH (1811–1878), Irish jesuit provincial ; studied at Rome ; professor of theology at Maynooth, 1838–50 ; teacher at St. Beuno's college and in the Roman catholic university of Ireland ; superior of Milltown Port, Dublin, 1859–78 ; Irish jesuit provincial, 1863–70 ; his 'Relations of the Church to Society' issued, 1892. [xii. 247]

O'REILLY, EDWARD (d. 1829), compiler of 'Irish-English Dictionary' (1817) ; published also 'Chronological Account of nearly four hundred Irish Writers,' 1820, and prize essays on the Brehon laws, 1824, and the authenticity of Macpherson's 'Ossian,' 1829. [xii. 247]

O'REILLY, HUGH (1580–1653), Roman catholic bishop of Kilmore, 1625–8, and archbishop of Armagh, 1628–53. [xii. 246]

O'REILLY, HUGH (d. 1695 ?). [See REILLY.]

O'REILLY, JOHN BOYLE (1844–1890), Irish revolutionist and author ; enlisted in 10th hussars, really as Fenian agent ; sentenced to death by court-martial, but his sentence commuted to penal servitude, 1866 ; escaped from West Australia in American whaler, 1869 ; after cruising in Indian Ocean settled in Boston, Massachusetts ; took part in O'Neill's invasion of Canada, 1870, and in organising rescue of the Catalpa of convicts in West Australia, 1876 ; edited the 'Pilot' and published four volumes of poems ...

Two pages from the concise version of the old *Dictionary of National Biography*, showing a mixture of the great, good and downright odd of Ireland and Britain. (The original old DNB was the *Dictionary of National Biography*, while the recently-revised version is called the ODNB, the *Oxford Dictionary of National Biography*.) (Courtesy of Oxford Dictionary of National Biography, OUP.)

Biographical dictionaries

The first great national biographical dictionary was the *Dictionary of National Biography*, whose initial editor was Sir Leslie Stephen (1832–1904), father of the novelist Virginia Woolf. The project began in 1882, encompassing the whole of the British Isles, thus including much Irish material: in fact, the first person under 'A' is Jacques Abbadie, the Huguenot dean of Killaloe, Co. Clare. Since then, most countries have produced biographical dictionaries. For small or newly-emerged states, such publications have become important symbols of nationhood. Biographical dictionaries also exist for many fields of endeavor — painters, architects, naval officers and so on, and for smaller geographical areas such as counties, provinces and cities.

Some dictionaries were very selective, but many aimed at widest possible sales by including almost anyone involved in business, local politics, the professions and arts. Most state date and place of birth, making them useful as genealogical tools. Many Irish migrants who made successes of themselves often appear in local biographical dictionaries with their places of origin clearly stated.

Wills

Wills were usually written towards the end of peoples' lives specifying who was to inherit what. Besides the obviously interesting details of personal possessions, paintings, books, land and so on, they help tie family trees together, sometimes providing details of people who missed being recorded in church, civil or census records. People generally named spouses and children, but you may also find parents, brothers and sisters, nieces and nephews, grandchildren and so on.

Wills tended to be written by people with property. The poor tended not to bother but this is not always so: if your ancestors were illiterate laborers they probably didn't leave wills, but once in a while you *might* find one.

Wills are a key source for establishing migrants' origins. You may not be able to find your migrant ancestor's baptism in Ireland, but if they wrote a will mentioning brothers and sisters, you can look for *their* baptisms instead. Sometimes migrants were kind enough to us to leave bequests to relatives still living in Ireland. In these cases their wills actually tell you where to look for their origins.

To make a will a legally-binding document it was taken, after the testator had died, to a probate court to be "proved" (making it legally vaild). This usually happened immediately after death but in some cases it was put off for several years, so a wide search is always advisable. Sometimes you'll find other records attached to wills, such as inventories of personal goods — wonderful material for broadening the family's history.

When seeking wills, you will also encounter administrations. When people died "intestate" — without leaving a will — letters of administration could be granted to the next of kin. Administrations give minimal genealogical information, but are still better than nothing.

Naturalizations

Each country had different rules or lack thereof, governing who was allowed to settle there. In many cases, people were allowed to enter and live in a country freely, with little or no interference from the state. If they wanted full legal rights, however, particularly in respect of bequeathing property, they had to become naturalized. Naturalization records will certainly tell you where your ancestor lived when they were naturalized, and where they came from — stating perhaps just "Ireland," but sometimes a precise place of origin will be given.

Shipping lists

International air travel is a new phenomena, and most people whose ancestors migrated by plane will know where they were from anyway. For genealogical purposes — and because Ireland is an island — the best records of migration are lists of passengers on ships.

These seldom give much detail, merely who migrated, when, and between which ports. They may state ages and other helpful details, but won't give either the ultimate destination or

---

Ché Guevara and Zorro

Ché Guevara, the epitome of South American revolutionary spirit, was the son of Ernesto Guevara Lynch. In Spanish culture, people generally add their mother's maiden name to their own surname, so in this case Ernesto's mother's family were Lynches, descended from Patrick Lynch, born in Galway in 1715. Ernesto once said of his son, "The first thing to note is that in my son's veins flowed the blood of the Irish rebels." Ché visited Ireland in 1965, enjoying an evening out at Hanratty's Hotel, Limerick, sporting a sprig of shamrock for St. Patrick's Day. He was less Irish, however, than that other great Latin-American maverick, Zorro, "the Fox," whose amorous adventures brought him to an untimely end in 1659. The great swashbuckler had in fact been born William Lamport in Co. Wexford in 1615.

Ships' passenger lists

The best sources for ships' passenger lists are in the country of arrival. TNA's lists (BT 32, described in information leaflet 71 and S. Colwell, *The National Archives: A Practical Guide for Family Historians,* National Archives, 2006) cover 1890–1960 but are arranged by date and port of departure. **www.irishorigins.com** has indexed those for 1890 to North America. While many migrated at their own expense, the government encouraged emigration to less hospitable or further parts of the Empire, such as Australia via the Colonial Land and Emigration Office (renamed Colonial Commission of Land and Emigration), which granted land and paid for journeys. Its records are at TNA, and may help if you are stuck:

CO 384: correspondence 1817–96 from and concerning settlers.

CO 327-8: registers for North America, 1850–96.

CO 385: emigration entry books 1814–71.

CO 386: records of the Commission for Land and Emigration, 1833–94.

A list of passengers from Ireland taken on board the ship *Alice Wilson*, which arrived in the port of New York on 4 August 1851 (courtesy of www.ancestry.com).

for they record journeys that changed your family's history forever. They can help establish your Irish roots too. The port of departure was often the nearest one to the family home, giving you a rough idea of the area of Ireland they came from. Migrants usually traveled in groups, so people of the same name in the ship's manifest may be related. People traveling in groups were often listed together, so the people above and below your ancestors in a list could be relatives. Looking at these people's origins could lead you to your own family's roots.

Local histories

Many settlements in the New World and Antipodes have only been there a handful of generations. A good number have had their histories written up, often using oral history and local records. These frequently include lists of the original inhabitants, with good genealogical details. Once you know where your Irish migrant ancestors first settled, contact the local libraries and archives to see what material may be available.

further reading

■ John Grenham, *Tracing your Irish Ancestors: The Complete Guide* (Gill & Macmillan, 3rd edn., 2006).

■ John O'Hart, *Irish Pedigrees* (Dublin 1892: GPC, 1999).

■ James G. Ryan, *Irish Records, Sources for Family and Local History* (Ancestry Incorporated [USA] and Flyleaf Press [Ireland], 1997, revised edn., n.d.).

Irish emigrants embarking for America at Waterloo Docks, Liverpool, July 6, 1850.

PART 2

Tracing back to Ireland: country by country

The spread of the Irish around the globe dates back to ancient times, but it reached epic proportions with the Great Famine. In this section, we will look at the seven countries to which they migrated in most numbers, following a rough chronological order — England and Wales, Scotland, the United States, Canada, Argentina, Australia and New Zealand. But these are not seven separate stories — all extended Irish family trees span each of these countries, and the accounts of invasion, transportation, colonization and economic migration are an extension of Ireland's own story.

On the steerage deck of an immigrant ship, 1907.

CHAPTER 3

England and Wales

Irish migration into England and Wales was fairly negligible until the 19th century, when many Irish Catholic laborers, called *spailpíns* (or "spalpeens" in English), flocked to mainland Britain to find work, to benefit from the Poor Law or simply to avoid famine.

*A *spailpín* trudges through the English countryside, seeking laboring work.*

The 1841 census records 60,000 Irish living on the mainland. Few wanted to stay permanently — many who came to Liverpool, for example, hoped to earn enough to pay for the passage to America. When they remained it was often accidental, not planned. Many came seasonally, and within living memory Irish people would walk from the ferry at Holyhead, Wales to wherever they could find summer work, culminating in hop-picking in Kent only to return with their wages to their families in Ireland. Many others came with their families, especially to settle in the industrial towns. Such migration often followed distinct patterns, i.e.:

• Yorkshire — many from Leinster and Connacht

• Bradford — mainly Dublin, Laois, Mayo and Sligo

• Leeds — mainly Mayo, Tipperary and Dublin

• Stafford — 40 percent from the Castlerea area of Co. Roscommon

The Great Famine brought in vast numbers, sailing to Liverpool, Swansea, Newport and Cardiff. Around 80,000 came in 1847 alone. The 1861 census shows a third of Cardiff's population was Irish. In Liverpool, where 300,000 people arrived in a mere six months, food was distributed from workhouse to 23,866 people *a day*. It was from Irish slums there that the typhus epidemic is thought to have started. After the Famine subsided, migration continued erratically: during World War II and in the 1950s when demand for manual labor was high, more Irish migrated to mainland Britain than to America.

Early migration

In the 4th century CE, western Britain was subject to constant raids from Ireland. The Úi Liatháin, kin to the Eóganacht of Munster, settled in parts of Wales and southwest Britain, while the Medieval Irish poem *The Expulsion of the Déisi* tells how Eochaid Allmuir ("from over the sea") of the Dési tribe from Co. Waterford, "with his descendants, went over the sea into the land of Dyfed, and his sons and grandsons died there. And from them is [descended] the race of the Crimthann over there." Linguistic and archaeological evidence in Dyfed supports this, and the old Welsh pedigrees proudly trace the kings of Dyfed and Brycheiniog back to Aed Brosc, son of Corath, son of this Eochaid of the Dési. The ultimate descendant of the Dyfed dynasty, Ellen ferch Llywarch in the 10th century, married Hywel Dda, King of Deheubarth, Gwynedd and Powys, ancestor of virtually everyone with Welsh princely blood in their veins.

The 13th-century English surnames Yreys, Irlond and Iryssh denote people from Ireland, but these may have been returning Cambro-Norman settlers, not native Gaels. This probably also applies to the MacWilliams, traders of Bristol who bought a landed estate at Stambourne, Essex, and are thought to be from the MacWilliam Oughter branch of the Burkes of Connacht. We know Irish beggars had become a problem by Tudor times because an Act of 1572 was framed to send them home. Later, besides the army, Irishmen were prominent in the navy, and many an Irish sailor found home in the squalid slums of 18th-century St. Giles's, London.

Archives

Each county has its own County Record Office, supplemented by local archives and local studies libraries. Details, often with access to their catalogs, are at **www.a2a.org.uk**. Over these is The National Archives (TNA) at Kew, on the outskirts of London and the National Library of Wales, Aberystwyth. The Mormon's Hyde Park Family History Centre (FHC), London, has the largest collection of Irish material on microfilm in Britain: copies of MMFs can be ordered to any local branch — see **www.familysearch.org**.

Societies

The SoG, London, has a lot of material for both English, Welsh and Irish research. As many Irish migrants were Catholics, it is worth joining the Catholic Family History Society and studying the publications of the Catholic Record Society.

Civil Registration

This is the mainstay of genealogical research back to July 1, 1837, when it started, and was thus operational just before the influx caused by the Great Famine. The records are arranged by

The birth places given in the 1881 census for a street in Farnworth, Lancashire, full of families of laborers and cotton mill workers. Rather unusually, Irish counties of birth are given and it's striking that all are in Connacht — mainly Galway, but also Sligo, Roscommon and Mayo. This underlines the fact that migrants often came in company and preferred to settle among people from their own ancestral area.

The Emigration Agents' Office where passage money was paid; Between decks on an emigration vessel; Departure of the *Nimrod* and *Athlone* steamers from Cork, with emigrants on board for Liverpool. From *The Illustrated London News*, May 10, 1851 (courtesy of National Library of Ireland).

the quarter of the year (March, June, September and December) in which the event was registered, and registration was usually within six weeks of the event.

Births record both parents' full names and father's occupation.

Marriages give ages of both parties, residences and occupations (many women's occupations are left blank, even if they actually worked very hard!), and names and occupations of fathers.

Deaths state name and address of an informant — often this will be a close relative. Deaths to June 1969 state age at death, and thereafter the date of birth.

The indexes are with the Registrar General at the Family Records Centre, but this is due to close. They are online at **www.genesreunited.com** and **www.findmypast.com**. A single index to the periods 1866-1920 and 1984-2002 is at **www.familyrelatives.org**, and an almost complete index for 1837-1901 is at **www.freebmd.org.uk**. You can order records from the Registrar General at **www.gro.gov.uk** or 0845 603 7788. You must purchase certificates — the information isn't released any other way — at £7.00 each, but if you know a detail that will definitely appear on the record, such as a father's first name, you can have the record checked and receive a partial refund if the document you ordered turns out to be the wrong one.

Censuses

British censuses have been taken from 1801, though only a handful before 1841, are any use to genealogists. The 1841 census lists everyone in each household, with occupations and ages rounded down to the nearest five years (someone aged 29 would be listed as 25). Those born in Ireland are marked "I," those from Scotland "S," while those born in England and Wales answered "Y[es]" or "N[o]" to the question "were you born in this county?" From 1851, precise ages, relationships to the head of household and places of birth are stated. Those within mainland Britain are usually accurate down to parish level, but the Irish-born are usually just recorded as "Ireland." The censuses from 1881 are more likely to give an Irish county or even parish; it's worth seeking Irish immigrants in all possible censuses.

CERTIFIED COPY OF AN ENTRY OF MARRIAGE   GIVEN AT THE GENERAL REGISTER OFFICE

Application Number G212416

191_7_. Marriage solemnized at *St Luke's Church Great Crosby* in the *Parish* of *Great Crosby* in the County of *Lancaster*							
Columns. No.	When Married.	Name and Surname.	Age.	Condition.	Rank or Profession.	Residence at the time of Marriage.	Father's Name and Surname.	Rank or Profession of Father.
120	First September 191_7_	William Petticrew Johnston	32	Bachelor	Manufacturer	Ardenza Knock Belfast	Samuel Johnston	Director
		Gladys May Archer	26	Spinster		Chesterfield Road Great Crosby	Charles Edward Archer (Deceased)	Gentleman

Married in the *Parish Church* according to the Rites and Ceremonies of the *Church of England* or after *Banns* by me, *F.G. Bartlett*

This Marriage was solemnized between us, *W.P. Johnston* / *Gladys May Archer* in the Presence of us, *Ernest C Johnston* / *Rebecca Archer*

CERTIFIED to be a true copy of an entry in the certified copy of a register of Marriages in the Registration District of **West Derby**
Given at the GENERAL REGISTER OFFICE, under the Seal of the said Office, the **23rd** day of **April 2007**

MXD 177831

CAUTION: THERE ARE OFFENCES RELATING TO FALSIFYING OR ALTERING A CERTIFICATE AND USING OR POSSESSING A FALSE CERTIFICATE ©CROWN COPYRIGHT
WARNING: A CERTIFICATE IS NOT EVIDENCE OF IDENTITY.

It is unusual to see Irish places of residence stated explicitly on mainland British Civil Registration certificates, but here's one: although he married in Great Crosby, Lancashire, William Petticrew Johnston, a 32-year-old manufacturer, was resident at "Ardenza," Knock, Belfast. The certificate names his Irish father, Samuel Johnston, a director. The fact that he was from Belfast and had a surname that is of Scottish origin makes it no surprise that he married in a Protestant, not a Catholic, church.

Unfortunately, many Irish migrants to mainland Britain viewed census takers with great suspicion, so claimed to have been born wherever they were living. The antidote is to seek them in several censuses, hoping to find the truth. The 1911 census will be released in 2012, that for 1921 in 2022 and so on according to the 100-year secrecy rule.

Censuses are at the Family Records Centre (soon to be moved to TNA), and are fully indexed and available online at **www.genesreunited.com** and **www.ancestry.com**, with transcripts of the 1881 census at **www.familysearch.org**.

1911 census

Before 2012, the 1911 census can be searched for specific addresses for £45 per search. See **www.nationalarchives.gov.uk/1911census** for more details.

Directories

Directories existed in England from the 17th century, becoming very detailed and widespread from the mid-19th century onwards. They list very few Irish laborers, but are useful for locating and tracking the movements of the slightly better off.

Religious registers

Anglican parish registers started in 1538, though few survive before 1600. Most are in County Record Offices and many — not all — are indexed at **www.familysearch.org**. Transcripts of a good number are at the SoG.

Protestants from Northern Ireland are more likely to appear in registers of Presbyterian chapels. Presbyterianism was widespread in England during the mid-17th century. Though made legal in 1698, it rapidly lost ground to Methodism in the next century. Surviving registers are mostly indexed in **www.familysearch.org** with the originals in

TNA series RG 10, as described in D.J. Steel, *Sources for Nonconformist Genealogy and Family History* (Phillimore for SoG, 1973). More information can be sought at United Reformed Church Archives.

Most Irish immigrants were Catholics. Catholicism survived Henry VIII's 16th-century Reformation, but rapidly dwindled to a hard core of nobles, gentry and their tenants. Since 1791 Catholic chapels were legalized: in many cases the first ones built in towns — Bradford, Halifax and Rotherham, for example — were for Irish famine migrants. Priests tended to be the younger sons of the surviving English Catholic gentry, many of them Lancastrian; it was not until the 20th century that the Irish Catholic priest (usually with a hip-flask of whiskey secreted in his cassock) became a familiar figure in England.

Registers are usually with the relevant church. All are cataloged by M. Gandy, *Catholic Missions and Registers 1700-1880* (M. Gandy, 1993) in six volumes covering England, Wales and Scotland and his *Catholic Parishes in England, Wales & Scotland: An Atlas* (M. Gandy, 1993). The major 19th century ones, such as those in Lancashire (where Catholicism had survived more comprehensively, and to which vast numbers of Irish immigrants came), have been published by the Catholic Record Society.

In 1853, municipal cemeteries were established and many Catholics chose to be buried there rather than in Anglican graveyards (as was the norm). Catholic priests could perform their ceremonies there, recording details in their own burial (or, more correctly, death) registers. In addition, look out for confirmation registers, lists of prayers for anniversaries of deaths, and lists of parishioners, called *status animarium* ("state of souls").

Newspapers

Newspapers started in 17th-century London and became widespread on a local level in the 19th century. Look for local papers in local archives where they are sometimes indexed. The best collection of local, national and foreign papers, including Catholic ones, is at the British Library Newspaper Library, cataloged at **www.bl.uk/ collections/newspapers.html**. News concerning everything from medal recipients to bankrupts appear in the *London Gazette* (1665–present), *Gentleman's Magazine* (1731–1868) and *The Times* (1785–present), the latter indexed in *The Times* Digital Archive, available in several good libraries including Guildhall Library,

---

Catholic marriages

English Catholic baptisms seldom list addresses or fathers' occupations, but during the 19th century many marriage registers from areas influenced by Continental priests, especially in London, started listing parents' residences, many of which were back in Ireland. Numerous Catholic marriages in Liverpool are indexed at **http://freepages.genealogy.rootsweb.com/ ~hibernia/mar/mar.htm**. The late Fr. Godfrey Anstruther's Catholic Marriage Index at the Institute of Heraldic and Genealogical Studies, Canterbury, has been fully transcribed by Peter Steward of the Parish Register Transcription Society. It covers mainly London and Essex from the earliest date of the registers (c. 1700) to about 1880 with some entries up to 1942. It is full of Irish families, for example:

12 June 1859 at Commercial Road, London, by W. Kelly Phillip Noble of 42 Berner Street, son of Henry and Mary Noble of Scherwin, Germany, married Joanna McGonigle of 161 Georges Street, daughter of James and Mary McGonigle of Kilrush, Clare, Ireland, witnesses Joseph Noble and Margaret Hughes.

An extraordinary 80 files of marriages and 11 of baptisms, all originally transcribed and indexed by Fr. Anstruther, now on a CD barely 2½ inches across.

London. Catholics newspapers include *The Tablet* (1840) and *The Universe* (1860). In addition, James Peter Coghlan (1732–1800), a London printer, filched *The Laity's Directory* publishing title from its founder, James Marmaduke, in 1760. Coghlan, who was Lancashire-born but clearly of Irish origin, maintained this vital organ of English Catholic life throughout the time of the Gordon Riots (1780) and when he died he left it to his wife's nephew and employee Richard Charles Brown (1776–1837), brother of the first Catholic bishop of Liverpool. Brown, my 4 x great-grandfather, ran it in partnership with Patrick Keating, styling themselves "Brown & Keating, printers to the R.R. the Vicars Apostolic." They continued *The Laity's Directory* until his death, and Brown's widow Jane (née Hemsworth) took it on for a few years. She gave up in the face of the rival *Catholic Directory* that continues to this day. These publications list many births, deaths and marriages for Catholics in England, including many of Irish origin.

Biographical dictionaries

The *Oxford Dictionary of National Biography* (OUP, 2004) is the best, covering all of Britain and Ireland up to independence. Also useful are the broader volumes of *Who's Who*. For prominent Catholics (Irish or not), see Joseph

Marriages. 13 jun 1919

LEICESTER—SAMUT.—On Tuesday, June 3, at St. George's Church, Worcester, with Nuptial Mass, by the Rev. Father Bernard Grafton (uncle of the bridegroom), Captain Philip Austin Leicester (late of the Worcestershire Regiment), eldest son of Alderman Hubert A. Leicester, K.C.S.G., J.P., and Mrs. Leicester, to Nella, eldest daughter of Captain C. Samut, R.A.M.C., and Mrs. Samut, of Valetta, Malta.

HUGHES—WALL.—On June 3, at Corpus Christi Church, Maiden Lane, with Nuptial Mass, by the Rev. B. P. Wall (brother of the bride), Patrick Hughes, M.B., B.S., son of Patrick Hughes (of Omagh, Ireland), and Ada Mary Wall, daughter of the late Daniel Wall and Mrs. Wall, of Isleworth.

Marriage announcements from *The Universe* in 1919, helpfully giving the Irish home of the Hughes family.

A scene of chaotic devotion in an Irish Catholic chapel — children play on the font, a young woman sways in prayer and on the floor an old lady mutters her rosary.

Gillow's *A Literary and Biographical History, or Bibliographical Dictionary of the English Catholics* (Burns & Oates, 5 vols., 1885–1902).

Wills

Back to January 12, 1858, wills have been proved centrally at the Principal Probate Registry (PPR). Searches can be made there: indexes forward to 1943 are also on fiche at many archives and Mormon FHCs.

Before 1858 wills were proved in church courts, as mapped in *The Phillimore Atlas and Index of Parish Registers* (Phillimore, rev. edn., 2003) and **www.genuki.org.uk**, and described in J. Gibson and E. Churchill, *Probate Jurisdictions, Where to look for Wills* (FFHS, 5th edn., 2002). Those with property in more than one jurisdiction or with the social pretension to be the sort of people who might, had wills proved in the next most senior court — usually

The will of Major General Thomas Hawkshaw of London and Dublin, dated October 11, 1817 and proved in the PCC in 1819, names various lands, daughters, friends and dependants, and his wife. Not atypically, he refers to their marriage settlement — "a certaine Indenture Deed or Settlement executed on the Marriage and by and between her late father Robert Percival of Nice Brook in the County of Meath Esqr and her Mother Frances Percival otherwise Armstrong the wife of the said Robert both since deceased..." — giving us the wife's parents and even her mother's maiden name! Note: this poor copy is normal — the sort of quality with which we often have to contend!

The will of my great-grandfather William Denning, an Irish immigrant, names both his wife and one Patrick O'Donoghue, who was actually a cousin of his, then living in Belfast.

I WILLIAM DENNING of The Lodge D'Abernon Chase Leatherhead in the County of Surrey Head Gardener and Bailiff hereby revoke all former wills and testamentary instruments heretofore made by me and declare this to be my last will and testament

1. I appoint my friends Patrick O'Donoughue of 178 Antrim Road Belfast Ireland and Joseph Kirgan of 3 Lower Lake Battle in the County of Sussex (hereinafter called "my trustees") to be the EXECUTORS and trustees of this my will

2. I bequeath to the said Joseph Kirgan the sum of ten pounds (free of duty) as a slight acknowledgment for the trouble he shall be put to in acting as an executor and trustees of this my will and I declare that my trustees shall be entitled to reimburse themselves all expenses incurred by them in connection with the administration of my estate

3. I bequeath to my wife Mary Denning (free of duty) an annuity of one hundred pounds for her life to commence from my death and to be considered as accruing from day to day but to be by equal quarterly payments the first payment to be made at the end of three months after my death and I bequeath to her my furniture and personal effects for her own use absolutely

the local bishop's — rising ultimately to the Prerogative Courts (of the Archbishops) of York and Canterbury. The latter — the PCC — included people, usually the wealthier sort, from all over the realm including those with property in both Ireland and the mainland, money in the Bank of England or who died abroad ("in foreign parts," often abbreviated to "pts") including soldiers and sailors. Between 1653 and 1660 under Cromwell, all wills in England and Wales were proved at the PCC too. Most Welsh wills are at the National Library of Wales. Those for York are at the Borthwick Institute and are largely covered by published indexes. All wills proved at the Prerogative Court of Canterbury (PCC) are indexed and accessible at **www.documentsonline. nationalarchives.gov.uk**.

Shipping lists

The journey across the Irish Sea was a domestic one, so virtually no passenger lists between Ireland and the mainland exist. Those that do are arranged by port and date and don't state places of origin anyway, making searches impractical and largely fruitless.

Other sources

Naturalizations: see p. 136 (naturalizations in Ireland).
Armed forces : see p 126.

further reading
■ A. Adolph, *Collins Tracing your Family History* (Collins, 2005).
■ M. Hartigan, *The History of the Irish in Britain: a Bibliography* (London, 1986).

Irish roots revealed

My cousins Dominic and Ruth Cassidy are a perfectly "normal" British couple: he was born in West London and she in Newport, South Wales. Digging into their roots, however, reveals recent ancestry from Germany, Scotland, Nigeria and Ireland. Dom's father, who sounds entirely English, is a Cassidy (*Ó Caiside*, a Fermanagh family, originally physicians and *ollamhs* — court poets — to the Maguire Princes of Fermanagh), while Dominic's equally very "English" great-grandmother was a Kilduff (*Mac Giolla Dhuibh*, descended, coincidentally, from the Princes of Fermanagh themselves). Dominic's mother's family of Bohane, long-since synonymous with Tunbridge Wells, Kent, were originally *Ó Buadhacháin*, traceable far back to his 3 x great-grandfather Patrick Bohane, born in Co. Cork about 1804 who became a marine store dealer in Pembroke, Wales. Ruth's mother's father was a Nigerian sailor who settled in Newport, while on her father's side her great-grandmother Mary Ann was brought over from Co. Waterford to Newport, Wales at the height of the Great Famine by her own mother, Jane White. Her family has a story that Jane "was so ill on the voyage she swore to settle in the first house she saw. This was not far from the truth," Ruth tells me, "for she settled in rooms in Canal Parade — a stone's throw from the river wharf where the family arrived."

Dominic Cassidy's maternal great-grandparents, pictured at Wadhurst, Sussex, were all English-born, but did not have very much English ancestry: Frank Bohane's roots lay in Co. Cork, Isabella Rietchel née Kilduff's father was from Co. Offaly, Julius Rietchel's father was from Saxony, Germany, and Helen Bohane née Brizard was of French extraction.

CHAPTER 4

Scotland

Scotland was originally called Alba. The Scots were Irish invaders and by the expansion of their kingdom to encompass the whole of Alba, the name Scotland was born.

Scots later migrated into Ireland due to the Plantations (see p. 201), but in the 19th century, there was a great backwash of Protestants and Catholics alike fleeing the Great Famine. By December 1846, Glasgow had acquired a population of 26,335 Irish paupers. Many moved on to the Grassmarket, West Port and Cowgate areas of Edinburgh where they lived crammed into the city's narrow wyndes and closes. In June 1847, anti-Irish rioting led to many being sent back to Ireland — but those who survived this trauma often had no choice but to return nonetheless.

This Scottish birth certificate shows that James Crowley was born on February 19, 1863, at Borthwick's Close, Cowgate, St. Giles's, Edinburgh, the son of James Crowley, a mason, and Helen, formerly Hunter, who married on November 25, 1851 in Co. Leitrim, Ireland (it turns out this date was inaccurate — but only by a day!)

Archives

The National Archives of Scotland (NAS), the General Register Office and National Library of Scotland (NLI) are all in Edinburgh, and there is an excellent network of local record offices and archives detailed at the Scottish Archives Network website, **www.scan.org.uk/**.

Civil Registration

This started on January 1, 1855. Births from 1855–1905, marriages from 1855–1930 and deaths from 1855–1955 can be searched and seen at **www.scotlandspeople. gov.uk**. Coverage is likely to be extended, but for the years not covered you can search at Scotland's General Register Office.

Births: mothers' maiden names appear in birth indexes from 1929. Certificates for 1855 and from 1861 onwards show the same categories of information as recorded in England and Wales, with the addition of date and place of parents' marriage — which, if it is in Ireland, is a massive advantage. Those for 1855 alone also record the ages and places of birth of the parents and details of the child's older siblings.

Page 80.

1863. BIRTHS in the *District* of *Saint Giles* in the *City* of *Edinburgh*

No.	Name and Surname.	When and Where Born.	Sex.	Name, Surname, & Rank or Profession of Father. Name, and Maiden Surname of Mother. Date and Place of Marriage.	Signature and Qualification of Informant, and Residence, if out of the House in which the Birth occurred.	When and Where Registered, and Signature of Registrar.
238	James Crowley	1863 February Nineteenth 3h. P.M. Borthwicks Close Cowgate Edinburgh	M.	James Crowley Mason — Helen Crowley M.S. Hunter 1851 November 25th Co. Leitrim	James Crowley Father	1863 March 2d At Edinburgh Wm Sutherland Asst Registrar D
239	Mary Smallan	1863. February Twenty First 3h. P.M. Campbells Close Cowgate	F.	Edward Smallan Masons Labourer — Rose Smallan M.S. McTague	Cross Smallan Her X Mark Mother Wm Sutherland Asst Registrar	1863. March 2d At Edinburgh Wm Sutherland Asst Registrar

Rightly or wrongly, the pedigrees of many prominent Scottish clans and of the Scottish kings themselves connect back to the ancient Irish genealogies and thus to the stem of Milesius, the traditional ancestor of the Gaels.

In the 3rd century CE, Eochaidh Dubhlen, son of the Irish High King, married Alechia, daughter of Updar, King of Alba (Scotland) and had three sons, known as the *Three Collas* (princes). Colla Uais, who died about 337 CE, was ancestor of Fergus Mac Carthann (sometimes incorrectly conflated with Fergus Mor Mac Erc — see below), father of Godfrith (d. 853), Taoiseach (Lord) of the Isles. Godfrith's descendants included Dughgall, ancestor of the MacDowells, and Somerled (d. 1164), Thane of Argyll and founder of the Kingdom of the Isles whose own 3 x great-grandson was Domhnall, ancestor of the MacDonalds. Meanwhile, the Campbells, Earls of Argyll claimed descent from Dairmuid Ua Duibhne, 4 x great-grandson of Fedhlimidh Rachtmar (d. 119 CE), 108th High King of Ireland (the father of the famous Conn of the Hundred Battles, legendary High King of Ireland).

The Medieval pedigrees of the Scottish kings, as recorded in both Scotland and Ireland, show their descent, rather confusingly, from two King Fergusses, both of Irish origin. The first (surely legendary) Fergus was the 3 x great-grandson of Fiacha Firma, son of Aeneas Tuirmeach-Teamrach (d. 324 BCE), High King of Ireland. Fiacha was abandoned at sea in a small boat but drifted to safety in Argyll, where he established the Irish colony-kingdom of Dal Riada. Later, when the Irish colonists were under attack from the native Picts his descendant Fergus returned to become the king.

By the 2nd century CE we hear for sure of the Irish kingdom of Dalriada that spanned northeast Ulster and the Argyll Peninsular of Scotland. It may have had its roots in that earlier Dal Riada or that may have been a legend created to give ancient legitimacy to the Ulster tribe's presence on the mainland. The later Scottish Dalriadan kings claimed descent from the second King Fergus Mor Mac Erc (d. 501 CE), son of Muireadach of Ulster (a grandson of Niall of the Nine Hostages — see p. 165) and his wife Erca, daughter of Lorne, descendant of the earlier Fergus (but note that somewhat contradictory pedigrees

make Fergus Mor son of a king called Erc who was in turn son of this king Lorne). Fergus Mor was sent to Scotland to help the Dalriadans against the invading Picts and ended up being elected king. He was the ancestor, through a line considered by many to be highly accurate, of Kenneth MacAlpin, King of Dalriada in 848-9 CE, who also ruled the Pictish kingdom to the east and thus became first king of all (or most) of Scotland, the ancestor of the subsequent Scottish monarchs. From Fergus Mor's brother Lorne, meanwhile, descended the Mormears of Moray, of whom the most famous was MacBeth (d. 1057) and the Earls of Moray and Ross.

The ancient genealogies make both Ferguses descendants of Milesius and thus of the Egyptian princess Scota (see p. 179), who in *Scottish* eyes was the eponymous founder of their race.

Kenneth MacAlpin, or Cináed mac Ailpín (b. after 800, d. 858), king of the Picts and the first king of the Scots, was the founder of the Scottish monarchy.

This Scottish death certificate shows that James Crowley died on December 9, 1895, at 61 High Street, Falkirk, Co. Stirling, aged 67, a journeyman mason (journeymen were day-laborers, rather than apprenticed master craftsmen). It says he was married to Helen Hunt and was the son of William Crowley, a deceased farmer, and Mary, formerly Wren. He died of senile decay (old age). The informant was his son James Crowley, then of Howeroad Cottage, Kilsyth.

Marriages: married women are indexed under both maiden and married names. Certificates include names of both parties' mothers and fathers, including mothers' maiden names. Women often kept their maiden names after marriage.

Deaths: ages are given in the indexes from 1868 and dates of birth from 1969. Mothers' maiden names are given from 1974. Certificates for 1855 alone record names of offspring, and those from 1855 to 1861 record place of burial. For 1855 and since 1861 they provide name of spouse and the deceased's parents, including father's occupation and mother's maiden name. This may identify a whole generation back in Ireland, though as everyone concerned is likely to have been dead this offers much scope for error.

Scott Crowley, a great-great-grandson of James and Helen, revisits Borthwick's Close. Grim as these dwellings are now, it's still very difficult to visualise them in the 1860s, crammed to bursting with desperately poor Irish families living in the most squalid conditions imaginable.

The General Register Office also has indexes to:

- consular births and deaths from 1914 and marriages from 1917.
- army births, marriages and deaths for Scots in British bases worldwide from 1881.
- deaths of Scots in the armed forces for the Boer War and World Wars I and II.
- births and deaths of Scots or children of Scottish fathers in British aircraft from 1948.

Censuses

These were taken every ten years between 1841 and 1901 and are indexed at **www.scotlandspeople.gov.uk**. They are almost identical to Ireland's and England's, but from 1861 they state the number of rooms with one or more windows, whether people were employers and if so how many people they employed. In 1841, births outside Scotland are identified "I" for Ireland, "E" for England and "F" (foreign) for everywhere else.

Directories

Edinburgh's directories started in 1773 and Glasgow's in 1783. For most poor Irish immigrants they're more useful for providing background on communities and chapels than naming individuals. As time passed, however, they became broader in their coverage and Irish families became more established, making directories an increasingly useful source.

Religious registers

In 1560, through the work of John Knox, Presbyterianism became Scotland's

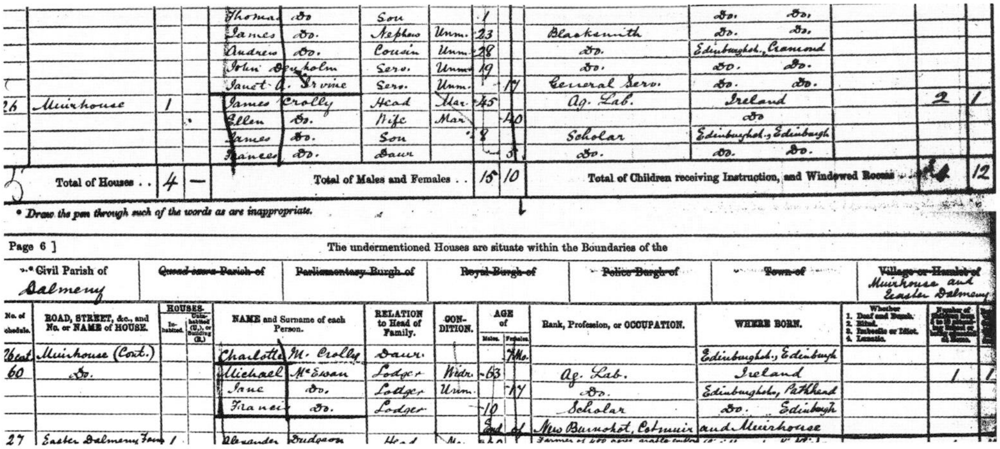

No. of Schedule	ROAD, STREET, &c., and No. or NAME of HOUSE	Houses Inhabited	Uninhabited	NAME and Surname of each Person		RELATION to Head of Family	CONDITION	AGE Males	AGE Females	Rank, Profession, or OCCUPATION	WHERE BORN		Number
				Thomas	Do	Son		1			Do.	Do.	
				James	Do.	Nephew	Unm.	23		Blacksmith	Do.	Do.	
				Andrew	Do.	Cousin	Unm.	28		Do.	Edinburghsh.,	Cramond	
				John	Dunholm	Serv.	Unm.	19		Do.	Do.	Do.	
				Janet A.	Irvine	Serv.	Unm.		17	General Serv.	Do.	Do.	
26	Muirhouse	1		James	Crolly	Head	Mar.	45		Ag. Lab.	Ireland		2 1
				Ellen	Do.	Wife	Mar.		40		Do		
				James	Do.	Son		8		Scholar	Edinburghsh.,	Edinburgh	
				Frances	Do.	Daur			5	Do.	Do.	Do.	
	Total of Houses . .	4	—		Total of Males and Females . .			15	10	Total of Children receiving Instruction, and Windowed Rooms		[illegible]	12

* Draw the pen through such of the words as are inappropriate.

Page 6] The undermentioned Houses are situate within the Boundaries of the

Civil Parish of Dalmeny | Quoad sacra Parish of | Parliamentary Burgh of | Royal Burgh of | Police Burgh of | Town of | Village or Hamlet of Muirhouse and Easter Dalmeny

No. of Schedule	ROAD, STREET, &c., and No. or NAME of HOUSE	Houses Inhabited	Uninhabited	NAME and Surname of each Person		RELATION to Head of Family	CONDITION	AGE Males	AGE Females	Rank, Profession, or OCCUPATION	WHERE BORN		Whether 1. Deaf and Dumb 2. Blind 3. Imbecile or Idiot 4. Lunatic	Number
26 cont.	Muirhouse (Cont.)			Charlotte	M. Crolly	Daur.			7 Mo.		Edinburghsh.,	Edinburgh		
60	Do.			Michael	McEwan	Lodger	Widr.	63		Ag. Lab.	Ireland			1 1
				Jane	Do.	Lodger	Unm.		17	Do.	Edinburghsh.,	Pathhead		
				Francis	Do.	Lodger		10		Scholar	Do.	Edinburgh		
								End of		New Barnton, Cotmuir	and Muirhouse			
27	Easter Dalmeny Farm	1		Alexander	Dudgeon	Head								

The 1871 census shows James and Helen Crowley (spelled James and Ellen Crolly) eight years after they were living in Edinburgh. They had made their way to Muirhouse, near Easter Dalmeny farm, Dalmeny, Co. Linlithgow, where James was working as an agricultural (i.e. farm) laborer. They occupied two rooms; three lodgers occupied a separate part of the same building.

established church. Presbyterianism differed from the CoE, CoI and Catholicism by scrapping the hierarchy of archdeacons, bishops and so on. Each parish was self-governed by elected elders meeting in "kirk sessions," choosing its own ministers. Representatives of neighboring congregations met in Presbyteries, which sent representatives to the General Assembly.

All surviving registers are indexed to 1854 at **www.scotlandspeople.gov.uk**. Some go back to 1553, but few survive before the mid-18th century. The newer editions of the *Phillimore Atlas* (see p. 38) include parish maps and dates of commencement of registers. Marriage registers generally record not the event itself but proclamations of intention to marry, which often amounted to much the same. Few parishes recorded burials, but the parishes' administrative records, the kirk sessions, often include "mort cloth dues" — the fee paid for renting out the kirk's black shroud for funerals.

Relatively few gravestones were erected or survive before the mid-19th century: much of what survives has been collected by the Scottish Genealogical Society. Some Scottish baptisms and marriages from different denominational records are at **www.familysearch.org**, but the index is far from complete.

Frederick Crowley (in the patterned sweater), grandson of James and Helen, with his family in Glasgow in the 1940s. Some 85 years after migration, this Irish family was thoroughly assimilated into Scottish life, but his children's names — Anthony, Valerie, Patricia and Brian — are still as Irish as they come.

Catholicism was made illegal in 1560 but remained a small, potent force. The risings of 1715 and 1745 contained strong Catholic elements. When the 1745 rising was crushed by the English, Catholics experienced severe persecution lasting until 1793. Most surviving pre-1855 Catholic registers are at the NAS, and those kept subsequently are with the churches: for a detailed guide see Gandy's books (see p. 36).

Newspapers

Scotland's extensive newspaper output can be examined at the NLS. *The Scotsman* (founded 1817) is now fully online to 1900 at **www.archive.scotsman.com**.

A late 19th-century Glasgow directory full of Irish names (courtesy of SoG).

(directory excerpt)

road & 5 West Princes street
Oatman Francis & Co. slaters, 14 Holmhead st.; T.N.4,330
Oatts J. Lumsden, writer (Lindsay, Meldrum & Oatts), 20 Queen's drive, Crosshill
Oatts William M. secretary Y.M.C.A. 70 Bothwell street; res. 81 Berkeley street
O'Brien Mrs. Agnes, clothes dealer, 20 Jail square
O'Brien Daniel, fent dealer, 219 Main st. Rutherglen
O'Brien Hugh, shoe maker, 57 West Scotland street, K P
O'Brien James, fish merchant & curer, 12 East Howard street & Fish market
O'Brien John, basket maker, 42 Elderslie street
O'Brien John, dairy, 6½ Stevenson street, C
O'Brien John P. produce broker (Horgan & O'Brien), 31 Rose street, Garnethill
O'Brien Joseph F. fish merchant (James O'Brien), 10 Abbotsford place
O'Brien Mrs. Margaret, laundry, 9½ Dale street, B
O'Brien Thomas, undertaker & coach & cab proprietor, 11 North Woodside road; T.N. 96; res.30 Northburn st
O'Brien William V. fish merchant (James O'Brien), 10 Abbotsford place
Ocean Accident & Guarantee Corporation Limited (James Beattie, res. sec.), 79 West Regent st. See advert
Oddy Benjamin, grocer, 49 Plantation st. Plantation
Odling Anselm & Sons Lim.marble masons,68 Bishop st.A
O'Donnell John, manager, 35 Rose street, Garnethill
O'Donnell Roger, dairyman, 56 George street
Oetzmann&Co.artistic furnishing depot,302Sauchiehall st
Ogden Charles, ironmonger, 266 Thistle street, S.S
OggBros.genl.drapers,milliners&c.2 to 20Paisley rd.we.K.P
Ogg George, draper (Ogg Bros.),22Bruce rd.Pollokshields
Ogg Henry, shopkeeper, 526 Rutherglen road, S.S
Ogg R. Alexander, draper (Ogg Brothers), 46 Melville street, Pollokshields
Ogg Robert Allan, warehouseman (Copland & Lye), Over-dale, Millbrae road, Langside
Ogg Wm. A. draper (Ogg Bros.) ...

Oliphant Thos.writr.(Oliphant&Jackson),Brownlea,Blntyre
Olive & Partington (Manchester), paper manufrs. (John A. Stewart, man.), 63a, St. Vincent street; T.A. "Partington"; T.N. 4,702
Olive (The) Tan Leather Co. tanners & curriers, 20 Henrietta place, C
Oliver Brothers, lard, grain & provision merchants, 61 & 63 Robertson street; T.A. "Olivers, Glasgow"
Oliver, Kirk & Co. tea merchants, 48 Robertson street; T.A. "Hindoo, Glasgow"
Oliver W. P.&Co.accountants, 75 Buchanan st.; T.N.3,811
Oliver Alexander, grain mer. (Oliver Bros.), 2 Royal ter
Oliver Cunningham, grain mer. (Oliver Bros.),2Royal ter
Oliver Francis, boot maker, 67 Main street, Tollcross
Oliver James, painter, 9 Wellshot ter.Main st.Shettleston
Oliver Jn. C. tea mer. (Oliver, Kirk & Co.), 2 Royal ter
Oliver Mrs. Margaret, draper, 54 Main street, B
Oliver Mrs. Mary, draper, 167 Ingram st.; res. 578 Cathcart road
Oliver Robert, bootmaker, 9 Rae pl. Main st. Shettleston
Oliver William P. accountant (W. P. Oliver & Co.), Hope bank, Dunoon
Ollendorf Henry, merchant, 109 Hope street; T.A. "Ollendorf, Glasgow"
Olswang Samuel, furniture broker, 36 Cook street, T
O'Malley Michael, bootmaker, 85 Bedford street, S.S
O'Malley Michael, ham curer & provision dealer, 76 & 104 Govan street, S.S
O'Malley Patrick, bootmaker, 659 Govan road, Govan
Omnet John, smith, 15 Norfolk street, G
O'Neil Miss Agnes, hardware dealer, 111 Bernard street
O'Neil Mrs. Annie, china &c. dealer, 24 Saltmarket & 132 King street, Trongate
O'Neil Charles, coal dealer, 593 Govan road, Govan
O'Neil James, dairy, 800 Springburn road
O'Neil James, draper, 368 Caledonia road, S.S
O'Neil John, greengrocer, 30 Gloucester street
O'Neil John, shopkeeper, 8 Eaglesham street, Plantation

Poor Relief

Where they survive, Poor Relief records can provide superb details on poor Irish immigrants. They date from 1845, though nothing survives for Edinburgh, Dundee or Aberdeen. However, the Glasgow area, where most Irish migrants went, is very well covered to 1948, specifically for Glasgow (from 1851), Barony (1861), Govan (1876) and other local parishes in Bute, Dunbartonshire, Lanarkshire and Renfrewshire. They are at the Mitchell Library indexed to 1900. Records can include name, age, marital status, religion, occupation; name, age and income of spouse; details of children, siblings and parents. They will say why the application was being made and, crucially, most state the place of birth which, if it is in Ireland, can be the clincher for your research.

Sometimes the solution was repatriation. *The Returns of Poor Removal from England, Wales and Scotland to Ireland, 1870-80* (HMSO), specially published for Parliament, contain many examples. In 1876, Mary Brown or Davidson, aged 60, was removed from Maybole, Ayrshire, described as "a perfect pest, often chargeable for short periods, cleared to Cootehill [Co. Cavan]." In 1875, the widow of Matthew Watson, 30, with children aged 8 and 6, who had been in Ayr for three years, was repatriated having gone "voluntarily to visit relatives in County Antrim."

Poor Relief was often distributed to the poor through workhouses. This workhouse at Barnhill, Glasgow, opened in 1853, was described in 1882 as "a very capacious asylum for the children of poverty and well adapted by its cleanliness, ventilation and position to mitigate the ills of their condition."

Wills

Inheritance of land was so strictly governed in Scotland that rather than bother writing wills (which bequeath land) people tended only to make testaments, dealing solely with moveable goods. These were proved by local commissary courts under the Principal Commissariot of Edinburgh, which also dealt with Scots owning goods in Scotland but who died elsewhere. From 1824 testaments were proved in county sheriffs' courts. All documents 1513–1901 are indexed and viewable at **www.scotlandspeople. gov.uk**. Those from 1901 are at the NAS.

Other sources

Biographical dictionaries: see p. 27, *Oxford Dictionary of National Biography*.
Naturalizations: see p. 136 (under Ireland).
Shipping lists: see p. 39 (under England).
Armed forces: see p 126 (under Ireland).

Poor Law records

This page from the Mitchell Library's Poor Law records tells us much about people in Scotland and also back in Ireland. The Irish parents of both the widow Catherine Stewart (née Clark) and her late husband Philip Stewart are given and we learn that both Catherine and Philip were from Co. Cavan, she being from "Billturbet," also called Annagh or Cloverhill, only three parishes away from my great-grandfather Denning's home parish of Drumgoon. This was found for the family tree of TV presenter Lorraine Kelly, which I traced for British TV show GMTV. Lorraine's great-great-grandmother Mary is listed further down the page already married to John Kelly. The reverse of the document, not shown here, states that Catherine made her living as a street hawker and stubbornly refused to go to hospital despite having been ill.

TV presenter Lorraine Kelly.

CHAPTER 5

United States of America

Today, thanks to the mass migration of the 19th century, over 40 million US citizens claim Irish roots, and 25 percent of them are pure Irish blood. The main destinations for immigration were California, New York, Massachusetts and Pennsylvania, with the cities of Boston, Chicago, San Francisco and New York having substantial Irish populations — the latter was one-third Irish by 1861 was nicknamed "the most Irish city in the world." The Irish rapidly dominated many police and fire departments and were a major element in the army, railroad building and politics.

A St. Patrick's day card — designed for Irish emigrants, it illustrates the strong association between America and Ireland, c. 1911.

Archives

The National Archives and Records Administration (NARA) has an excellent collection of census returns and ships' passenger lists. The Library of Congress has a vast collection of published family histories, cataloged at **www.lcweb.loc.gov**. The foremost compendium of printed pedigrees is F.A. Virkus, *The Abridged Compendium of American Genealogy, First Families of America, a Genealogical Encyclopedia of the United States* (7 vols., 1925-42, GPC reprint, 1987). The Mormons' Family History Library (MFHL), Utah (see p. 19), is second to none for American research and, because of its magnificent microfilm collection, is one of the best places for tracing Irish ancestry too.

Most original records are held locally, such as at county court houses. It's always important to learn when communities were founded, and where its founders came from, as this can explain lack of early records and suggest where else to look when following the trail back to Ireland.

Societies

America has a plethora of genealogy societies. Of note are the National Genealogical Society, The Irish Genealogical Society International, which publishes *Septs*, and TIARA (The Irish Ancestral Research Association). The site **www.irishabroad.com/yourroots/** has much for Americans with Irish roots.

Colonization of America

According to *The Voyage of Saint Brendan*, St. Brendan, who was from Munster, sailed west in the 6th century CE and landed in "a spacious land with apple trees bearing fruit… they took as many of the apples as they wanted and they drank from springs, and then for forty days they wandered over the land but they could not find an end to it." Examining the legend in *Land to the West* (Collins, 1963), Geoffrey Ashe concluded that while the legend could not be proved definitively, it could well be correct.

After its rediscovery by Columbus in 1492, the English made several failed attempts to colonize North America until Virginia was established in 1607. Many records of early settlers, including their near-perpetual disputes with London, are in the published State Papers (Colonial) series. The practice of sending "rogues, vagabond and sturdy beggars" to the Americas, initially the West Indies, started in 1597. Cromwell sent many of his opponents there in the 1650s to work as laborers or, really, slaves.

The Transportation Act (1717) regularized the system, and by 1770 some 30,000 people, a third of whom were Irish, had been sent to the Americas. Indeed, one of North America's grievances that led to the Revolutionary War of 1773–84 was that they had become a dumping ground for convicts. Many Irish immigrants — from both free and convict backgrounds — were, understandably, on the revolutionary side: 13 of the Declaration of Independence's signatories, along with the man who printed it, had Irish roots.

By 1790, the USA numbered 3 million people of whom 44,000 were Irish-born, 150,000 were of Irish parentage and an unknown number more had earlier Irish roots. The Great Famine caused a huge population movement from Ireland to America. Because they brought disease with them, Irish immigrants weren't always welcome: New York's Staten Island quarantine station was attacked and burned down by angry neighbors in 1858.

Immigrants arriving at Ellis Island, New York Harbor, c. 1900.

President Kennedy

Several recent presidents, including Ronald Regan and Richard Nixon, were of Irish origin but none was more famously Irish than John F. Kennedy (1917–63). His great-grandfather Patrick Kennedy (1823–58), of Dunganstown, Co. Wexford, married Bridget Murphy, probably of Owenduff, Co. Wexford. In fact, all the president's great-grandparents were Irish. His middle name, Fitzgerald, is from his mother Rose Elizabeth Fitzgerald (1890–1995), whose paternal grandfather and maternal grandmother were Fitzgeralds from Bruff, Co. Limerick. Their surname suggests descent from the Cambro-Norman Geraldines (see p. 195).

An enumerator filling in an 1870 census form (sketch by Thomas Worth, 1839–1917).

Civil registration

Civil registration for births and deaths started in the late 18th century in certain cities such as New Orleans (1790), and on a state level in the 19th century, beginning with Massachusetts (1840), the latest to start being Georgia (1919). Marriages were performed by clergymen or justices of the peace; licenses were issued by county clerks and civil registration only started in the late 19th or early 20th century. Each state differs in its start dates, accessibility of its records and the amount of information recorded. The best sources are www.cyndislist.com under the individual state, and A. Eakle and J. Cerny, *The Source: A Guidebook of American Genealogy* (Ancestry, new edn. 1996 by L. Szucs and S. Luebking). At best civil registration records can tell you how long an immigrant had lived in America, whether they were naturalized, and where they came from, though this will usually just be the country, not exact place, of origin.

Some civil registration is becoming available at www.ancestry.com. The US Social Security Death Index (1962–96), available at www.familysearch.org, includes dates of birth. It's an excellent way of tracing where the descendants of immigrants ended up.

Censuses

There have been censuses every ten years since 1790. All are searchable to 1930 at www.ancestry.com (with 1880 free at www.familysearch.org too). Up to 1840 they recorded heads of households with numbers but not names of other people present, divided into sexes and age groups — frustrating for lack of detail, but not entirely uninformative. From 1850, all names and ages are recorded along with place of birth and the relationship to the head of the household is stated from 1880. Much of the 1890 census was accidentally burned. From 1880–1920 the countries of birth of everyone's *parents* is stated as well. Those for 1900 state how long people had been in America. Those for 1910 indicate on which side veterans of the Civil War had fought. Censuses will tell you who was from Ireland, but don't state precise places of origin.

Directories

Flourishing from the 19th century, these are especially strong for cities where many Irish migrants went and list much of the working population. They are a great source for tracking ancestors year by year, thereby working out roughly when they arrived, and identifying possible relatives living nearby.

Religious registers

In fortunate cases these go back to the foundation dates of communities. Most are with their churches or church archives and most are on MMF. Some records, especially marriages,

SCHEDULE 1.—Free Inhabitants in *Dist 2th City of Springfield* in the County of *Sangamon* State of *Ill.* enumerated by me, on the *14* day of *July* 1860. *J. H. Clemie* Ass't Marshal.

Post Office *Springfield*

1	2	3	4	5	6	7	8	9	10	11	12	13	14	
1		John B. R. Worthen	5	m					Ills					1
9	997 976	Lotus Niles	40	m		Secretary	7000	2500	N.Y					9
12	1001 988	Henry Carrigan	58	m				30000	300	Ireland				12
13		Susan	50	f					"					13
14		Hugh	24	m		Livery Stable			"					14
15		Henry	12	m					Ills		1			15
16	1002 989	Abraham Lincoln	51	m		Lawyer	5000	12000	Ky					16
17		Mary	35	f										17
18		Robt. S.	16	m					Ills		1			18
19		Willie W.	9	m					"		1			19
20		Thomas	7	m					"					20
21														21

American writer F. Scott Fitzgerald (1896–1940) was of Irish descent; his father was Edward Fitzgerald, and his mother was Mary (Mollie) McQuillan, the daughter of an Irish immigrant.

Judy Garland (1922–69) described herself as Irish and Scottish. In fact her father's family (the Gumm family) was a mixture of English, Irish, Scottish, French Huguenot (Protestant) and German. On her mother's side, her great-grandmother, one of thousands of orphans as a result of the Irish Famine, was raised in a Dublin convent.

may identify migrants' places of origin. Church archives, more so Protestant ones, may also contain letters of recommendation written by the migrant's clergyman back home.

Newspapers

Much is available in local and state repositories and increasingly online. Especially in the late 19th and early 20th centuries, obituaries for migrants *or their descendants* often state the place of origin. Also worth seeking are reports of ships' arrivals and adverts for people in America or Ireland seeking relatives. Such adverts from the *Boston Pilot* (1831–1916), for example, are published by the New England Historic Genealogical Society as *The Search for Missing Friends*. Catholic newspapers flourished locally in the 19th century, including *Philadelphia's Erin* (1822) and the *Catholic Advocate and Irishman's Journal* (1823). By 1911 there were 321 of them: see www. newadvent.org/cathen/11692a.htm

James Denning, 81, Pioneer Livestock Man, Succumbs

James Denning, 81, prominent Idaho livestock man, died Monday at 10:25 a. m. at a local hospital following a lingering illness.

A colorful figure of the west for nearly half a century, Mr. Denning operated his ranch on Medicine Lodge river until December, 1943, when he sold his interests and retired, moving with his wife to Idaho Falls where they have since made their home.

He was born at Coothill, Cavin county, Ireland, June 15, 1863, the son of James and Elizabeth Denning. At the age of 21' he came alone to the United States and remained in New York for about 10 years in the employ of Senator W. A. Clark.

He then came west with Senator Clark to Butte, Mont., and after being there a short time came to Arco with one of the senator's sons and together they formed a partp in the cattle business.

Later he became affiliated with ank Swauger in the livestock iness at Arco. They then pured a ranch on Medicine Lodge started raising sheep. A few rs later the partnership was ssolved and Mr. Denning continued operating alone.

Married in New York

In 1908 he returned to New York and on March 2 of that year he was united in marriage to Miss Elizabeth McCabe of the metropolis.

They returned to the west and a ew years later he combined his interests with those of Sam Clark and sons and together they operated as the Denning and Clark Livestock company for several years.

After Mr. Clark's death, several years ago, Mr. Denning took over the entire ranch property and livestock, operating it until he retired about a year ago.

member of the Catholic ch, Mr. Denning was a fourth degree member of the Knights of Columbus at Salt Lake City.

He was also affiliated with the Elks lodge 1087 at Idaho Falls.

Besides his widow, he is survived by one sister, Mrs. Annie McMahon of New York City. The body is at the McHan and Buck Funeral home. Services will be announced later. Burial will be in New York.

ABOVE: My great-great-uncle James Denning settled in Idaho, where his newspaper obituary provides an excellent biography with precise details of where and when he was born and who his parents were. His mother, however, was in fact called Rose, not Elizabeth.

ABOVE RIGHT: James Denning and his wife, pictured probably not long before he died.

Biographical dictionaries

There are many of these for cities and states, and overall the *Dictionary of American Biography* (Charles Scribner's Sons, 1996).

Wills

Most wills were proved in local county courthouses (which also house local legal records); many are on MMF.

Naturalizations

These often state residence and occupation, the ship of arrival and date and rough place of birth, though seldom in any detail — usually you'll just find "Ireland." They are normally at the court where the naturalization took place. From 1868, however, they were issued at Federal Naturalization Centers, though detailed records only date from 1906. L.D. Szucs, *They Became Americans* (Ancestry, 1997), goes into detail. The NARA have pre-1906 federal naturalization indexes for Maine, Massachusetts, New Hampshire and Rhode Island up to 1906, and for all states from 1906 until 75 years ago (i.e. 1932 for people searching in 2007). Citizenship applications up to 1941 and passport applications 1795-1919 are on MMF.

Shipping lists

The best overall guide to passenger lists for ships between Ireland and America is www.genealogybranches.com/irishpassengerlists.

Some lists of Irish people leaving for America have been published, especially B. Mitchell, *Irish Passenger Lists, 1803-06, Lists of Passengers Sailing from Ireland to America Extracted from the Hardwick Papers* (GPC, 1995) (about 4,500 people) and B. Mitchell, *Irish Passenger Lists 1847-71, Lists of Passengers Sailing from Londonderry to America on Ships of the J. & J. Cooke Line & the McCorkell Line* (GPC, 1988) (about 27, 500 people).

Generally, the best records are at the port of arrival. Some have been published and are indexed in P.W. Filby and M.K. Meyer, *Passenger and Immigration Index* (Gale Research Co., 3 vols., 1981) with annual supplements to 2000, now also on CD (to 1999) from Family Tree Maker's Family Archives (#354).

Records of immigration and passenger lists at the American end are mostly at the NARA. Customs passenger lists date from 1820 and will only state the country of origin, but the Immigration Passenger Lists that started in 1883 will state the last place of residence — in many cases the actual place of birth.

For the Great Famine, see I.A. Glazier and M. Tepper, *The Famine Immigrants, Lists of Irish*

Immigrants arriving at the Port of New York 1846-51 (GPC, 7 vols., 1893-6). Over 600,000 Famine immigrants, named in passenger lists and New York port arrivals, are indexed at **www.ancestry.com**. The database **www.irishgenealogy.ie/famine_ship** is a record of ships arriving 1846-51. Many Irish came through New York's Castle Garden 1830-92 (see **www.castlegarden.org**) and Ellis Island 1892 and 1924 (**www.ellisisland.org** — these can also be searched *without* knowing the migrant's initials at **www.jewishgen.org/ databases/EIDB/ellis.html**).

Army records

Most pre-20th-century army records concern the Revolutionary War (1773-84) and Civil War (1861-5). Army service and pension records are in state archives (especially for Confederate states) and at the NARA (as described in Meredith S. Colket Jr. and Frank E. Bridges, *Guide to Genealogical Records in the National Archives* (National Archives and Records Administration, 2001). A useful guide to Civil War records is **www.illinoiscivilwar.org/cwgeneal.html**. There are also social societies, such as the Daughters of the American Revolution, whose membership is for those who can prove descent from revolutionary soldiers, including many Irishmen, and whose archives are therefore rich sources.

Land records

Land records are among the most useful American sources. Originally, land was granted by the monarch and after the Revolution, by the federal government. Subsequent land transfers were recorded in deeds and re-grants which tend to be recorded comprehensively, mostly in county courthouses. In areas where religious records are sparse or lost, evidence of landownership and transfer is often a key element to proving an American family tree.

Sentenced to transportation

Many Irish criminals, even those who committed what we would now consider rather petty misdemeanors, ended their days on the gallows. For the rest, the usual punishment was transportation to British colonies. Many 17th- and 18th-century settlers in America and the Caribbean until the American War of Independence, were in fact transportees.

The main sources for transportation have been collated and indexed in:

- P.W. Coldham, *The Complete Book of Emigrants in Bondage 1614-1775* (GPC, 1990).
- J.C. Hotten, *The Original Lists of Persons of Quality, Emigrants, Religious Exiles, Political Rebels, Serving Men sold for a term of years, Apprentices, Children stolen, Maidens pressed and others who went from Great Britain to the American Plantations 1660-1700 from MSS preserved in the State Paper department at the PRO* (GPC, 1962).
- W.M. Wingfield, *The Monmouth Rebels 1685* (Somerset Record Society, 1985) — for men sentenced to transportation after the Monmouth rebellion in Somerset, England, in 1685.

further reading

- A.K. Bradley, *History of the Irish in America* (Chartwell, 1986).
- J.P. Colletta, *They Came in Ships* (Ancestry, 3rd edn., 2002).
- The Mormons' *Irish Research Outline* (1st edn., 1993).
- D. Radford and K. Betit, *Ireland: a Genealogical Guide for North Americans* (The Irish at Home and Abroad, 4th edn., 1997).
- L.D. Szucs, *They Became Americans: Finding Naturalization Records and Ethnic Origins* (Ancestry, 1998).

CHAPTER 6

Canada

By 1867, 20 percent of Canada's population — some 174,000 people — had Irish roots. In 2001, this figure had risen to 3,822,665 people, some 13 percent of the total population. Brian Mulroney (b. 1939), Prime Minister of Canada (1984-93), for example, was the son of Benedict Mulroney who migrated from Bagenalstown, Co. Carlow.

Archives

The National Archives are in Ottawa. Each province has a provincial archive.

Civil registration

Civil registration started in the Canadian provinces as follows: Nova Scotia, 1864 (but excluded births and deaths between 1876 and 1908); Ontario, 1869; British Columbia, 1872; Saskatchewan, 1878; Manitoba, 1882; New Brunswick, 1888; Newfoundland, 1891; Alberta, 1897; Prince Edward Island, 1906; Yukon and Northwest Territories, 1896 and Quebec, 1926.

Records are with the provincial Registrars General and, Quebec excepted, access is usually only by application — see **www.cyndislist.com** under each province. Some records have been transferred to Provincial Archives, however, such as the 19th- and early 20th-century ones for Ontario and some earlier ones for British Columbia and Alberta. **www.ancestry.com** now has some Ontario and British Columbia Civil Registration online.

Censuses

Early censuses include one for Nova Scotia from 1770 and of heads of household for Ontario (1842, 1848 and 1850) and Quebec (1825, 1831 and 1842). Canada has had full censuses every ten years from 1851, though those for 1851 and 1861 are mainly concerned only with Ontario, Quebec, Nova Scotia, New Brunswick and Newfoundland, the lands further west not yet having been colonized. The whole of Canada, such as it was, is covered by censuses from 1871 onwards and those up to 1901 are available for searching. The 1881 census is at **www.familysearch.org** and 1901 is online at **www.collectionscanada.ca/02/020122_e.html** and **www.automatedgenealogy.com/census/cache/NationalSummary.jsp**.

Directories

Those for Montreal date from 1819, with many for the cities from the mid-19th century. They are fairly inclusive in terms of householders,

Composite illustration of British emigrants en route from Liverpool, England, to Canada, published in the *Illustrated London News*, November 15, 1884.

Colonization of Canada

Canada was colonized from the 17th century by the British in Newfoundland and the French in Quebec. In 1670, the British founded the Hudson's Bay Company, to promote trade and colonization. British control spread, especially due to the Seven Years War between England and France. The capture of Quebec achieved by General James Wolfe (see p. 54) at the cost of his own life led to British control of all Canada.

The Irish came in the highest numbers in the 18th and 19th centuries — as free settlers (as opposed to convicts). From about 1807, merchants shipping timber to Britain for the navy realised they could make money carrying settlers the other way and tried to encourage migration. In 1825, the government commissioned Peter Robinson to bring 2,000 new settlers from Ireland to Peterborough, Ontario, where they were given land, a cow, and implements including kettles and three bushels of seed potato. Colonization of Canada continued throughout the 19th century and in some senses it is still ongoing.

Migration between Canada and America has been constant and researching Irish roots in one country often involves looking in the other as well. Because the passage to Canada was cheaper than to America, many Irish, especially Famine migrants, went there and then tramped south. They were seldom welcomed, for they often carried diseases acquired in Ireland or on the voyage. In fact, quarantine stations had operated at Grosse Isle at the mouth of the St. Lawrence River from 1832, but they were far too small for the Famine years. With ships lining up right down the St. Lawrence, the system collapsed and fever-ridden Irish refugees flooded into Quebec, Montreal and St. John's.

Records of US-Canada border crossings between 1895 and 1956 are now on **www.ancestry.com**.

however humble, sometimes listing occupations as well as addresses.

Religious registers

Copies of many of Canada's surviving church registers of all denominations including Catholics and Presbyterians are on microfilm at the National Archives of Canada. The earliest are from 1620 in Quebec, but many started much more recently, when settlements (with churches) were founded in the wilderness. In New Brunswick, marriages were also reported to county clerks, and records up to 1888 are at the Provincial Archives. Marriages often name both sets of parents. All Prince Edward Island baptisms 1777-1906 are indexed and online to 1886 at **www.gov.pe.ca/cca/index**.

Newspapers

There are good collections at the National Archives, provincial archives and libraries, many of which have collections of clippings of genealogical interest, such as the Alberta Provincial Archives' "old timers" clippings 1956-9, relating to people who had settled there

Eviction was an ever-present threat for many Irish families impoverished by crop failures. In the quest for a new life, Canada was a favored destination — passage there was cheaper than to America. Here, we see (ABOVE) an evicted family at Glenbeigh, Ireland, in 1888, and (BELOW) evicted Irish folk in Powell's celebrated painting (c. 1871).

This page from the *Ottawa Citizen* lists deaths and provides details of family relationships. In the case of **Stanley Moore** it shows that his parents were from Northern Ireland.

How Irish was Captain Wolfe?

Although born in Kent, England, James Wolfe (1727–59), the great British general who was killed while successfully capturing Quebec from the French, had Irish roots. His father was General Edward Wolfe (1685–1759), whose brother Captain Walter retired to Dublin, and whose sister Margaret married George Goldsmith, a cousin of the writer Oliver Goldsmith. John Ferrar's *History of Limerick* (1787) makes Edward a grandson of Captain George Wolfe of Limerick, a Royalist who fled to England, but the genealogist and herald Sir Anthony Wagner argued that this was not true, and that Edward's father was actually an earlier Edward Wolfe, an army officer of Dublin. When James II came there, Wolfe was thrown out for being a Protestant but later rejoined under William III. Records at the Deeds Registry, Dublin, show,

"that in 1686 Edward Wolfe of the City of Dublin, later a Major, had a lease of a moiety of the lands of Kilmurry and Kilmekanoge in the half barony of Rathdowne, County Wicklow, for the lives of himself, his wife Margaret and his son Edward and that on his death at some date before 1715 his son Walter Wolfe was substituted for him in the Lease, while in 1715, his daughter Margaret Goldsmith and her son George were also added to it."

Wagner thought it most likely that this senior Edward was the son of an earlier Edward. A petition in the Cromwellian State Papers by Jane, widow of Lieutenant-Colonel Edward Wolfe, states that the latter accompanied Cromwell to Ireland in 1649, but died six months later at Youghal, Co. Cork, leaving her with six small children. So much for the earlier link to Limerick, though as Edward MacLysaght (see p. 155) points out the Irish Wolfes were all ultimately of Cambro-Norman origin anyway.

General James Wolfe, lying mortally wounded during the siege of Quebec, 1759.

B12 The Ottawa Citizen, Monday, August 26, 1991

DEATHS

Continued from previous page

MOORE, Stanley Stuart
At home after a lengthy illness on Saturday, August 24, 1991, Stan Moore of Ottawa, age 59 years. Beloved husband of Ann Marie Honkanen. Dear son of George and Margaret Moore of Northern Ireland. Brother of Helen (wife of George Lesley) of Toronto and Ann (wife of Ken Hedley) of Northern Ireland. Survived by seven nieces and nephews and close friends. Friends may call at the Tubman Funeral Home, Westboro Chapel, 403 Richmond Road at Roosevelt, 7 to 9 p.m. Sunday, Monday, Tuesday. Cremation. Those who wish may make memorial donations to the Canadian Cancer Society.

Deaths

McCULLOCH, Cecilia Anne
Peacefully in hospital, on Saturday, August 24, 1991, Cecilia McCulloch; beloved wife of the late Thomas Arthur McCulloch. Dear mother of Allan (Martha), Peter (Yvonne), Ross and Marilyn (Gill). Loving grandmother of Jessica, Jennifer, Christopher, Julie, Kim, David, Michael, Tracey, Stephen, Kiri and great-grandmother of Devon and Dylan. Private family service. Memorial contributions to the Heart and Stroke Foundation of Ontario would be appreciated. Funeral arrangements by the Central Chapel of Hulse, Playfair & McGarry, 233-1143.

McMULLIN, May
In hospital on Saturday, August 24, 1991, May McMullin, in her 68th year. Loving mother of Michael and his wife Lynn. Dear mother-in-law of Roger and Laurie Bonis. She will be greatly missed by her family and friends. Special thanks to the nursing staff of the Riverside Hospital. Friends may call at the Central Chapel of Hulse, Playfair & McGarry, 315 McLeod Street, on Tuesday, August 27, 1991, from 1 to 3 p.m. Service in the Chapel at 3 p.m. Interment Capital

before 1905. Some material is online (see **www.cyndislist.com**).

Biographical dictionaries

The main one is the *Dictionary of Canadian Biography* (University of Toronto Press/OUP, 1966–91).

Wills

These are divided between provincial probate registries and local county or judicial district offices. Details are on **www.cyndislist.com** and in Baxter's guide (see "Further Reading" on p. 55).

Naturalizations

As Ireland was part of the British Empire, no naturalization was needed.

Land grants

There are many petitions and grants of land in the Canadian National and particularly the provincial archives, as described by Baxter. Those for Quebec and Ontario date from the 17th and 18th centuries respectively. B.D. Merriman, *Genealogy in Ontario, Searching the Records* (Ontario Genealogy Society, 3rd edn., 1996) is particularly useful for Irish settlement there.

A scene at Grosse Isle, Canada, on the St. Lawrence River. Fearful that a tide of Irish immigrants might engulf them, Americans insisted that some immigrants be diverted to Canada. By the spring of 1847, the St. Lawrence was jammed with vessels loaded with immigrants awaiting processing at the Grosse Isle Quarantine Station.

Shipping lists

The main collections of ships' passenger lists are at the National Archives of Canada. They date, sporadically, from 1745 and are complete from 1865 for Quebec and Halifax. Usually, you need to know the port and rough date of arrival. The lists may not tell you much more, though it's helpful to see with whom your ancestors arrived, as they seldom left home alone. Some provincial archives have records of organized parties of immigrants, such as Peter Robinson's (see p. 53). **www.irishorigins.com** has a growing database of British and Irish arrivals in Canada for 1890.

Hudson's Bay Company

The provincial archives of Manitoba contain the records of the Hudson's Bay Company, founded in 1670, and copies are available on film elsewhere, including TNA. Wills of employees date from 1717 and ships' logs from 1751, but few personnel records exist before 1770. Thereafter they can be extremely useful.

Empire Loyalists

There were undoubtedly people with Irish roots among the 70,000 Empire Loyalists who settled in Canada from America after Britain lost the American Revolutionary War in 1784. They made claims (now at the National Archives of Canada's audit office) for loss of land. The United Empire Loyalists' Library is an excellent starting point for research. For the most part, however, the Irish in America were very happy *not* to support the British Crown!

further reading

■ A. Baxter, *In Search of Your Canadian Roots: Tracing Your Family Tree in Canada* (GPC, 1999).

■ C. Houston and W. Smyth, *Irish Emigration and Canadian Settlement* (University of Toronto Press, 1990).

■ D. MacKay, *Flight from Famine: The Coming of the Irish to Canada* (McClelland & Stewart, 1992).

■ R. O'Driscoll and L. Reynolds, (eds.) *The Untold Story: The Irish in Canada* (2 vols., Celtic Arts of Canada, 1988).

CHAPTER 7

Argentina

In all, about 45,000 Irish people migrated to Argentina in the 19th century, resulting in some 800,000 people there now having at least some Irish blood.

Three brothers, Carlos Miguel MacAllister, Horacio Alfredo MacAllister and Nelson Rodolfo MacAllister, pictured in Pergamino City, Buenos Aires (1955). As third generation Irish descendants, they kept their Irish surname but under the law their first names had to be Spanish.

Archives

Argentina's main archives are in Buenos Aires, particularly the Archivo General de la Nacion and Bibliotheca Nacional, with other central and provincial archives as identified below.

Societies

The Instituto Argentino de Ciencias Genealógicas, Buenos Aires, is the country's main genealogical society.

Civil registration

Birth, marriage and death records are called *partidas*. Civil registration started in 1886 for Buenos Aires City, in 1890 for Buenos Aires Province and other parts of Argentina around the same time. Each municipality has a *Registro Civil*, with duplicate records at the relevant Judicial or Provincial Archives. Most Irish migrant families appear in the records of Buenos Aires Province. Births include ages and nationalities (so, before 1922, the Irish were "British"). Early birth records sometimes list grandparents' names. There are also *recognitions* of children by their fathers. Marriages list all four parents' names and nationalities.

Irish family reunions are taking place the world over. This MacAllistair clan gathering took place in May 2005 at the Hurling Club in Buenos Aires, and comprises MacAllistars from Argentina and Co. Dublin, Ireland.

Migration to Argentina

Irish missionaries and Wild Geese (see p. 207) were instrumental in the Spanish conquest of South America and its subsequent settlement. Dublin-born Hugh O'Connor (1734–97) became Hugh Oconór in the *Regiment de Aragon* and Viceroy of New Mexico, fighting the Apaches and Comanches and founding Tucson, Arizona. Ambrose O'Higgins (1721–1801) from Ballina, Co. Sligo, followed a similar route to become Viceroy of Peru, ennobled as Baron de Ballenary and Marquis de Osorno. His son Bernardo O'Higgins (1780–1846) was the Liberator of Chile, where a province now bears his name. Under these luminaries, many Irishmen fought in South America's wars. The army Simon Bolivar used to liberate Bolivia included many Irishmen. The Irishmen of the St. Patrick's Battalion who died in the Mexican-American war of 1847 are commemorated by a memorial in Mexico City.

The first Irish to reach Argentina were probably the Galway-born sailors who participated in Ferdinand Magellan's circumnavigation of the globe in 1520. Later Irish participants in the Spanish colonization of Argentina included Dr. Michael O'Gorman (d. 1819), who founded the Buenos Aires' school of medicine. The British Army that temporarily invaded Argentina in 1806–7 included several hundred Irish soldiers who remained there, farming the rich pampas lands just as their ancestors had done in the Irish Midlands.

William Brown, born in Co. Mayo in 1777, arrived in Buenos Aires in 1812 and went on to found the Argentinean Navy. Later, General John Thomond O'Brien (1796–1861) from Baltinglass, Co. Wicklow, became aide-de-camp to José de San Martín, the general who liberated Argentina and Chile from European rule. In 1827, O'Brien visited Ireland to encourage people to settle in Argentina, hoping both to bolster the Argentinean economy with skilled sheep farmers and also to recreate a sort of Gaelic Eden, far from the rapacity of the British Empire. Irish merchants too, such as Patrick Cullen and the Sheridan brothers, encouraged migration on board their ships that returned otherwise empty from Liverpool. However, the length and dangers of the voyage put off most until the Famine years. In 1889, a smaller wave of 1,772 poorer people, mainly from Dublin and Limerick, came on the *City of Dresden*, encouraged by the Argentine government's promise of free passage and land. The promise of land was broken and many of the immigrants found themselves destitute. The "Dresden Affair" discouraged further significant migration. "Buenos Aires is a most cosmopolitan city," ranted the Catholic Archbishop of Cashel in *The Freeman's Journal* in 1889, "into which the Revolution of 1848 has brought the scum of European scoundrelism. I most solemnly conjure my poorer countrymen, as they value their happiness hereafter, never to set foot on the Argentine Republic however tempted to do so they may be by offers of a passage or an assurance of comfortable homes."

The 1889 intake aside, most Irish immigrants were younger children of middling tenant sheep farming families from the Irish Midlands: half were from Co. Westmeath, with significant contributions from Longford, Offaly, Wexford, Clare, Cork and Dublin. They settled mainly in the rich pastures around the mouth of the River Plate, near Buenos Aires and Santa Fé, spilling over into modern Uruguay with some becoming merchants in Buenos Aires itself.

A strong sense of Irish identity was maintained by mutual self-help, intermarriage and the deliberate policy of their priests. They founded a Gaelic Athletic Association and Hurling Club, supported the struggle for Irish independence and were known collectively by a misnomer, *gauchos ingleses*. "In no part of the world," proclaimed *The Southern Cross* (January 16, 1875), "is the Irishman more respected and esteemed than in the province of Buenos Aires; and in no part of the world, in the same space of time, have Irish settlers made such large fortunes."

Under Argentinean law, all children had to be registered with Spanish names. The first generation of Irish born there tended to give their children Hispanicised Christian names, such as Tomás for Thomas, but in normal life they used the Anglicized versions. Thomas Bulfin (1863–1910) from Co. Offaly wrote a very influential collection of stories of pioneering Argentina (*Tales of the Pampas*), and here all the Irish characters have Anglicized names — "Patrick Delaney," "Joseph Hagan," and so forth. However, the second and subsequent generations tended to use their Spanish names in Spanish.

Immigrants transported by horse-drawn wagon, Buenos Aires, Argentina.

Life on the Pampas

John Brabazon (1828–1914) came from a Protestant landed family in Mullingar, Co. Westmeath. His uncle was killed by Catholics for being "a Protestant dog," so John left for a better life in Argentina, reaching Buenos Aires in 1845. He rode to El Arazá, Chascomús, where he built his *puesto* and established a flock of sheep. Over the next 20 years he worked as "sheep-farmer, ditch-digger, builder, carpenter, wholesaler, stock farmer and merchant," and hunted with the Indians in his spare time. John became a Catholic to marry Honor MacDonnell in Buenos Aires, but she and her sisters were murdered by outlaw gauchos. His second marriage was to Mary Wallace, and he became a Justice of the Peace in Necochea, Buenos Aires Province in 1890 and died there in 1914. He recorded his adventures in a manuscript *The Customs and Habits of the Country of Buenos Ayres from the year 1845* which was published in 1981.

Censuses

Censuses were taken nationally in 1869, 1895 and 1914 and for Buenos Aires alone in 1855, the latter being the only significant area of European settlement. These and other local censuses, which include age, occupation and nationality, are at the Archivo General de la Nacion and provincial archives.

Religious registers

Church registers, mainly Catholic, are generally held by churches. A fire in 1955 destroyed many of the early Buenos Aires registers, but most for the 19th century — the key period of Irish

370

TABLA IV-1

Irlandeses e hiberno-argentinos censados en 1895 en la Provincia de Buenos Aires

Nombre	Edad (años)	Nacionalidad o lugar nac.	Estado civil	Ocupación o actividad
MacCarthy,Cornelius	11	inglesa	-	-
" ,Ann	9	id	-	-
" ,John	7	id	-	-
" ,Maria Elena	5	argentina	-	-
" ,Catalina	3	id	-	-
✗ " ,Timoteo	0	id	-	-
Darcy,Margaret	36	inglesa	viuda	cocinera
" ,Patricio	3	argentina	-	-
Callaghan,Daniel	60	irlandesa	casado	jornalero
" ,Ellen	55	id	id	-
" ,Thomas	22	id	soltero	-
" ,John	19	id	id	-
" ,Fermin	15	argentina	id	-
Moran,Juan	47	id	casado	estanciero
" ,Catalina	33	id	id	-
" ,Mario	8	id	-	-
" ,José	7	id	-	-
Casey,Patricio	36	id	casado	puestero
" ,Teresa	30	id	id	-
" ,Juan	4	id	-	-
8.-BARADERO a)Zona urbana				
Whelan,Isabel	56	argentina	casada	-
" ,Maria	18	id	soltera	-
" ,Elisa	14	id	id	-
" ,Timoteo	12	id	-	-
" ,Patricio	10	id	-	-
" ,Brigida	9	id	-	-
O'Rourke,Julián (1)	41	id	casado	hacendado
" ,Maria Esther	10	id	-	-
" ,Carmen	7	id	-	-
" ,Felisa	5	id	-	-
" ,Maria	4	id	-	-
" ,Manuela	1	id	-	-
" ,Patricio	1	id	-	-
b)Zona rural				
Brennan,Eduardo	38	argentina	casado	estanciero
" ,Catalina FitzSimons	38	id	id	-
" ,Maria	9	id	-	-
" ,Margarita	8	id	-	-
" ,Miguel	6	id	-	-
" ,Tomás	4	id	-	-

This extract from the 1895 Irish-Argentinean census for the province of Buenos Aires shows the acquisition of Argentinean nationality and Spanish first names among some Irish families, especially younger members (courtesy of Irish Seamen's Relatives Association).

migration — survive. Gravestones often identify precise places of origin in Ireland. Generally, they must be looked for in graveyards, as few have been transcribed.

Newspapers

The Irish community in Argentina was deliberately held together as a bastion against the British by its priests, led by Fr. Anthony Fahy (d. 1871) and his successor Fr. Patrick Joseph Dillon. Dillon founded *The Southern Cross* for this purpose in 1875, and it remains a focus for the

A crowded dining room at an immigrant hotel, Buenos Aires, Argentina.

Trounced by Evita

One Irish family rose to the very top of Argentinean society. Edelmiro Julián Farrell was born on February 12, 1887 in Villa de los Industriales, Lanús, Buenos Aires, son of Juan Farrell (b. 1846), who was in turn son of Matthew Farrell (d. 1860) from Co. Longford. Edelmiro joined the army and went to Italy to train under Mussolini's fascists. He then became a major general back in Argentina, and assisted in Pedro Ramierez's coup that made a president out of Arturo Rawson. Ramierez soon replaced Rawson, but was himself deposed in a pro-German coup at which point, in March 1944, Edelmiro Farrell became President of the Argentine Republic.

At the end of the war, Farrell began losing popularity to his vice president, Col. Juan D. Perón (1895–1974). Perón's overwhelming support from the poor and the younger element in the army was greatly enhanced by his charismatic wife Eva Duarte, known to the world as Evita. After the election of February 1946, Farrell conceded power to Perón. He lived on peacefully until his death at the Kavanagh Building, Buenos Aires, on 31 October 1980.

Evita, or Madame Eva (Maria) Duarte De Perón (1919–52), makes a rousing address during demonstrations by the General Federation of Labor to persuade President Perón to stand for re-election.

Joined-up genealogy

Eduardo Coghlan (1912–97) compiled two monumental works on Irish-Argentinean genealogy, *Los Irlandeses en la Argentina: Su Actuación y Descendencia* (Buenos Aires, 1987), and *El Aporte de los Irlandeses a la Formación de la Nación Argentina* (Buenos Aires, 1982). The former includes details of some 4,000 migrants and their families, using ships' passenger lists, the 1869 and 1895 censuses and much personal knowledge.

The website **www.Irishgenealogy.com.ar** is run by Dr. Rodolfo Martin MacAllistair. It contains a rich treasury of Irish-Argentinean pedigrees, many based on Coghlan, and is of much use and interest for people tracing Irish-Argentinean families.

Dr. Rodolfo Martin MacAllistair's family migrated to Pergamino, Argentina, in 1866, from Donabate, Co. Dublin. His pedigree, one of many on his site **www.irishgenealogy. com.ar**, was reconstructed mainly from gravestones, but also from photographs, family letters and civil registration. His brother Max, who lives in New York, is working on tracing back further, from Northern Ireland to Scotland, for the family were originally Galloglasses (see p. 200).

Dr. MacAllistair's great-grandfather, Charles MacAllistair y Fox, born in 1874 in Pergamino, Argentina, of Irish parentage. Besides owning a farm, "Santa Rose," Charles was the public relations agent for a British railway-building firm in Argentina. Though he spent his life in Argentina, he retained a lifelong love of his ancestral home, Donabate, Co. Dublin.

community. It is full of announcements of births, baptisms, marriages, deaths and funerals. *The Buenos Aires Standard*, founded in 1861 by the Mulhall brothers, published arrival lists. The newspaper's archive is at the Biblioteca Nacional.

Biographical dictionaries

The *Dictionary of Irish Latin American Biography* is online at **www.irishargentine.org/ bios1.htm**.

Wills

Although wills were seldom made, most families can be traced back through *sucesiones*, created when people died to enable their heirs to inherit property. They were made at local courts. All wills and *sucesiones* to 1900 are in the Fondo Documental of the Archivo General de la Nacion, with those from 1900 in the relevant provincial archives. The Mormons have filmed an "alphabetical and chronological Index of

A farm in Argentina, typical of the many established by Irish immigrants – indeed it does not look very different from a farm in Ireland at the time.

Bunk beds lined up in an immigrant hotel, Buenos Aires, Argentina.

Sucesiones" for all Argentina, 1600–1920 (letters C–K, 1614822 Items 1–2, and all other letters 1614822 Items 3–6).

Naturalizations

Records of migrants' naturalizations 1880–1929 are at the Centro de Estudios Migratorios Latinoamericanos, but while many Irish people were naturalized, the records do not state places of birth.

Shipping lists

The National Immigration Office holds many passenger lists that often give age, nationality, occupation and marital status.

further reading

■ M.J. Geraghty, 'Argentina: Land of Broken Promises,' *Buenos Aires Herald*, 1999, at **www.irlandeses.org/dresden.htm**.

■ A. Graham-Yooll, *The Forgotten Colony: A History of the English-Speaking Communities in Argentina* (Hutchinson, 1981).

■ A.C. White, 'Researching the Irish in Argentina,' *The Irish at Home and Abroad*, vol.. 5, no. 1, (1st quarter) 1998, p. 26–30.

CHAPTER 8

Australia

Australia's states and state capital (Canberra) were established in their present form in 1901. Many Australian politicians have been of Irish origins: they include Charles Gavan Duffy (1816-1903) from Co. Monaghan, Premier of Victoria, who had previously served a term in jail for his part in the struggle for Irish independence. Six of the seven Australian prime ministers between 1929 and 1949 had Irish ancestors, and more recently P.M. Paul Keating had relatives in Co. Galway.

Ned Kelly (1854-80) was born near Melbourne to Irish parents. His father, John "Red" Kelly, had been deported to Australia convicted for the alleged theft of two pigs, arriving in the penal colony of Van Diemen's Land in 1842. Ned gained his own criminal reputation from an early age, and was arrested for various crimes including robbing two banks. He was eventually hanged at Melbourne Jail in 1880. In this picture he is wearing his famous bucket helmet in a shoot-out.

Archives

The National Library of Australia includes Australia's Oral History Collections and the Register of Australian Archives and Manuscripts. The National Archives of Australia has branches in each state, which can be located through **www. naa.gov.au** (**www.nla.gov.au/raam/**). The Society of Australian Genealogists is in Sydney.

Civil registration

The dates of commencement in each state are: Tasmania, 1838; Western Australia, 1841; South Australia, 1842; Victoria, 1842; New South Wales, 1856; Queensland, 1856; Northern Territory, 1870; Australian Capital Territory, 1930. There are cumulative indexes (some of which are called "Pioneers Indexes") to most older civil registration records, on CD in most libraries and archives — an example is the *Victoria Pioneers Index* (1837-88). Records are held by state registrars. The amount of information varies from state to state, but generally records are more detailed then their equivalents in Ireland.

Birth records usually identify older siblings and say when and where the parents married.

Marriages generally state ages and places of birth — very handy for Irish immigrants — and all four parents of the bride and groom.

Deaths can show the deceased's parents' names, children and burial details. Those for

Early settlers

Captain James Cook discovered Australia in 1770. When the American Revolutionary War stopped the British sending convicts to America, it was decided to use Australia instead. The First Fleet of some 1,350 convicts set sail from Portsmouth, England, in May 1787 and arrived at Sydney Cove, New South Wales (NSW), the following January. On board were two Co. Offaly men, Captain David Collins and John White, the colony's new judge advocate and chief physician respectively.

The first convict ship from Ireland left Cobh, Co. Cork, in 1791, holding 159 prisoners. In the subsequent risings, many were arrested and loaded onto convict ships without trial, so that by 1798, 653 Irish convicts were living in New South Wales. Transportation to NSW ceased in 1840, but continued to 1852 in Tasmania. It started in Western Australia in 1850. Transportation from Ireland was halted altogether in 1853, but continued between mainland Britain and Western Australia to 1868. The very last ship's inmates included 63 Fenians (Irish nationalists), who had been tried in Britain.

By 1868, some 162,000 convicts had been transported. Of these about a quarter were Irish, although many "from England" probably had Irish roots too.

Many free settlers came too. The passage to Australia was too expensive for most Irish fleeing the Famine, but many still went there for the 1851 Gold Rush. Others were semi-free, such as the 4,000 orphan girls aged 14–19 who were sent from the Irish workhouses in the 1840s — their records are in the relevant state archives. About 500,000 free settlers had come by 1900, most of these between 1848 and 1886, and particularly from Munster. Tom Power of the Great Irish Famine Commemoration Committee, estimates that about 40 percent of Australians now have Irish roots — some 8 million people in all.

New South Wales from 1856 onwards give even more — the parents' ages appear on birth certificates, for example, and the place of marriage on death certificates. Check that the specific information you want is likely to be on a record before going to the trouble of seeking it — but the level of detail seldom makes the exercise a wasted one.

Censuses

There are population lists between 1788 and 1859 for Tasmania and NSW. There was a full census in 1828, including ages but not specific places of birth (published by the Library of Australian History, 1980, with copies in the main archives). A small section of the 1841 census of heads of households survives for NSW and is at **www.records.nsw.gov.au/ archives/1841_census_1068.asp**. Thereafter, all censuses have been destroyed, except for partial ones for NSW, 1885 and 1891. Those for 1901 and 1911 are at the National Library of Australia and the State Records Authority of NSW. The one for 1916 will be released — in 2100! An overview of population lists, which

D 63745

Registration of Births, Deaths and Marriages Act, 1973.

CERTIFIED COPY

DEATH REGISTERED IN NEW SOUTH WALES, AUSTRALIA

Surname of deceased	KELLY
Other names	Michael
Occupation / Sex and Age / Marital status	Farmer / Male 86 years / —
Date of death / Place of death	27th April, 1922. / HAMPTON, Shire of Blaxland.
Usual residence	—
Place of birth	Limerick, Ireland. / About 80 years in N.S.Wales.
Father - Surname / Other names / Mother - Maiden surname / Other names	KELLY / Daniel / KEOGH / Catherine
Place of marriage / Age at marriage / To whom married / Children of marriage	Hartley, N.S.Wales. / 23 years / Ellen Hartigan / Catherine 61 years, Daniel 59, James 57, Mary 55, Joseph 49, Ann 47, Susan A. 44. Living. One male and one female deceased.
Informant	James Kelly, Son, / 73 Hassans Walls Road, / Lithgow.
Cause of death	Senile decay.
By whom certified	John Malcolm (Registered).
Particulars of burial or cremation	28th April, 1922. / Roman Catholic Cemetery Lowther.
Particulars of registration	J. M. Bonthorne / District / Registrar, — Date 28th April, 1922. Number 538

I, Kevin Jack Irvine hereby certify that the above is a true copy of particulars recorded in a register kept by me.

Lithgow

The death certificate of Michael Kelly from NSW. Note that the information it gives on the Kelly family's Irish roots — Michael's county and his parents' full names — has been recorded here 80 years after the family emigrated. It might therefore be slightly inaccurate — but it is a far more detailed record than you would find if he'd stayed in Ireland! Michael's 3 x great-niece Jacqui, who is married to genealogist Jeremy Palmer (www. anzestry.com), has traced the Kellys back to Shanagolden, Co. Limerick, an area largely depopulated by the Famine: Lord Monteagle paid for many of his tenants to migrate, but the Kellys seem to have had to fund their voyage themselves.

are partial census substitutes, is at http://members.iinet.net.au/~perthdps/convicts/census.html.

Directories

The best substitutes for censuses are electoral lists and directories, listing householders, tradesmen and professionals in local and state archives.

Religious registers

Many early registers are with state civil registrars. A comprehensive guide is Nick Vine Hall, *Parish Registers in Australia, a List of Originals, Transcripts, Microfilms and Indexes of Australian Parish Registers* (N. Vine Hall, 2nd edn., 1990). Associated burial grounds can be found through Vine Hall's *Tracing Your Family History* (see p. 65). The Mormons have indexed many Australian religious registers on www.familysearch.org. Catholic ones are best accessed through relevant churches or diocesan archives.

Newspapers

Australian newspapers started in 1803 with the *Sydney Gazette and New South Wales Advertiser*. The state archives have excellent collections, as does the Dixson Library, NSW. Newspapers to 1900 — and much other useful genealogical material — are well surveyed in Sir J. Ferguson's, *Bibliography of Australia 1780-1900* (Angus & Robertson, 1941-69). For Catholic newspapers — relevant to most with Irish Catholic ancestry — refer to diocesan and archdiocesan archives. Many contain birth, marriage and death announcements, as well as details of arrivals and accounts of voyages.

Biographical dictionaries

The *Australian Dictionary of Biography* is online at www.adb.online.anu.edu.au/biogs/A060227b.htm. Also useful is H.W. Coffey and M.J. Morgan's *Irish Families in Australia and New Zealand 1788-1979* (H.W. Coffey, 1979-94, 4 vols.).

Wills

These were proved by state probate courts, and are detailed along with finding aids in Vine Hall's *Tracing Your Family History*.

Convicts and free settlers

Always contact the relevant state archives and local family history societies because they hold a lot of biographical material and finding aids for immigrants and look on the Internet to see if an Australian immigrant's ancestry has already been investigated. If not, they can be traced back through the records of their transportation and trial in the British Isles, especially the Colonial Office records at TNA, though the latter are often pretty brief and places of origin are seldom stated. Often, simply knowing where the trial took place gives at least a rough geographical area from which the convict is likely to have come.

Dublin Castle has records of the 40,000 Irish convicts transported from Ireland to Australia 1788-1868, including the convicted rebels of 1798. Copies were given to Australia by the Irish *Taoiseach* (chief) as part of the 1988 Bicentennial celebrations. They can be searched at www.nationalarchives.ie/search01.html and in Australian state archives. The Internet site

Two Irish girls

The Second Fleet of convict ships to leave Britain for America in 1790 included Mary Butler and Mary Desmont, who were apprehended in Covent Garden Market, London, with a basket containing nine pecks of French beans in August 1789. A passer-by became suspicious when he overheard them speaking Irish and they were accused of having stolen the beans. Mary Butler found love in New South Wales in the unusual person of John Randall, one of the handful of black transportees, and had three children by him.

www.pcug.org.au/~ppmay/convicts.htm lists convicts arriving from 1791 to 1831, who are not in previously mentioned website.

Because they tended to be poor, many Irish people living in England and Wales fell on the wrong side of the law and were among the convicts transported to Australia. Scots (and people in Scotland of Irish descent) who were sentenced to transportation were sent on English ships, so appear in the records at TNA too. For these, see D.T. Hawkings, *Criminal Ancestors: A Guide to Historical Criminal Records in England & Wales* (Sutton, 1992). This lists TNA sources for those sent to Australia, the main one being the registers of convict transportation 1787–1867 in HO 11, which are sadly unindexed.

The state archives, especially for NSW, Tasmania and Western Australia, have indexed their Convict Indents, which include date and place of trial and, latterly, the place of origin.

Besides convicts, many free settlers went to Australia, where they were granted or (later) sold land. Records of land grants are an important part of Australian research, and are covered in detail by Vine Hall. Those who came as assisted immigrants — people whose journey was paid for — are particularly well covered by indexes produced by the relevant state archives. For example, the University of Wollongong (**www.library.uow.edu.au/ archives/collections/irish.html**) has an online index of assisted Irish immigrants to NSW, 1848–67. These often state the person's age and ship, which leads you to passenger lists.

Australia's state archives hold excellent collections of ships' passenger lists (arranged by port of arrival), many of which have been indexed. They can be frustratingly brief, but at their best give the port and date of departure, age and country or place of birth.

Migrants on board a ship bound for a new life in Australia (picture courtesy of National Library of Ireland).

Magazines

Australia and New Zealand are well served by Irish-interest magazines, especially *The Ulster Link* for the northern Irish, and *The Australian Journal of Irish Studies* of the Centre for Irish Studies in Perth. *Irish Links* is sadly no longer being published, but back issues are in many libraries and archives around the world. It is a goldmine of information for its articles about Irish research, the information it contains on individual Irish families who settled in Australia and also as a means of finding out who may have researched your Irish-Australian family tree already.

further reading

■ **Nick Vine Hall**, *Tracing your Family History in Australia — A National Guide to Sources* (**www.vinehall.com.au**, **2002**).

■ **Nick Vine Hall**, *Tracing your Family History in Australia — A Bibliography* (**www.vinehall.com.au**, **2002**).

Vine-Hall writes that, of the 30 most popular family stories he's heard in his career as an Australian genealogist, "I think we are Irish!" is the most frequent.

CHAPTER 9

New Zealand

Some 17 percent of the population of New Zealand has predominantly Irish roots, though many more have a line or two of Irish ancestry. Captain William Hobson, who first proposed and later signed the Treaty of Waitangi with the Maoris, thereby founding the modern state of New Zealand, came from Co. Waterford. James Edward Fitzgerald (1818–96), a leading early statesman whom some consider to have been the country's first prime minister, was the grandson of Col. Richard Fitzgerald of Kilminchy Castle, Queen's County, MP for Boyle, who was shot in a duel in 1776.

Archives

The main archives are in Wellington, with a network of 12 provincial archives. The New Zealand Society of Genealogists (NZSoG) is in Auckland.

Civil registration

This started for Europeans in 1848 and was compulsory from 1856 (it was voluntary for Maoris, and not compulsory until 1913). Records are searchable at the Registrar General's office in Wellington and via microfilm copies elsewhere, such as branches of the NZSoG and the SoG, London.

RIGHT: **British naval commander William Hobson (1793–1842), who was appointed as first governor of New Zealand.**

FAR RIGHT: **Signing the Treaty of Waitangi with the Maori chiefs, which secured England sovereignty over the country.**

European colonization

New Zealand was first colonized by Europeans from the new Australian colony of New South Wales in the 1790s. It became a Crown Colony in its own right in 1840. Immigration was boosted by the discovery of gold, attracting many settlers from NSW and also direct from Ireland and Britain, especially when migration was promoted by the New Zealand Company and similar organizations. Some 2,000 Irish immigrants arrived each year between 1870 and 1914, 80 percent of whom were from Munster (especially Co. Kerry) and Ulster, but the influx waned after that.

A New Zealand Company advertisement for emigrant workers, 1848. The Company was offering assisted (rather than free) passages to people "of good character" (courtesy of Hocken Collections, University of Otago).

Births: from 1876 state date and place of the parents' marriage, and parents' ages and places of birth, which may identify Irish roots. From 1916, previous children of the marriage are listed too.

Marriages: from 1867 include details of subsequent divorce: they state parents' names from 1881, together with the places of birth of both parties marrying.

Deaths: from 1876 state where the deceased was born; how long they had been in New Zealand; full names of both parents, together with the father's occupation; name and age of husband or wife and place of marriage, together with ages and genders of offspring.

Censuses

New Zealand's censuses were mostly destroyed once their statistical purpose had been fulfilled. The few early ones that survive are at the NZNA.

Directories

The best holdings for these and electoral registers are at the Alexander Turnbull Library in the NZNL.

Religious registers

The earliest Anglican registers date from the 1820s, with slightly later starting dates for Catholic and Methodist ones. Some are with the churches where they were created, but most are in relevant diocesan archives, with all Presbyterian records in their archives in Dunedin. Most gravestones have been transcribed and are on microfilm at branches of the NZSoG.

Newspapers

These are excellent sources for birth, marriage and death (BMD) announcements, obituaries, arrival of new settlers and descriptions of incoming voyages. They are in archives and libraries and many are indexed, as detailed by Bromell (see p. 69). Notices of estates of deceased people, specifying how much money they were worth and the names of the beneficiaries, were published regularly in the *Provincial Gazette*, later called the *New Zealand Gazette*. Most BMD

A typical homestead of settlers in New Zealand, c. 1906.

The New Zealand Ireland Connection website **www.geocities.com/Heartland/Prairie/ 7271/immlist.htm** was established by Angela McCarthy in 1997. It is a major contact point for New Zealand families tracing Irish roots, and for others seeking Irish relatives who went there. It also features a bibliography for the Irish in New Zealand, including Dr. McCarthy's own books, *Irish Migrants in New Zealand, 1840-1937: 'The Desired Haven'* (2005) and *Personal Narratives of Irish and Scottish Migration, 1921-65: 'For Spirit and Adventure'* (2007), which focuses on 20th-century migration. Angela's 19th-century ancestors hailed from Cork, Fermanagh, Donegal and Derry. Her paternal grandfather Gerard McCarthy arrived in New Zealand in 1938, but then vanished. Angela eventually discovered that he died in Christchurch following a stroke. From his death certificate and street directories she traced a daughter of his caretaker, who sent her his photograph and crucifix.

notices have been indexed and are accessible in local libraries. The Internet site **http://paperspast. natlib.govt.nz/** is the NZNL's Digitized Collection of Newspapers.

Biographical dictionaries

See G. Scholefield, *Dictionary of New Zealand Biography* (Department of Internal Affairs, 2 vols., 1940), now also at **www.dnzb.govt.nz /dnzb/** and E. Graydon, *People of Irish Descent: Biographical Notes on New Zealanders of Irish Descent* (E.M. Graydon, 1992).

Wills

Before 1842, wills were proved in NSW and after that in the Supreme Court of New Zealand, later called the High Court. Probate files, usually containing a will, have been transferred to the National Archives and its regional offices.

Naturalizations

As Ireland was part of the British Empire, no naturalization was needed.

Shipping lists

A substantial collection of passenger lists is at the NZNA with many lists also in provincial and

REGISTER OF ADMISSION,

Register Number.	Former Reg. No. of Pupil readmitted.	Date of Admission or Readmission.	Name in full (Surname first).	Date of Birth.	Name and Address of Parent or Guardian. (Customary order.)
69.			McCrossan, Katherine Mary	10.1.1905	Denis McCrossan Grosvenor St, Dn.
70.			McGrath, Adelina Maura	14.11.1905	John Vincent McGrath Dowling St,
71.			McKendry, Josephina Rita	27.7.1904	Jas. F. McKendry, Scotland St, Dn
72.			Millar, Nora	25.5.1903	John Millar, Hotel, Dunedin
73.			Mooney, Eileen Margaret	31.10.1904	T. Mooney Roslyn, Dunedin
74.			O'Connor, Dorothy Gertrude J	11.2.1905	Patrick O'Connor, Woodhaugh
75.			O'Neill, Agnes Margaret	17.3.1904	Mrs Herman Cepsilom St, Dn.
76.			O'Neill, Josephine	15.12.1905	Eugene Jos. O'Neill. High St, Dn
77.			O'Neill, Helen Mary	9.5.1907	
78.			Rodgers, Constance Helen	29.11.1905	C. Rodgers Arthur St, Dunedin
79.			Sligo, Ada Mary	30.3.1907	Wm. F. Sligo Madaggan St, Dn
80.			Sutherland, Ivy Rose Arlington	25.8.1904	Geo. Alex Sutherland, Howard St, Dn
81.			Tanner, Rosie Vera	3.4.1907	Louisa Tanner, Dowling St, Dn.
82.			Tanner, Eileen May	3.4.1907	
83.			Thomas, Stella Constance	25.6.1904	P. Thomas, Cromwell, C. Otago
84.			Todd, Sheila Margaret	29.1.1907	Chas. Todd Anderson's Bay Dn
85.			Woods, Irene Esther	18.6.1905	Francis J Woods Belleknowes Dn
86.		1905	Mulholland, Madge	28.12.1898	Hugh Mulholland St Kilda
87.		1904	Leslie, Margaret Josephine	15.3.1898	Mrs Leslie, Lawrence.
88.			Millar, Tessa	4.5.1900	Mr Millar Oban Hotel Dn.
89.			McEwen, Eileen	7.8.1898	Mr McEwen Port Chalmers
90.			Walsh, Annie	6.1.1903	Mrs M Walsh, King Edward St, S.D.
91.			McKeefry, Annie	7.5.1900	Mr McKeefry
92.		July 1914	Graham, Rose	30.6.1897	Mrs M Graham Waipiata
93.		Mar. 1912	McKendry, Una	5.5.1902	Mrs E McKendry, Scotland St, Dn
94.		1911	Bastings, Mary	4.6.1902	Mrs M Bastings, Hotel, Dn.
95.		1914	O'Meara, Mary	4.8.1899	Mr O'Meara Nightcaps

School registers can be an excellent source of genealogical information. Many of the names are obviously Irish in this "Admission Progress Withdrawal Register" (APW) from St. Dominic's College, a Catholic girls' school in Dunedin (c. 1907). APWs can date from 1879 onwards, though sadly not all Catholic schools kept them. When they exist, they can give you the pupil's name, date of admission, date of birth, parent's name and address, the pupil's progress, date of leaving, previous school and destination on leaving (APW AG-265-A-001/004, courtesy of Hocken Collections, University of Otago).

local archives, though places of origin are seldom stated. A.G. Peake, *National Register of Shipping Arrivals, Australia and New Zealand* (Australian Federation of Family History Organizations, 3rd edn., 1993) is a detailed guide.

The New Zealand Company's records of applications made by people seeking financial help to emigrate are in TNA: series C 208 has the Company's records for 1839-53. For the years after that, see H. Morris and B. Hafslund, *New Zealand Assisted Passenger Lists 1855-71, From Here to There* (W. and F. Pascoe Pty, 1994), which usually state places of origin. The NZNA have records of immigrants to 1973, indexed to 1910.

Land records

Most immigrants to New Zealand came for land, so appear in the excellent national and local land registers. The NZNA has extensive holdings of deeds, surveys, maps and claims. There are also local deed registries, dating from 1841, and land registries from 1870 many of which have excellent indexes: details of all these records are in Bromell (see below).

further reading
■ A. Bromell, *Tracing Family History in New Zealand* (Government Printing Office Publishing, 1988).
■ www.ireland.co.nz, The New Zealand Irish directory.

PART 3

Tracing your roots in Ireland

This is the beginning of your research using Irish sources to trace where your family were living in Ireland, their occupation and as much as possible about them and their ancestors.

Wool spinning in an Irish cottage, Carrick, Co. Donegal.

CHAPTER 10

Introducing Ireland

If all has gone well, you have found an ancestor in Ireland you wish to investigate. If you're lucky, you'll know where in Ireland they were living, but in many cases "Ireland" is as much as you will have found. So what next? This chapter introduces the various sources of information available in Ireland.

How to find the place of origin within Ireland

The technique is to find out through "localizing" where families of the right surname were living at the time your ancestor left. In the case of common surnames, you may be able to localize further by seeing where first names used in the first couple of generations of your migrant family appear in families of the same surname in Ireland.

Localizing sources include Griffith's Valuation (see p. 84), Tithe Applotments (p. 88), statistical surveys of surname distribution such as Matheson's (p. 89), the Civil Registration (see p. 90) and knowledge of where surnames originated (p. 89 and 146). Once you have localized the surname, you can explore records for that area, such as civil registration and religious registers, to find the birth or baptism of your ancestor. If looking in the most likely area fails, look in the next most hopeful, and so on. If records for what appears to be the right area have not

"Making themselves known: ancestors prompt the genealogist" — a lively evocation of Irish genealogy by a leading Irish genealogist, Justin Martin of Dublin.

survived, seek possible living relatives by tracing down lines of the same surname, towards the present. People living in Ireland today may have written or oral history that could confirm that your migrant ancestor belonged to their family.

A new localizing technique is DNA testing (see p. 212). If you find an exact DNA match with someone of the same surname and they know where their ancestor was from, the chances are that yours was from the same place too.

Irish sources

Whether or not you've found your ancestor's place of origin yet, don't leap on the next plane to Dublin. Much Irish research can be done online and using the Mormons' microfilmed records, which can be ordered to any FHC (see p. 33). These include most civil registration indexes, many religious registers and much of the holdings of the Genealogical Office (GO) and Deeds Registry. Most Irish County Heritage Centres (CHCs) insist on their staff undertaking research themselves, reporting back by post or email. It often pays to hire professional searchers to search in the Dublin and London repositories, for some records essential to Irish research are on the mainland.

By doing all you can from home, you can then make best use of your time in Ireland, when you can examine records you couldn't access remotely or want to study personally. You can visit where your ancestors lived — an irreplaceable experience — and allow Irish luck to play its part. Who knows what extra information — an unexpected family grave, or a chance meeting with a distant relative — awaits you on the shores of the Emerald Isle?

Professionals

Irish genealogy has two professional bodies: the Association of Professional Genealogists in Ireland and Association of Ulster Genealogists

Visit Ireland

Éire's currency is the Euro, and Northern Ireland's is the Pound Sterling. You may need an electricity adaptor (easily available in airports) for laptops and other electronic gadgetry. Take good maps — the Ordnance Survey's 1:50,000 "Discovery" series is excellent, though you can buy larger-scale maps locally that will show footpaths and individual buildings. Also advisable are waterproof shoes (or boots for the countryside) and an umbrella.

and Record Agents. Lists of record agents are at **www.nationalarchives.ie/genealogy/researchers.html** and **www.proni.gov.uk/research/searcher.htm**. Quality lurches wildly from highly professional to absolutely awful, but you can often anticipate quality through the promptness and presentation of an initial response to your enquiry — if you wait two weeks and receive a slapdash response from someone, don't hire them!

Societies

There are many name and clan societies who collate data on their surnames and hold reunions in their ancestral Irish homes. They can be found at **www.celts.org/clans/** or by making a simple Internet search under the name plus "genealogy," "clan society" or "family association." Family history societies offer journals, meetings, talks, mutual help and advice. Most for Ireland and the Commonwealth belong to The Federation of Family History Societies (FFHS). Of particular note are:

- Guild of One Name Studies (GOONS). This includes some Irish surnames **www.one-name.org/register.shtml**.
- The Irish Genealogical Research Society (IGRS) **www.igrsoc.org**. Established in 1936 to collate sources that might help the loss of records in 1922, its library in London is open on Saturdays 2–6 pm. It publishes *The Irish Genealogist*. A list of back issues is on its website.

For a key to abbreviations used, see p. 9.

- The Genealogical Society of Ireland, housed in a converted Martello Tower, publishes the *Genealogical Society of Ireland Journal*.
- The Irish Family History Society publishes *Irish Family History*.
- The Ulster Historical Foundation (12 College Square East, Belfast, BT1 6DD, 028 90 332288), **www.ancestryireland.com**, has a large collection of searchable databases containing over 2 million names. It runs the Ulster Genealogical Historical Guild and publishes *Familia, the Ulster Genealogical Review*.
- The North of Ireland Family History Society publishes *North Irish Roots*.

Magazines

Besides the journals of societies (above) there are a number of commercial magazines including *Irish Roots Magazine* and *The Irish Ancestor*, which was edited by Rosemary Ffolliott and ran from 1969 to 1986. It can be purchased whole on CD from Eneclann (see p. 75). The following British Isles genealogy magazines also publish much to do with Ireland: *Your Family Tree*, *Family History Monthly*, *Practical Family History*, *Family Tree Magazine* and *Ancestors*.

Books

Two useful guides to Irish material are *Periodical Sources for the History of Irish Civilisation*, which covers periodicals from all over the world published up to 1970 and R. Hayes, *Manuscript Sources for the History of Irish Civilisation* (14 vol., Hall & Co, 1965) with a supplement to 1975 covering unpublished material in archives around the world. Copies of both are at the NLI.

Almost comprehensive guides to Irish records are provided by James G. Ryan, *Irish Records, Sources for Family and Local History* (see p. 9) and John Grenham, *Tracing your Irish Ancestors: The Complete Guide* (see p. 9). The latter's contents are also online at **www.ireland.com/ancestor**. Both list sources on a county-by-county basis, including censuses, census substitutes and religious registers. These excellent works largely duplicate each other, though each has a small amount of information not found in the other. By studying both you can build up a checklist of sources for your ancestral parish(es). Ryan provides slightly more detailed coverage of Protestant Nonconformist records. His potted county histories are excellent: if your ancestors

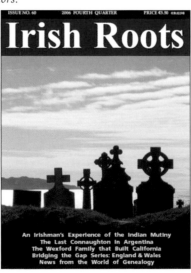

are from Co. Roscommon, for example, it's worth knowing that,

"in the Cromwellian resettlement of Ireland, the county was one of those set aside for occupation by the 'delinquent proprietors', i.e., those landowners who had been dispossessed of land in other parts of the country. The number of non-native settlers in the county has therefore been very low."

CD-ROMs

The foremost Irish CD publishers are Eneclann/ Archive CD Books (Ireland) — though of separate origins, Eneclann owns the latter — with an ever-growing catalog of available material.

Websites

These are the best websites to date (2007):

- **www.irishorigins.com** is a subscription-based online service with an ever-growing list of databases, including Griffith's Valuation (see p. 84). It includes a discussion group and the Irish Origins Library of rare vintage photos, maps and books, including the Children's Employment Commission report of 1842,
  "a government publication containing evidence on the employment of children. An amazing and fascinating insight into conditions of work and peoples' lifestyle in 1842 in their own words."

- **www.irishfamilyresearch.co.uk**, a subscription-based site with all manner of lists, directories and other sources covering all Ireland.

- **www.rootsweb.com/~fianna** includes some random transcripts of records and a guide to research.

- Some library websites containing free transcriptions of local material, see especially **www.clarelibrary.ie** and **www.waterfordcountylibrary.ie**.

Good internet message boards

- http://groups.google.com/group/ soc.genealogy.surnames.ireland
- www.rootsweb.com/~jfuller/gen_mail_ country-unk-irl.html
- http://groups.yahoo.com/search? query= Irish+ancestry
- www.curiousfox.org.uk

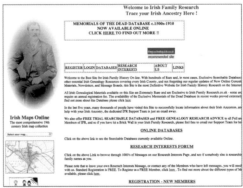

- **www.censusfinder.com/ireland.htm**, providing links to many 1901 and 1911 census subscriptions, earlier fragmentary transcriptions, and directories, musters and much more.
- **www.rootsweb.com/~jfuller/ gen_mail_country-unk-irl.html** has Irish resources and mailing lists.
- **www.irelandroots.com/** has message boards arranged by county.
- **www.surnamesources.eshire.net/ index.html** a pay-to-view site run by Lorna Peel, containing much unusual material.
- **www.askaboutireland.ie**, an extraordinary resource for pictures and information about Irish history and roots.
- **www.otherdays.com**, providing links to Irish genealogical sources.
- **www.celticcousins.net/ireland** has useful transcriptions of directories, religious registers, even some will abstracts, mainly for Counties Clare, Galway, Limerick, Mayo and Roscommon.
- **www.cyndislist.com/ireland.htm** has approaching 200,000 links.
- **www.genuki.org.uk/indexes/IRLcontents. html** has many links to Irish resources.
- **www.irelandgenweb.com**, the site of the Irish Genweb project.
- **www.rootsweb.com/~nirwgw** has county listings for Northern Ireland.

- **www.genealogylinks.net/uk/ireland** has listings for Ireland.
- **www.doras.ie**, Eircom, the Irish telephone company, has a large listing of Irish genealogy sites.

Biographical dictionaries

See A. Webb, *A Compendium of Irish Biography* (Gill & Sons, 1878) and J.S. Crone, *A Concise Dictionary of Irish Biography*, 1937 (Kraus Reprint, 1970).

Archives

When you visit Ireland, you'll find many archives in Dublin and Belfast. Make sure you can visit the County Heritage Centres (CHCs — see p. 77) and local archives and libraries for your home county.

The best archive guide is S. Helferty and R. Refaussé, *Directory of Irish Archives* (Four Courts Press, 2003).

Dublin

Most Dublin repositories — the NLI, NAI, Trinity College, the GO and the archaeology and history section of the National Museum of Ireland — are all within easy walking distance of each other in the heart of this elegant city and the others are within an easy bus or taxi ride. The NAI, created in 1988 from the merging of the State Paper Office (1702) and Public Record Office (1867), was housed in the Four Courts until 1990, when it moved to its present home in Bishop Street. The NAI and NLI include a Genealogy Advisory Service (GAS), staffed by members of the Association of Professional Genealogists in Ireland. The NLI has the Lawrence Collection of 19th-century photographs, due to be available free at **www.nli.ie**. The GO's collections are searchable in the NLI. The National Museum of Ireland has several regional bases, including the County Life section in Co. Mayo, where your ancestors' lives in mid-19th century Ireland are brought vividly to life.

This picture from the National Folklore Collection shows a woman enjoying her pipe by a traditional kitchen hearth in Co. Galway, 1935 (courtesy of National Folklore Collection, UCD).

Also in Dublin is University College's Department of Folklore. This is a rich repository for the folklore that underpins and informs all Irish genealogy. Particularly interesting is the Schools Collection, created by 11–14-year-olds in 1937–8, recording stories, legends, grandparents' memories of the famine years, customs and even jokes. The children did not explicitly record genealogical information, but their words contain much incidental information about their families.

Belfast

The main repositories, the Registrar General's Office, the Central Library, the Presbyterian Historical Society, the Ulster Historical Foundation and the Linen Hall Library are all in close proximity in central Belfast. The PRONI is a short bus or taxi ride away to the south. Also worth a visit is Belfast Central Library, which has many privately produced family histories, electoral registers, relevant Parliamentary Papers and sections of Griffith's Valuation.

The County Heritage Centres

The main record-holders in each county are the CHCs. These were established by the government in the 1980s (primarily to provide employment for those who withdrew from school) under the Irish Genealogy Project, renamed the Irish Family History Foundation, www.irish-roots.net. Their website provides links to the participating centers. Irish Genealogy Ltd. is its coordinating body. Both sites contain useful addresses and links.

The project's aim was to transcribe and computerize all surviving religious registers, and the task is nearly complete. You can only access their records by paying CHC staff for a report, something best done well in advance of visiting Ireland. The CHCs are still worth visiting because the many resources available on the open shelves. Some centers are starting

to make material available online; leading the way are Counties Antrim and Down, with www.ancestryireland.co.uk.

Also worth visiting are local libraries, whose umbrella sites are www.library.ie (south) and www.ni-libraries.net (north).

Local forges.

There are three forges in our Parish, Mr. Mac Garry's, Mr. Lacey's, and Mr. Malone's. Mr. Mac Garry's is situated at the corner of Clonard St. Mr. Malone's beside the guards barracks in Dublin St. And Mr. Lacey's beside the canal. The Lacey's and Malones are smyths as long as the people can remember. There is a little stream beside Mr. Lacey's forge. On Mr. Lacey's forge there is a slated roof. There is one fire place and a big belbown bellows. The implements he has are, the hammar, anvil, nails, and a pliers. He puts shoes on the horses and asses. He makes gates for fields. The only work that is done outside is putting the rim on the wheel of a cart. The forge water will cure warts. Sometimes people meet in the forge for a chat. There was a little forge in Balrothery owned by Patrick Farrell. As King Billy was going on his way to Dublin after the Battle of the Boyne he shod King Billy's horse there. This is proved by an old headstone over farrell's grave which may be seen to this day. There is a pincers, hammar, and shoe carved on it.

Collected by John Matthews
Clonard St
from Mr Lacey
Dublin   age 59

Unexpected genealogical clues come from documents such as this one from the Schools Collection at the Department of Folklore — an essay written in 1937/8 by John Matthews, a pupil of Saint Peter and Paul's Boys National School, Balbriggan, Dublin, who collected the information from a Mr Lacey, also from Dublin, who was 59 at the time (document NFCD 783:335, courtesy of National Folklore Collection, UCD).

further reading

■ The Flyleaf Press publishes detailed guides Tracing your… Ancestors for Cork, Dublin, Donegal, Kerry, Mayo, and also Longford & its People.
■ S. Irvine and N.M. Hickey, Going to Ireland: A Genealogical Researcher's Guide (Trafford Publishing, www.trafford.com/robots/97-0002.html, 1998), is handy to take on a trip to Ireland.

CHAPTER 11

The divisions of Ireland

Most Irish records are arranged by locality and most people within them are identified by where they lived. Understanding how the country was divided is especially important due to the deep bond that existed between people and the land.

Townlands

Generally, the Irish call hamlets and villages "towns" and their surrounding land "townlands." The roughly 64,000 townlands are Ireland's smallest official administrative divisions. They are based on the Gaelic *bally betagh*, the area controlled by a single *sept* or family, itself composed of 16 *ballyboes* (*ballyboes* were composed of six *sessiaghs*), originally supposed to be the land needed to keep a cow. In fact, townlands vary enormously in size from less than an acre (roughly 4,000 square meters) to several thousand, the smaller usually being the most fertile. They were standardized by the Ordnance Survey in the 1830s, when some older names were lost or demoted to being "sub-denominational." Townlands are grouped, usually 5 to 30 of them, into Civil Parishes.

The *General Alphabetical Index to the Towns, Townlands and Parishes of Ireland* (created 1851, published ten years later in 1861, repr. GPC, 2006),

Killybegs, a small and lovely town in Co. Donegal, Ireland, pictured about 1900.

available in the Dublin searchrooms and online as the *IreAtlas Database*, **www.seanruad**.com, is the best guide. This tells you the parish, barony, Poor Law Union, county, and sometimes the acreage and alternative names for any townland. It lists the townlands within any of the wider administrative units (which, incidentally, tells you the names of the civil parishes within baronies, Poor Law Unions, and so on). The index is also at **www.Ireland.com/ ancestor/placenames**, which will just tell you the civil parish, union and county for any townland and (for a fee) shows you the entry in Lewis's dictionary (see p. 80).

Useful too is Y. Goblet, *Index to the Townlands in the Civil Survey 1654-6* (Irish Manuscripts Commission, 1954), G.B. Handran, *Townlands in Poor Law Unions: a Reprint of Poor Law Union Pamphlets of the General Registrar's Office with an Introduction, and Six Appendices relating to Irish Genealogical Research* (Higginson Books, 1997) and B. Mitchell, *Townland Maps of Ireland* (Pennsylvania, 1988) covering Armagh, Donegal, Londonderry and Tyrone.

Parishes

Ireland's troubled religious history is reflected in the structure of its parishes. Early Irish Christianity was based on monasteries, and the system of parishes administered by priests and responsible to bishops only started effectively in the 12th century. Many parishes were based on traditional family territories.

The Protestant Reformation had little effect until 1560, when Elizabeth I changed the Catholic Church in Ireland into the Protestant Church of Ireland (CoI), with herself as its head. The old parishes became Protestant ones, and on these the later Civil Parishes were based. The Reformation took until the end of the 17th century to implement in most of Ireland beyond the Pale (the area around Dublin settled by

Gaelic place names

Irish place names can be confusing due to variant spellings and Anglicization. The best guide is P.W. Joyce, *Irish Local Names Explained* (1884, repr. 1979), while for original research John O'Donovan's maps and name books at the NLI and Ordnance Survey Office, Dublin, help link modern and ancient place names together. Some frequent Gaelic place name elements are:

Achadh – field
Árd – height
Baile – farm, town or general place
Beg – small
Carraig – rock
Cashel/Cathair – stone fort
Ceapach – plot of land
Ceathramha – quarter
Cill – church
Cluain – field cleared from a forest or bog
Cnoc – hill
Cúil – corner
Currach – marsh or moor
Doire – oak wood
Druim – ridge
Dún – fort of stone and earth
Eanach – marsh
Garran – shrubby wood
Garrdha – garden
Glean – glen
Gort – field
Leitir – hillside
Lios – enclosure
Moin – bog
Mor – big
Muine – shrubby wood
Mullach – summit
Pairc – field or demesne
Rath – earthen fort
Tulach – mound

English incomers from the 15th century). At times, the Catholics had the upper hand. During the Civil War in the mid-17th century, the Catholic lords formed a Confederacy at Kilkenny, and a bellicose Papal legate, Rinuccini, encouraged the massacre of many Protestant settlers. With the defeat of Catholic forces loyal

The dreadful treatment of the Irish people, both leading up to the Famine and also in the centuries of British rule that preceeded it, spawned many sorrowful ballads, such as this piece of sheet music from about 1840, "The lament of the Irish emigrant — a ballad."

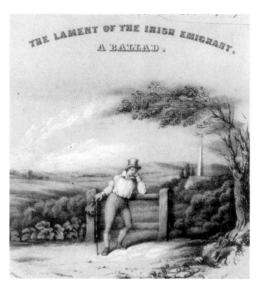

to James II in 1691, however, the struggle was lost and in 1695 the first of a series of Penal Laws was passed, aiming to disarm Irish Catholics, sever their ties with Europe, prevent them from worshipping and remove their secure tenure of land. Most importantly, in 1704, the Act to Prevent the Further Growth of Popery forbade Catholics to buy land, inherit it from Protestants or take out leases of 31 years or more, and decreed that Catholic estates should be

Ireland's Catholic dioceses, grouped into the four Provinces of Armagh, Cashel, Tuam and Dublin.

subdivided between all the male heirs, leading inevitably to great families being reduced over a few generations to the status of peasants.

The Catholic bishops, archdeacons and members of religious orders were expelled officially in 1697-8. The parish priests, however, were allowed to stay provided they registered with the authorities. In practice, the authorities left them alone, and very little effort was made to turn the Catholic peasantry into Protestants.

Having lost control of the now Protestant parishes, the Catholic priests formed new ones based around their existing congregations. As time passed, larger Catholic parishes were subdivided, so the older ones will often cover wider areas than later ones and families may therefore be found in more than one register. Divisions up to 1837 are described in Lewis's *Topographical Dictionary of Ireland*. For those after 1837 you must rely on local research and be aware that early records for your family may be in a neighboring, older register.

Some Catholic and Civil parishes shared the same name, though not necessarily the same area. Others had different names, or several alternative ones, as noted in Grenham (see p. 9).

If you know the townland, you can find the right Civil Parish using the Townlands Indexes, best searched at **www.seanruad.com** or **www.Ireland.com/ancestor/placenames**. The latter links to Lewis's dictionary (see above), which states the relevant Catholic parish(es) and Protestant non-conformist chapels. There is no list of what townlands fell directly within Catholic parishes, but there is a map in the NLI's *Index of Surnames* (also called the *Householder's Index*), superimposing Civil and Catholic parishes. You can often guess using the Catholic parish maps in Grenham, now online at **www.ireland.com/ancestor/browse/counties/rcmaps/**.

For parish registers, see p. 103 and 108.

Dioceses

Parishes are grouped into Archdeaconries, several of which formed dioceses, presided over by bishops. They date back to the 12th century. From 1560, the CoI got the old palaces and legal rights. Although Catholic bishops were banished in 1697, Catholic priests grouped their new parishes under the old dioceses and sometimes amalgamated two small dioceses into one new one for convenience.

Baronies

Townlands, and to a broad degree parishes, were grouped into Ireland's 270 baronies. Their roots lie in the old Gaelic Lordships, the lands of the *tuaths* ("people") of ancient Ireland. Much manipulation by the Cambro-Norman settlers (see p. 195) followed but their borders were largely fixed by the 16th century. They became units for local government and taxation but are now redundant.

Counties

Ireland's counties are composed of groups of baronies. Some counties correspond roughly to old Gaelic kingdoms, but the "shiring" of Ireland — creating a county and appointing a sheriff with legal, military and administrative power over it — was a Cambro-Norman practice, starting with Co. Dublin in the late 12th century. The practice spread outwards as English control widened. Antrim and Down, for example, were "shired" about 1300, and Westmeath in 1543. Sir Henry Sydney shired Connacht into Galway, Mayo, Sligo and Clare between 1568 and 1578, the latter having been the old O'Brien kingdom of Thomond (Clare was transferred to the province of Munster in 1639).

Provinces

Ireland's four provinces were Connacht in the west, Ulster in the north, Leinster in the east and Munster in the south. They have their roots in the ancient *Cúig Cúigí* ("five fifths"), allegedly created by the *Fir Bolg*, as described on p. 192.

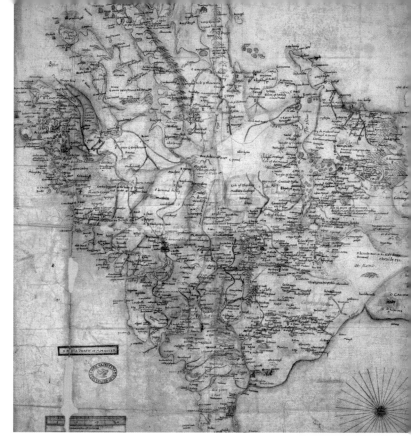

Modern Ireland and the Four Courts

Throughout the 19th century, Ireland's ongoing struggle for freedom, accompanied and fuelled by an ever-increasing awareness of Gaelic history, culture and — dare one say, genealogy — continued to grow. In America, Irishmen joined the Fenian movement, promoting freedom at all costs for their kin back home. The Home Rule movement gathered strength among MPs in the Westminster Parliament, supported by the likes of Gladstone, but it was not until after World War I that Britain finally released its grip on Ireland. The Easter Rising of 1916 was suppressed, but the War of Independence of 1919-21 forced the British government to negotiate with the self-appointed *Dáil Éireann* (Irish Parliament). The war ended with the Anglo-Irish Treaty of December 1921 and the

A map of the province of Munster. This was drawn about 1572, before the convention of showing the north at the top became established. Here, in fact, the southern-most tip of Ireland is shown at the top of the page, so in modern terms it is upside down!

Saorstát Éireann (Irish Free State) was created in March 1922. On June 28, however, civil war erupted between the provisional Government's Irish Free State Army under Michael Collins and the anti-Treaty forces of the Irish Republican Army. The latter barricaded themselves into the Four Courts, home of the Public Record Office.

Writing in 1911, H.A. Crofton commented in *How to Trace a Pedigree* "the searcher in Ireland

The Four Courts on fire as a result of the civil conflict in June 1922.

Maps online

- **www.irishhistoricalmaps.com**
  A commercial site offering reproduction maps including the first large-scale (6 inch-to-the-mile) survey of Ireland, 1837–46, used as the basis for land valuation and taxes.
- **www.osi.ie**
  The Ordnance Survey of Ireland's own map site.
- **www.ireland.com/ancestor**
  Includes a substantial collection of maps.
- **http://homepage.ntlworld.com/tomals/index2.htm**
  Moderately poor-quality scans of Samuel Lewis's county maps of the whole of the British Isles.
- **www.cyndislist.com/maps.htm**
  Entitled "Maps, Gazetteers and Geographical Information," this section of the popular genealogy site contains many links to sources for maps, including some Irish ones.
- **www.proni.nics.gov.uk/geogindx/geogindx.htm**
  The PRONI's geographical Index of Northern Ireland, listing counties, baronies, Poor Law Unions, dioceses (parishes grouped under a bishop), parishes and townlands.
- **www.clarelibrary.ie/eolas/coclare/history/parliamentary_gazeteerJl845.htm**
  Clare County Library's transcription of Clare places in the *Parliamentary Gazetteer of Ireland* of 1845.
- **www.irishorigins.com**
  Dublin City 1847 Ordnance Survey Town Plans, the first detailed town plans of Dublin, and still in use today.
- **www.ireland.ie/mapping/advancedsearchbymap.aspx**
  Allows you to zoom into any part of Ireland.

has most need of all to be grateful to the powers that be... for, practically speaking, all Irish wills can be found in Dublin... situated in the 'Four Courts'." Here too, on June 28, 1922, could be found barricaded in the IRA under Ernie O'Malley. After shelling the building on the 28th, the Free State Army stormed it the next day. The Public Record Office, in the western block, had been used as an ammunition store and as fire spread the gunpowder exploded and many records concerning our Irish roots were destroyed — but do not despair, for much still remains!

Although the civil war lasted until May 1923, the Irish Free State Constitution was enacted in December 1922, with Northern Ireland opting out and remaining part of Great Britain. The Irish Free State changed its constitution and was renamed *Éire* in 1937. It remained nominally part of the British Empire until (under the Republic of Ireland Act, 1948) it became an entirely independent republic in 1949.

Until 1922, Ulster comprised Antrim, Armagh, (London)Derry, Down, Fermanagh, Tyrone, Cavan, Donegal and Monaghan. In 1922, Northern Ireland was created, incorporating the first six of these counties only, ruled by the Crown but with its own governing body in Belfast.

The once-proud lion and unicorn of the royal family of Great Britain, now dismantled and firmly caged up under the Spanish Arch in Galway City.

Temperance Movement

All Irish families were affected one way or the other by national politics and also by social trends such as the Temperance Movement. Fr. Theobald Matthew (1790–1856) launched a crusade against drinking that by 1842 resulted in an astonishing 5 million people taking the teetotal pledge. Yet there were plenty of exceptions. This sketch from Thackeray's *Irish Sketchbook* shows "two Irish ladies" whom he found standing next to the entrance of some caves on the seashore at Kingsdown, Dublin, in 1842.

"They said they had not acquiesced to the general Temperance movement that had taken place throughout the country; and indeed, if the truth must be known, it was only under promise of a glass of whisky apiece that their modesty could be so far overcome as to permit them to sit for their portraits."

CHAPTER 12

Griffith's Valuation and Tithe Applotments

A page from Griffith's Valuation for Cootehill, Co. Cavan, including my 2 x great-grandfather James "Dinning" and a couple of his relations (courtesy of the Commissioner of Valuation, Valuation Office, Dublin).

Griffith's Valuation is now easily available online. It is a mid-19th-century survey of Irish land occupiers. It is usually paired with the Tithe Applotments of the 1820s and '30s. Together, they are one of the best ways of localizing surnames and working out where in Ireland your ancestors may have originated.

In these records you may find a migrant ancestor at home before he left Ireland. If he married abroad and named his father on his marriage record, you may find the father listed in Griffith's in the family's ancestral home. Even if you don't find a known ancestor, finding the parishes in which the surname was prevalent can lead you to the right religious registers in which your ancestor's baptism might be found.

Even if you know your family's home townland, these records are still wonderful for filling in details about their lives. In the absence of older religious records, they may even be the earliest certain mention you have of your people at all, making them doubly valued.

Surveying Ireland

In Tudor times, mapmakers such as Richard Lythe (1567–71) and Richard Bartlett (1601–2) surveyed and mapped Ireland largely to help military campaigns. In the 17th century, maps helping the English define and thereby acquire landholdings were created, particularly the remarkably accurate Down Survey of Sir William Petty (1623–87). The Irish Bogs Commission (1809–14) created detailed maps to enable engineers to drain bogs and create new farm land. In 1824, the government's map-making body, the Ordnance Survey, began its authoritative surveys of Ireland.

Townland Valuations

Among the Bogs Commission's surveyors was Richard Griffith. He became Boundary

---

VALUATION OF TENEMENTS.   21

PARISH OF DRUMGOON.

No. and Letters of Reference to Map.	Townlands and Occupiers	Immediate Lessors	Description of Tenement	Area (A. R. P.)	Land (£ s. d.)	Buildings (£ s. d.)	Total Annual Valuation of Rateable Property (£ s. d.)
	DRUMMAN. (Ord. S. 17.)						
1	John M'Crackin	Richard Coote (minor)	Land	2 3 19	4 10 0	—	4 10 0
2	Ellen M'Cabe	Same	Land	5 1 4	7 10 0	—	7 10 0
3	John Sheeran	Same	Land	5 3 29	6 10 0	—	6 10 0
4	Samuel Fisher	Same	Land	7 2 37	7 15 0	—	} 15 10 0
5			Land	5 3 36	7 15 0	—	
6	John M'Fadden	Same	Land	7 1 31	7 0 0	—	7 0 0
7	John Dunne	Same	Land	3 0 6	3 0 0	—	3 0 0
8	Peter Murphy	Same	Land	2 3 30	3 0 0	—	3 0 0
9	John Porter	Same	House, office, and land	7 1 28	8 0 0	0 10 0	8 10 0
10	John M'Nally	Same	House, office, and land	32 0 25	33 15 0	1 15 0	35 10 0
11	Terence M'Nally	Same	Land	2 2 29	3 5 0	—	3 5 0
12	Charles M'Enroe	Same	Land	2 0 39	2 10 0	—	2 10 0
13	Bernard M'Cabe	Same	Land	3 1 29	4 10 0	—	4 10 0
14	William Egginton	Same	Land	4 1 29	4 15 0	—	4 15 0
15, 16	John M'Cabe	Same	Land / Caretaker's ho. and ld.	1 3 6 / 4 1 15	2 5 0 / 5 0 0	— / 0 15 0	} 8 0 0
17				2 1 19	2 5 0	—	
18	William Steward	Same	Land	5 2 11	6 15 0	—	} 9 0 0
19	John M'Crackin	Same	Land	3 2 30	4 15 0	—	4 15 0
			Total,	111 1 12	124 15 0	3 0 0	127 15 0
	DRUMROOGHILL. (Ord. S. 17.)						
1	Philip Smith	Richard Coote (minor)	House, office, and land	4 2 21	3 5 0	0 5 0	3 10 0
2	John M'Nally	Same	House, office, and land	18 2 22	12 5 0	0 15 0	13 0 0
3	John Embersley	Same	House, office, and land	3 3 4	2 10 0	0 10 0	3 0 0
4	James Dale	Same	House, office, and land	3 2 30	2 10 0	0 10 0	3 0 0
5	Philip Dinning	Same	House, offices, and land	13 3 30	9 0 0	0 15 0	9 15 0
6	James Dinning	Same	House, office, and land	5 2 0	3 15 0	0 10 0	4 5 0
7			Land	0 3 22	0 10 0	—	
8 a,b	Stephen Gilmore	Same	House, office, and land / Cottier's house	18 3 10	13 5 0	1 0 0 / 0 10 0	} 19 5 0
9	Francis Conlan	Same	House, office, and land	5 2 37	4 0 0	—	
10	John Leary	Same	House, office, and land	14 2 12	10 0 0	0 10 0	10 10 0
11			House, office, and land	13 3 21	8 0 0	0 15 0	8 15 0
12	Owen Leary	Same	Land	2 2 7	1 5 0	—	
13			Land	1 2 7	1 0 0	—	} 6 5 0
14	Catherine Boylan	Same	House, office, and land	3 2 38	2 15 0	0 15 0	
15	William Dinning	Same	House, office, and land	8 0 10	5 10 0	0 10 0	6 0 0
16	James Creeth	Same	House, office, and land	8 2 38	5 15 0	0 10 0	6 5 0
17	Daniel M'Aveeny	Same	Caretaker's ho., off., & ld.	14 0 35	9 10 0	1 10 0	11 0 0
18	John Kennedy	Same	House, office, and land	3 2 11	2 10 0	0 5 0	2 15 0
19	John Cahilly	Same	Land	3 2 11	2 5 0	—	2 5 0
20	Thomas Connolly	Same	Land	6 2 27	4 10 0	—	4 10 0
21 a			House, offices, and land	14 1 16	9 5 0	3 10 0	12 15 0
b	School-house	No rent (see Exemptions)					
22	Catherine Smith, Mary Smith, Anne Smith	Richard Coote (minor)	House, office, and land	10 0 30	6 15 0	0 10 0	7 5 0
23	Jane Brady	Same	House, office, and land	12 0 3	8 10 0	0 15 0	9 5 0
24	Joseph Malone	Same	House, office, and land	9 0 7	6 5 0	0 10 0	6 15 0
25	William Gilmore	Same	House, office, and land	15 2 21	10 10 0	0 10 0	11 0 0
26	Richard Coote (minor)	In fee	Land	6 0 38	3 5 0	—	3 5 0
			Total of Rateable Property,	224 0 31	149 0 0	15 5 0	164 5 0
21 b		Richard Coote (minor)	**Exemptions:** School-house	—	—	0 5 0	0 5 0
			Total, including Exemptions,	224 0 31	149 0 0	15 10 0	164 10 0
	DUNG. (Ord. S. 17.)						
1 a,b	Hugh Smith, sen.	Richd. Coote (minor)	House, offices, and land / Cottier's house	21 0 15	12 15 0	2 5 0 / 0 5 0	} 15 5 0

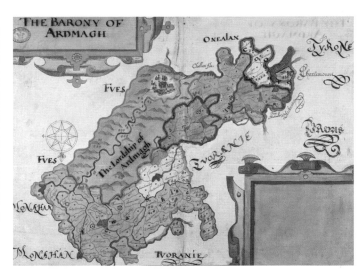

A map of Armagh, from about 1609.

A reconstructed peasant cottage at Dún Aran, Inishmore.

Commissioner in 1825 and following the Townland Valuation Act, 1826, Commissioner for Valuation, with the mandate of mapping the land and fixing boundaries. Griffith started by making detailed plans of each individual building in Londonderry in 1831. Realizing the scope of his survey was too great, he lowered his aim to mapping buildings worth £3 and later £5 or more, thereby excluding many small houses and cottages. However, between 1844 and 1864, valuations were extended to all buildings. The results were published as *The General Valuation of the Rateable Property in Ireland* — "Griffith's Primary Valuation."

The NAI and PRONI hold voluminous original records made by the surveyors in the field. Their "house books" recorded the buildings and occupiers. "Field books" were concerned with soil quality and list occupiers from 1844. The NAI also has "tenure books" that detailed landlords and leases; records of rents paid; "quarto books" covering towns; "perambulation books" made by the surveyors exploring areas on foot; and books recording mills. The NAI and PRONI have full catalogs, most of which are on MMF.

The Valuation Office has maps showing the location of most properties and additional surveyors' notebooks. Its "Cancelled Land

Books" update Griffith's original data right up to 1968 by annotating copies of the original printed surveys, showing alterations in owners, occupiers or the status of the buildings. This was done continuously with a major general revision in 1935. Northern Ireland's are at PRONI up to the early 1930s only.

These are goldmines for genealogy and home history alike, and are immensely useful for tracing branches of the family tree forward. The records may show when the last member of the surname lived in the family home or confirm that descendants were still there in the 1960s.

Griffith's Primary Valuation

The most accessible of these records are Griffith's Primary Valuation, made between 1847 and 1864 to assess rateable values of all properties. Townland by townland (and by street and ward in towns), Griffith's surveyors recorded the occupier; his immediate landlord (who may or may not have been the overall owner); descriptions of each property in terms of "house" (dwellings and also public buildings such as churches), "offices" (sheds, shops, factories, cornsheds, cowsheds, pigsties, etc.), "mill," "forge," "yard," "garden," "land," "bog" or "mountain." They detailed both area and annual value (i.e. what rent could reasonably be charged). Brick and slate houses were rated higher than mud and thatch. Each property was identified by an Ordnance Survey map sheet number. The returns are arranged by townland and parish, initially within baronies and later by Poor Law Union. The results were published by county.

Often more than one person in a townland had the same name. Surveyors distinguished between them in a variety of ways. "Senior" and "junior" (or just one of these terms, with the other left undesignated) invariably denoted father and son. Otherwise, surveyors used the

Griffith's cracks the case

The Crowleys were one of many families who settled in Scotland due to the Great Famine and its aftermath. When James Crowley was born at Borthwick's Close, Edinburgh, in 1863, his birth records his parents as James Crowley, mason, and Helen née Hunter, and states that they married on November 25, 1851 in Co. Leitrim, Ireland. When James senior died in Stirling in 1895, the informant — his son James — stated that his parents were William Crowley, a deceased farmer, and Mary née Wren.

Co. Leitrim was affected severely by the Famine, its population tumbling from 155,000 in 1841 to 112,000 in 1851, of whom 20,000 had died and the rest emigrated. The key to finding the Crowley's origins was through Griffith's Valuation, which surveyed Co. Leitrim in 1856. Luckily, there was only one William 'Crawley' listed, occupying a house, "office" (farm buildings) and land totalling 20 acres, 3 rods and 10 perches — showing him to be a small farmer, rather than a poor cottier — worth £11, tenanted from William Richard Ormsby-Gore (who became 2nd Baron Harlech). He lived in the townland of Killyfad in the parish of Annaduff and barony of Mohill. This was probably the right William, but proof was needed. A letter to the parish priest at Annaduff confirmed that James and Helen had indeed married there and reconnected the Scottish Crowleys firmly to their Irish roots.

An extract from Griffith's Valuation, 1856, for Co. Leitrim, showing William Crawley (courtesy of the Valuation Office, Dublin).

VALUATION OF TENEMENTS.

PARISH OF ANNADUFF.

No. and Letters of Reference to Map.	Names. Townlands and Occupiers.	Names. Immediate Lessors.	Description of Tenement.	Area. A. R. P.	Rateable Annual Valuation. Land. £ s. d.	Rateable Annual Valuation. Buildings. £ s. d.	Total Annual Valuation of Rateable Property. £ s. d.
b	GORTINEE— continued. James Gormly,	Michael Boyle, Same,	House, House			0 5 0	0 5 0
1 a	(Ord. S. 35.) Thomas Shanley,	Wm. Rhd. Ormsby Gore,	House, offices, and land,	8 1 23	4 15 0	0 15 0	5 10 0
2 a	John Shanley,	Same,	House, offices, and land,	31 2 6	16 15 0	1 5 0	18 0 0
b	Bridget Oates,	John Shanley,	House,			0 10 0	0 10 0
3 a	William Crawley,	Wm. Rhd. Ormsby Gore,	House, offices, and land,	20 3 10	10 0 0	1 0 0	11 0 0
4 a			House, offices, and land,	14 0 0	7 0 0	1 0 0	
5	John Cronogue,	Same,	Land,	2 1 4	0 15 0		10 0 0
6			Land,	5 3 24	1 5 0		
4 b	John Kerny,	John Cronogue,	House,			0 5 0	0 5 0
a	Patrick Sweeny,	Wm. Rhd. Ormsby Gore,	House, office, and land,	20 2 11	7 5 0	1 0 0	8 5 0
b	Barney Sweeny,	Same,	House & small garden,			1 0 0	1 0 0
8 a	Matthew Healy,	Same,	House, office, and land,	6 3 2	2 10 0		3 10 0

Gaelic custom of adding the father's first name after the name (such as "James Crowley [Patrick]," i.e. James son of Patrick Crowley), or an occupation or physical observation (e.g. "tall"/"short"). To distinguish similarly-named women, the maiden name might be given in brackets.

An ancestor's absence from Griffith's does not mean they were absent or dead. Griffith omitted the very poorest in their makeshift hovels, while for buildings with multiple occupants the "householder" would usually be one of several, chosen at random. According to Griffith's rules, *"when a portion of a farmhouse has been given up by a farmer to his mother or father, and no rent is paid for it to the farmer; or where a father or mother in giving up a farm to their son [or daughter] retains a portion of the house for his or her dwelling-house during his or her lifetime, such occupation does not form a distinct tenement,"* so the parent's name is not listed.

"Reps of" show that the person named had died and their legal representatives were settling the estate. "In Chancery" indicates a dispute following the landholder's death: some Chancery records survive at the NAI. "Free" often denotes squatters.

The landholding's size determined how people were described. The "cottier or laborer" had less than 5 acres (2 hectares) and usually an annual tenancy (which was renewed automatically and could only be changed by mutual consent or litigation). The larger, more comfortable farmers had over 30 acres (12.1 hectares), normally with leases for lives (lasting for the lifetimes of three named people, usually tenant, wife and son). The small tenant farmer fell in between, with either type of lease. Those holding land "in fee" owned it outright, and were usually owners of the whole townland. If you find the owner, you can see if their estate papers survived, which *may* mention tenants.

Land measurements

- *Irish acre* — as used in tithes — 7,840 square yards.
- *English acre* — as used in Griffiths. This started as the area a team of oxen could plow in a morning but became fixed at 4,480 square yards (the *Scottish acre* was 6,100 square yards).
- *English mile* — 8 furlongs or 1,760 yards.
- *Furlong* — 40 rods or 220 yards.
- *Hide/carucate/plowland* — the area a team of oxen could plow in a year, which varied from 60 to 180 acres depending on the soil.
- *Rod/pole/perch* — 16½ square feet or 5½ square yards.
- *Rood* — 40 square rods.
- *Square mile* — 640 English acres.

When cottages were part of a farm, the farmhouse was labelled "a" and the cottages "b," "c," etc.

When the tenant held land in one townland but lived in another, the name of the townland of residence was given after their name. When a group of tenants is bracketed together, lettered "a," "b," etc., this denotes a "rundale" holding, whereby the tenants shared the land and rent; often, even if they had different surnames, they might be descendants of a single original tenant.

The original published books are at the NAI

Sir Richard Griffith was born in Naas, Co. Kildare, in 1784, and trained as a geologist. He was made a baronet in 1858 and died, having completed his great surveying work, in 1878 (picture courtesy of Engineers Ireland).

Paying tithes was massively unpopular with Catholics, who were forced to give a tenth of their very hard-earned income to maintain the CoI. The "war" started in 1830 when the Catholic parishioners of Graiguenamanagh, Co. Kilkenny, withheld their tithes. The next year the protest, widely encouraged by the Catholic clergy, spread throughout south Leinster and Munster. Although protests were supposed to be peaceful, several incidents erupted into violence and at Newtownbarry, Co. Wexford, in June 1831, the local yeomanry shot 14 protestors, while that December at Carrickshock, Co. Kilkenny, protesters killed an official and 12 policemen. The resultant Tithe Rentcharge Act of 1838 converted tithes into a charge payable by landlords, not tenants, thereby effectively abolishing the hated system.

The Church of Ireland clergy who lost revenue due to the "war" compiled lists of "Tithe Defaulters" which provide extra details about many ordinary people. The NAI has 127 surviving lists, mainly for Counties Kilkenny and Tipperary, and partial coverage of Carlow, Cork, Kerry, Laois, Limerick, Louth, Meath, Offaly, Waterford and Wexford. It is online at **www.originsnetwork.com** and for sale at **http://home.alphalink.com.au/~datatree/ datree5.htm**.

and genealogical libraries such as the SoG and also on microfiche. The only absolutely full set exists online at **www.irishorigins.com**, which links the returns to relevant Ordnance Survey and original valuation survey maps.

As a final caution, the genealogist John Grenham reminds us (in *Your Family Tree*, May 2005) that Griffiths is "a snapshot of the immediate aftermath of a cataclysm [the Famine], rather than the stable picture of a settled society that it can often appear to be."

Tithe Applotments

In old Ireland, a tenth of everyone's annual produce was handed over to the CoI. Sometimes it was paid to a landowner who paid the clergyman a proportion, keeping the rest himself.

In 1823, the Duke of Wellington's government introduced the Tithe Composition Act, allowing tithes to be paid in money (a system that had already started in practice) and a great survey was conducted to determine how

much the occupiers of land should pay. The survey was made over 15 years, up to 1838, when the payment of tithes was cancelled.

The records are arranged by townland and list all occupiers, detailing the size of their landholding and the tithes deemed to be payable. This was based on the average price of oats and wheat between 1816 and 1823, with the land's quality taken into account. Translating figures back into anything meaningful about your ancestors is obviously difficult, but you can easily see how *relatively* well- or badly-off they were compared to their neighbors, while quality of land was graded between 1 (very good) and 4 (very poor). Note that "and Partners" or "and Co." actually usually means a number of tenants holding land in common — not a "company' in the modern sense.

The records omit all who were not occupying land, while some areas, thanks to ancient quirks in the law, were simply exempt. From 1736, grazing land in Munster — mostly owned by landowners — was exempt, yet the tiny potato patches of the peasantry were not. Grenham points out, though, that by unfairly taxing the poor, the records have become more (not less) valuable to posterity.

Original records are at the NAI and on MMF. Those for Northern Ireland are also on film in the PRONI.

Indexes to Griffiths and the Tithe Applotments

The NAI has an index, widely available on microfiche, stating the barony in which surnames occur (and the number of instances of each surname per barony for Griffith's). Thus, "Crowley G5 T" indicates five Crowleys in Griffiths and an unspecified number in the tithes in the barony concerned. The online indexes to Griffiths now suggest which parishes are worth a search in the tithes, too. As a localizing tool, of course, the NAI index is quite useful in its own right.

Irish Ancestors (**www.ireland.com/ancestor**) has the old surname indexes online. A free but apparently incomplete index is at **www.failteromhat.com**.

Northern Ireland's tithes are fully indexed on CD-ROM as *International Land Records: Tithe Applotment Books, 1823–38* (Family Tree Maker, 1999).

Various parishes' returns have been transcribed on the Internet. For listings see **www.ireland.com/ ancestor/browse/links/counties.htm** and **www.genealogylinks.net/ireland**.

Surname distribution

In Ireland, understanding how surnames arose and what they mean is often a major clue to where families lived. Gaelic surnames arose under the ancient clan system (see p. 148). Although the English destroyed the latter, it is remarkable how little they affected the original distribution of surnames. Often, despite war and famine, surnames are still commonest in the areas where they originated.

This is of course tremendously useful for working out roughly where an Irish ancestor is most likely to have originated. They might not have, but if all else fails, localizing the surname and then looking in local records for evidence of your known ancestor may become your best bet.

The great Irish surname-historian Edward MacLysaght found that,
"Gaelic names are still mainly to be found in the part of the country to which their sept belonged: thus practically all Conneelys and Keadys come from Co. Galway, Teahans and Sugrues from Kerry, Lehanes and Riordans from Co. Cork... this is the case even with names which have become very numerous and are inevitably found in Dublin and the larger towns..."

In his *Irish Families* (see p. 155) MacLysaght includes a list (p. 205–8) of the most stable — Lavelle, for example, is almost exclusively found in Co. Mayo, MacGahan in Co. Louth, Mac Fall in West Antrim and East Derry, and so on. His book includes useful surname distribution maps that can also be bought as a single map of Ireland: *Irish Family Names Map* (Bartholomew, n.d.).

Also useful is the *Special Report on Surnames in Ireland* (published in 1894 and reissued in 1909). Nicknamed "Matheson" after the Registrar General who compiled it, Robert E. Matheson (1845–1926). It was reprinted at the back of *Irish Genealogy: A Record Finder* and is now online at **www.ireland.com/ancestor**. It lists all surnames for which five or more births were registered in 1890 with a breakdown by province and notes on the counties where it was most common. Asterixes show that variants were included in the total number of births given, while the number of births under the specific spelling shown is given in brackets. For a more finely-tuned approach, however, simply search for your surname in the early 1864 and 1865 civil registration registers and see where it was most common.

Another indication of where surnames were — though this is more for interest than practical use — is when they became incorporated into place names. Those starting *Bally-*, *Dun-*, *Clon-* and *Letter-* are often followed by the name of the family whose farm, fort, field or hillside it happened to be. Beware, though, as sometimes the name will be that of a saint, not a family.

further reading

■ James R. Reilly, 'Is there more in Griffith's Valuation than just names?', **www.leitrim-roscommon.com/GRIFFITH/Griffiths.PDF**.

CHAPTER 13

Civil Registration

If you have found your ancestor's place of origin in Ireland, you can now seek them and their immediate ancestors in Civil Registration and religious records. If you are still not sure, your attempts to localize the surname will at least have suggested the parishes in which their roots are likeliest to have lain. You can now seek evidence that your ancestors did live there through Civil Registration and religious records.

Youghal Church, Co. Cork, in the 19th century, still being used for wedding services despite being partly in ruin.

Civil Registration started on April 1, 1845 for non-Catholic marriages, and on January 1, 1864 for all births, marriages and deaths.

The post-1864 system was based on the Irish Poor Law which, in 1838, had divided Ireland into 163 Poor Law Unions. From 1864, these doubled up as Superintendent Registrars' districts. During the 1850s, each Union was divided into (usually) six or seven Dispensary Districts. From 1864, these doubled up as Local Registration Districts. The district medical officer usually acted as the local registrar. The Poor Law districts were not based in the traditional administrative divisions of Ireland but were created from the catchment areas of market towns. Therefore, neither these nor the resulting registration districts recognize old county boundaries, but instead reflect areas focused on the markets, which affected people's daily lives.

You can discover which registration district covers a given parish or townland using the sources shown on p. 78-9.

The local registrars compiled the records of all non-Catholic marriages (from 1845) — effectively all Protestants and Jews — and from 1864 of all births, marriages and deaths. These were sent to the Superintendent Registrar responsible for the Union. The records were collated and forwarded to the General Register Office in Dublin, where they were copied and compiled into a national index. The original records were then sent back to the Superintendent Registrars.

Searching the indexes

The Registrar Generals' records have all been indexed on computer. They will become available on the Internet — see the Registrar Generals' websites for details — something that has been due to happen "next year" for several years running. At the time of writing, however, the indexes must still be searched manually. This can be done for a daily fee at the Registrar General's searchroom in Dublin. However, it's best to get all your searching done before you visit Ireland.

At present, **www.familysearch.org** indexes the birth indexes from 1864 to 1874 and the Protestant marriages 1847-64. Some local material is also coming online, for example:

- **www.sci.net.au/userpages/mgrogan/cork**: some Civil Registration material for Co. Cork.
- **www.waterfordcountylibrary.ie**: deaths for Waterford 1864-1901, freely searchable.

For a small fee you can request searches and buy copies of records by postal application to the Registrar General. It costs €2 (2 euros) for a five year search or €20 for a day. Once an entry is found that looks right, you pay a further €4 for a print-out (with extra for postage). Full certificates for official use (such as passport applications) cost €8, and short-form ones giving minimal detail also cost €8 if the reference number is known, and €10 if it is not. For genealogy though, you can order a photocopy of the entries (containing exactly the same information as the certificates), costing €4 each.

Most indexes and the records themselves are also on MMF, which you can order to any FHC or inspect free at Dublin City Library and South Dublin County Library, Tallaght. The drawback is that they are incomplete (and apparently will remain so), as follows:

Births: *Indexes 1864-1921: Republic 1922-58 and NI 1922-59. Registers 1864-March 1881 and 1900-13: Republic 1930-55 and NI 1922-59.*

A page from the website www. familysearch.org.

Marriages: *Indexes 1845-1921: Republic 1922-58 and NI 1922-59. Registers 1845-70: NI 1922-59.*

Deaths: *Indexes 1864-1921: Republic 1922-58 and NI 1922-59. Registers 1864-70: NI 1922-59.*

The records can *also* be searched via the 163 Superintendent Registrars, most (but not all) of whom give access to their holdings. Their addresses can be found in telephone books, under the heading "Health Services Executive." You can usually search the original register books, thereby finding all the events that took place locally for your family. By searching only one area, however, you will miss any events that took place anywhere beyond that local jurisdiction. Some registrars' records are now deposited at CHCs (see p. 77), such as Kerry's. However, under Éire's Civil Registration Act (2004), the Superintendent Registrar's records may soon be centralized.

Some CHCs have created databases of their local registrar's records. These include Counties Clare, Derry, Mayo and Tipperary South.

Northern Ireland

All records for Northern Ireland from 1922 onwards are with the Registrar General of Northern Ireland (RGNI) and on MMF.

The original centralized records up to 1922 are in Dublin. The RGNI has computerized indexes to all marriage records for its six counties from 1845, and copies of Dublin's birth

This Irish marriage certificate from Newtownards (now in Northern Ireland) shows the 1917 marriage of Ada Margaret, daughter of Samuel Parkhill, a harbor master. Though born in Carrickfergus, Samuel had run away to sea and jumped ship in China where he became Harbor Master in the Imperial Maritime Customs service at Chefoo. Although Ada Margaret was sent back to be brought up by Samuel's family in Ireland, she had been born in China, and was in fact half Chinese!

and death records for the six counties from 1864. The marriage records from 1864 are with the district registrars, whose records are now with local councils, with database copies at the CHCs.

You can search the indexes at the GRONI — book well in advance — for £10 per day, with extra charges depending on how many records you want to see, or you may pay extra for an assisted search with a member of staff. If you know when the event took place you can order certificates online at www.groni.gov.uk for £5.50 if you know the reference number and £11 if you know the precise details but not the reference number. Some material is going online, such as the Ulster Historical Foundation's index for Antrim and Down births and marriages 1864–1921 (deaths to follow) at www.ancestryireland.co.uk.

The indexes

Births, marriages and deaths are indexed separately. They provide name, registration district, volume and page number. Protestant marriages from 1845, and all events from 1864 to 1877, are indexed annually. From 1878, indexes are quarterly, January–March (called the "March Quarter"), April–June ("the June Quarter") and so on. From 1903 to 1927, in 1933 alone and from 1966 to 1995, births reverted to being indexed annually. In all years indexed annually, late registrations are given after "Z."

- From 1903, dates of birth and mothers' maiden names were added to the birth indexes. By triangulating this and the registration district, you can often pick out all offspring of a particular couple. Mothers' maiden names but not dates of birth, are shown 1928–65; both are shown from 1966 onwards.
- Marriages and deaths are indexed quarterly right up to 1965. Marriage indexes from 1966 are annual and give the precise date and spouse's surname. Death indexes from 1966 are annual and give precise date, age and marital status.

All post-1995 records are indexed on computer and can be checked by the staff.

What the records say

Clergymen conducting weddings sent (or were supposed to send) details to the registrars. The onus to register births and children's deaths lay with the parents or, failing them, anyone who knew of such events. Deaths could be registered by anyone, but were usually done by relatives or medics. The informant's name and residence will appear on the record. The records tell you:

Births: date and place; name; gender; full name and residence of father; full name before and (if applicable) after marriage of mother; residences of unmarried mothers; father's occupation or social rank. From 1997, mother's occupations are included.

Marriages: date and place; full names of bride and groom; whether single (bachelor or spinster), widow or widower; occupation or rank — usually, women's jobs were left out even if they actually worked very hard; residences (and, from 1957, the couple's intended place of residence after marriage if within Éire); names and occupations of the fathers; sometimes it was stated if the fathers were deceased; signatures of two witnesses, often close relatives, most often siblings of the bride or groom; ages of the couple marrying, but sometimes in terms simply of "minor" (under 21), or "full age" (21 or over, or claming to be so despite being under 21). There are plenty of cases of people claming to be older than they really were though sometimes in the case of an older woman marrying a younger man, the

The Barry family in Ballyin, Lismore, Co. Waterford, in 1926, including my great-grandmother Mary, second from left: the old man is her brother John Barry. They were born in Ballyin in 1871 and 1865 respectively.

older party might adjust his age down a bit! For Catholic weddings from 1856 in most of Dublin it's worth also checking the church registers which often state the mothers' maiden names and parents' places of residence.

Deaths: date and place; full name; gender; whether married or widow[er]ed; age; occupation or rank; cause of death. If the informant was a child of the deceased this is usually stated: other relationships usually are not.

Signed "X"

An "X" after someone's name usually denotes illiteracy, though sometimes they could write but were too deferential to contradict a registrar who had assumed they couldn't — or they had simply injured their hand!

The record of my great-grandmother Mary Barry's birth on August 4, 1871 at Ballyin, Lismore, Co. Waterford, daughter of Patrick Barry, farmer of Ballyin and his wife Mary Morrissey. Patrick didn't sign with a cross, and oral tradition suggests the family had received a fairly good education in hedgerow schools. They were said to be "coat" not "shawl," indicating they could afford decent clothes.

Superintendent Registrar's District _Lismore_   Registrar's District _Lismore_

18 _71_. Births Registered in the District of _Lismore_ in the Union of _Lismore_ in the County of _Waterford_ in the

No.	Date and Place of Birth.	Name (if any).	Sex.	Name and Surname and Dwelling Place of Father.	Name and Surname and Maiden Surname of Mother.	Rank or Profession of Father.	Signature, Qualification, and Residence of Informant.	When Registered.	Signature of Registrar.	Baptismal Name, if added after Registration of Birth, and Date.
	Nineteenth						Church Lane Lismore	"	Registrar	
47	Fourth August 1871 Ballyin	Mary	Female	Patrick Barry Ballyin	Mary Barry formerly Morrissey	Farmer	Patrick Barry Father Ballyin	Eighth August 1871	Edmond Barry MD Registrar	
	Thirtyfirst									

Up to 15 percent of events, especially births, were not registered. Sometimes births were registered late, but to avoid the fines the parents made up a later date of birth. A lot of people reached adulthood without a birth certificate and, finding they needed one, made their own late registrations. These appear separately at the end of the index volume for the year (or quarter of the year) when the birth took place — a nuisance to have to look for, but of course, a lot better than nothing.

Other General Registration records

The Registrar General in Dublin also has various records relating to births, marriages and deaths of Irish-born people, or people with an Irish parent outside the British Isles. Generally,

The Little Irish Girl.

As I went out one evening
  From Tipperary town,
I met a little colleen
  Among the heather brown.
"Oh!" says I, "Perhaps you're
  lonely?"
  She toss'd her pretty curl :
"Well, maybe I prefer it !"
  Och ! the dear little girl !

Says I, "Perhaps your married ?"
  Says she. "Perhaps I'm not."
Says I, "I'll be your gossoon !"
  Says she, "I'll not be caught !"
"Oh ! your eyes are like the ocean,
  And your heart is like a
  pearl !"
Says she, " Well then, I'll keep it !"
  Och ! the dear little girl !

Prior to marriage came courtship — though it was not always successful. In this postcard, a young buck tries to seduce a pretty Irish colleen. "Your heart is like a pearl," he croons. "Well then, I'll keep it!" she retorts smartly.

only those intending to return to Ireland would use this registration method — migrants almost always used the registration system of their country of settlement.

The GRO, London, has information for British people abroad, which until 1922 included many Irish (and afterwards many British people of Irish origin). These records are searchable at **www.1837online.com** and at the FHC, London.

Consular records of birth, marriage and death of British subjects registered with British consuls from July 1, 1849, are with the GRO, London. From 1864, events concerning Irish-born people were sent to the GRO, Dublin; the entries can only be searched by GRO staff. After 1922, events concerning citizens of the Irish Republic occurring abroad were recorded in the country concerned, although a few overseas deaths of Irish citizens still appear in British consular records, including three 1952 deaths and a 1926 birth. The Irish GRO tells me it maintains a Foreign Birth Register restricted to applications from those working in the Diplomatic Service abroad or Irish subjects in countries where no local system exists.

The GRONI has registers for children with one or more Northern Irish parent whose birth or death was registered with a British consul from January 1, 1922 and marriages for people born in Northern Ireland from January 1, 1923. There is a separate register for births, marriages and deaths of Northern Irish people abroad registered with British High Commissioners from January 1, 1950.

Birth and death at sea from July 1, 1837 was recorded by the GRO, London. The GRO, Dublin also holds births and deaths at sea from 1864 for children with at least one Irish-born parent. These were registered separately from 1864 but from 1886 they appear at the back of the regular

Most Irish peasants never got as far as Lourdes. This shrine at Mulhudart County, Dublin, is visited here by pilgrims (in 1920) who believed its holy water would cure all sorts of ailments. Over the entrance is a shrine dedicated to the Blessing Virgin, whose apparition is said to have been seen there.

birth indexes. The GRONI has registers for children with one or more Northern Irish parent born or died at sea from 1 January 1922. The NLI has registers of seamen who died between 1887 and 1949, giving their name, age, rank, official number, name and type of ship, port of registry, place and cause of death, and from 1893 their last place of abode on land.

Army births, marriages and deaths: see p. 127.

Lourdes

Marriages of 15 Irish couples conducted at the Catholic shrine of Lourdes, France, between 1939 and 1967, are at the GRO, Dublin.

Pre-1837 records

TNA has miscellaneous births, baptisms, marriages, deaths and burials of British subjects abroad in department RG: see www.catalogue.nationalarchives.gov.uk.

India

From the 17th century to 1947, many British (and thus Irish) families spent time in India, often as soldiers. Their baptisms, marriages and burials, together with copious directories and government records concerning individuals and

families are at the British Library's Oriental and India Office Collections. For memorial inscriptions of the Irish in India, see E. Hewson (comp.) *The Forgotten Irish Memorials of the Raj*.

Adoption

Northern Ireland's adoption records are at GRONI (from 1931). Éire's are at the GRO, Dublin (from 1953) and The Adoption Board. In Éire only non-identifying information will be released to adoptees, and original birth certificates are kept secret. The Federation of Services for Unmarried Parents and their Children maintains an unofficial Adoption Contact Register, and advises on tracing natural parents without the State's help.

further reading
■ M. Holme, 'The Irish and India: Imperialism, Nationalism and Internationalism' in Bielenberg's *The Irish Diaspora* (see p. 17).
■ C. and M. Watts, *Tracing Births, Deaths and Marriages at Sea* (SoG, 2004).

CHAPTER 14

Censuses

The Barrys of Ballyin, as enumerated on April 2, 1911. Note that the older generation, including John's brother Bartholomew, could speak Gaelic and English. By implication, their sister, my great-grandmother Mary, who was then in England, must have been able to speak some Gaelic too — I never realized this before.

Irish censuses are a fantastic source for early 20th-century family history and contain valuable information on people born throughout the 19th century. Earlier survivals can, in rare cases, take you back into the 18th century.

Although censuses were taken every year from 1821, those between 1861 and 1891 were pulped by the British government to save space during World War I. Those for 1821–51 were largely destroyed in the Four Courts fire of 1922. Despite this, some data for each census from 1821 onwards (except 1881 and 1891) has survived, as

noted below. Those for 1901 and 1911 have survived and are of great use both for tracing back from recent Irish ancestors, and working forward to find relatives of migrants. They can also be used to eliminate false possibilities: if you find the birth of someone you think was your ancestor who migrated abroad before 1901 but they're still there in the censuses, then unless they had gone home for a visit, the birth wasn't the right one after all.

Bear in mind that, besides accidental omissions, policemen and people in mental hospitals were recorded, but only by their initials.

CENSUS OF IRELAND, 1911. — Form A, return of the Barry family.

FORM B. 1.—HOUSE AND BUILDING RETURN.

County, *Waterford* Parliamentary Division, *West Waterford* Poor Law Union, *Lismore* District Electoral Division, *Ballyin* Townland, *Ballyin upper*

Parliamentary Borough, City, Urban District, Town or Village, Street, Barony, *Coshmore & c. Coshbride* Parish, *Lismore*

Note A.—When a Towaland or Street is situated in two Parliamentary Divisions, or in more than one District Electoral Division or Parish, or is partly within and partly without a Parliamentary Borough, City, Urban District, Town, or Village, a *separate* Return should be made for each portion.

No. of House or Building.	Whether Built or Building.	State whether Private Dwelling, Public Building, School, Manufactory, Hotel, Publichouse, Lodging-house, or Shop, &c.	Number of Out-Offices and Farm-steadings as returned on Form B. 2.	Is House Inhabited?	WALLS.	ROOF.	ROOMS.	Windows in Front.	CLASS OF HOUSE.	No. of distinct Families in each House.	Name of the Head of each Family residing in the House.	No. of Rooms occupied by each Family.	Total Number of Persons in each Family.	Date on which Form A was collected.	Number of Persons who were sick on 2nd April 1911.	Name of the Landlord of any on whose Holding the Home is situated, whether that name appears in column 13 or not.	No. of Rooms or Building of a Land-holder.
1	Built	Private dwelling	9	Yes	1	0	3	4	8	2nd	1	John O'Gorman	4	11	1911 3rd	—	John O'Gorman	2
2	Built	Private dwelling	4	Yes	1	0	2	3	6	2nd	1	John Hale	3	10	3rd	—	John Hale	3
3	Built	Private dwelling	4	Yes	1	0	2	3	6	2nd	1	John Barry	4	12	3rd	—	John Barry	8
4	Built	Private dwelling	2	Yes	1	0	2	2	5	3rd	1	John Murray	3	3	3rd	—	Michl Broderick	1
5	Built	Private dwelling	4	Yes	1	0	2	3	6	2nd	1	Margt Creedon	4	3	3rd	—	Duke of Devonshire	1
6	Built	Private dwelling	3	Yes	1	0	2	2	5	3rd	1	Cornelius Morrissey	2	1	3rd	—	Cornelius Morrissey	9
7	Built	Private dwelling	5	Yes	1	0	2	3	6	2nd	1	Michael Hale	3	4	3rd	—	Michael Hale	4
8	Built	Private dwelling	2	Yes	1	0	2	3	6	2nd	1	Mary Nugent	2	5	3rd	—	Mary Nugent	6
9	Built	Private dwelling	7	Yes	1	0	2	3	6	2nd	1	Wm Kneen	3	5	10th	—	William Kneen	5
10	Built	Private dwelling		Yes	1	0	2	2	5	3rd	1	Ellen Fitzgerald	2	3	10th	—	John O'Gorman	2

1911 and 1901

These censuses were taken on Sunday, March 31, 1901, and Sunday, April 2, 1911. They are available on microfilm at NAI and on MMF. Copies of the 1901 census for Northern Ireland are at the PRONI.

The returns were compiled by enumerators going from door to door collecting forms that each household was supposed to fill in and filling in forms for the illiterate. For each address, you will find on "Form A" the names of everyone at home; relationships to head of household; occupation; age; marital status; county of birth; religious denomination; whether able to read and write; whether able to speak Gaelic, English or both; and whether "'deaf and dumb;' 'dumb' only; blind; 'imbecile' or 'idiot;' or 'lunatic.'" In 1911, married women (not widows) were asked how long they had been married, how many of their children were born alive and of these how many were still living — details sometimes volunteered by widows too.

Ages were often artificially rounded up or down to the nearest ten years. Many ages in 1901 were less than they should have been, and people often aged more than ten years by 1911 —

"Form B" showing Ballyin's buildings and occupiers in 1911. This tells me that my great-great-uncle John Barry's home had four outbuildings. The house itself was of stone, brick or concrete, as opposed to wood and mud, but it was thatched, not roofed with slate or tiles. It had four rooms, with three windows facing the front, making it a "second class" house. The Barrys, numbering 12, were the sole occupiers, and the head, John Barry, was the landholder (presumably thanks to the late 19th-century Land Acts; the major local landowner, the Duke of Devonshire, only held one house in the townland). His house was pretty average for the townland (though his granddaughter remembers it as the most attractive!). The townland included two Hales, relations of John's wife Ellen, and Cornelius Morrissey, presumably a relation of his mother Mary Morrissey, and quite likely occupying her family home.

John and Ellen's children, "the Barry Boys," my grandmother's first cousins as photographed by her on a visit to Ballyin in 1926. My Irish cousin Ann Black remembers the now-ruined cottage: most of it seemed to comprise bedrooms, while in the kitchen was a *chez-longue* and a fireplace large enough to walk into, which contained "the machine," some sort of contraption that worked the bellows.

Changes

The 1926 Irish Free State census was due to be released in 2026, but the new Heraldry Bill may make it available now. The 1901 and 1911 censuses are due to go online (by 2009, they say!), thanks to a partnership of the NAI, NLI and the Canadian Archives: see **www.national archives.ie/genealogy/censusrtns.html** for up-to-date information.

probably to "qualify" for old age pensions, which were introduced in 1908. Therefore, ages give an idea of when people were born, but should be used as rough guides only.

In both 1901 and 1911, "Form B" recorded the number of rooms occupied; details of how the walls and roof were made; number of rooms; number of windows at the front of the house; how many families lived in each house; and who the landholder was, which can be useful for seeking estate records.

Seeking families

Parts of the censuses from 1911 back to 1821, where they survive, are already appearing online. The fabulous site **www.censusfinder. com/ireland.htm** has over 750 links to sites including, for example, **www.irishorigins.com**, which includes the 1901 returns for Dublin's Rotunda Ward and the 1851 survivals for Dublin City. Non-computerized indexes are summarized in Grenham's county source lists (see p. 74).

In the absence of indexes — or, crucially, if you ever suspect the indexes are inaccurate — you can search manually. The returns are arranged by county and within these by District Electoral Divisions, in which enumerators were assigned small areas to walk around recording each family they encountered. At the start of each enumeration book, which you'll find when you scroll through the microfilms, you will find a short description of the route taken and a list of surnames of heads of households.

The 1901 *Townlands Index*, available in the NAI and on MMF 865092, states which townlands were within which Division and provides their numbers (the 1911 *Census Catalogue* in the NAI provide numbers for 1911

Anthony Trollope on Ireland

Fiction as well as fact can add color to your family history. Anthony Trollope's Irish novels such as *The MacDermots of Ballycloran* (1843–7) paint a vivid picture of life in early 1840s Ireland. This section indicates, by implication, why census enumeration may never have been very thorough in the Aughacashel area:

"Aughacashel is a mountain on the eastern side of Loch Allen, near the borders of the County Cavan—uncultivated and rocky at the top, but nevertheless inhabited, and studded with many miserably poor cabins, till within about a quarter of a mile of the summit. The owners of these cabins, with great labor, have contrived to obtain wretchedly poor crops of potatoes from the barren soil immediately round their cabins. To their agricultural pursuits many joined the more profitable but hazardous business of making potheen [illicitly distilled whiskey], and they were, generally speaking, a lawless, reckless set of people—paying, some little, and others no rent, and living without the common blessings or restraints of civilization: no road, or sign of a road, came within some miles of them..."

Anthony Trollope (1815–82).

Transcripts

Edmund Walsh Kelly, a genealogist, made detailed extracts of the 1821–51 censuses for parts of Waterford and Kilkenny, especially the latter's barony of Iverk. Much of this was published in the *Irish Ancestor*, as detailed in Ryan and Grenham (the latter is also at **www.ireland.com/ancestor/browse/counties/index.htm**).

too). To find all the townlands within a parish, see the 1841 *Townlands Index* (also called the *Addenda to the 1841 Census*) in the NAI searchroom. Towns and cities could span several District Electoral Districts and the 1901 *Census Catalogue* usually indexes them down to street level. The cities of Cork, Dublin, Dun Laoghaire (Kingstown), Limerick and Belfast have been street indexed (copies in the searchroom and on MMF 6035493, 4 and 5). Otherwise, just scroll through the returns for the relevant area. This useful exercise will show you what the area was like and you may spot other families of the same surname who were probably relatives. To focus your search, you can seek an address from birth certificates of children born about the right time, for example, or, for tradespeople and the better-off, from directories (see p. 100).

Censuses before 1901

Surviving returns are mainly in the NAI and PRONI, all of which are cataloged by Ryan and Grenham (also online at **www.ireland.com/ancestor/browse/counties/index.htm**). In general:

1891: nothing survives.

1881: nothing survives.

1871: only for Drumcondra and Loughbraclen, Co. Meath (NLI).

1861: only for Catholics in Enniscorthy, Co. Wexford (NLI).

1851: survivals are mainly for Dublin (at www.irishorigins.com) and Co. Antrim (at the PRONI and NAI) and pensions (see p. 100). It lists name, age, occupation, relationship to head, date of marriage, whether able to read or write, denomination, members of the family not present and those who had died since 1841.

1841: only returns for parts of Killeshandra, Co. Cavan, survive (NAI) and pensions (see p. 100). It lists name, age, occupation, relationship to head, date of marriage, ability to read or write, members of the family who were not present, and those who had died since 1831.

1831: copies survive in Walsh Kelly's extracts (see "Transcripts" on this page). Copies were also made for the 1834 religious census and a few fragments of these survive, mostly for Co. Derry (NAI, PRONI and Derry's Genealogy Centre). A little is online, such as **www.rootsweb.com/~nirldy**, for Dunboe. Some further copies for individual parishes are in Catholic archives. It lists name, age, occupation, relationship to head, acreage landholding and (for the 1834 copies) religion.

1821: survives for small parts of Counties Armagh, Cavan, Fermanagh, Galway, Meath and Offaly (King's), as detailed in Grenham. It lists names, ages, occupations, relationships to head of household, acreage landholding and number of storeys of the home.

Pre-1821: there are no earlier censuses, but there are various lists that genealogists call "census substitutes" as described later in this book (see p. 130).

Irish homes

The 1841 census graded Irish homes in four categories. The lowest were windowless mud huts. Furniture in such dwellings was beyond most people's means: in one Donegal townland there were only 93 chairs and 243 stools between 9,000 people.

Old age pensions

When these were introduced for people over 70 in 1908, everyone eligible had been born before General Registration had started in 1864. As evidence of age, therefore, they were allowed to submit extracts from the 1841 and 1851 (and rarely 1821) censuses. These extracts are in two series (called "Green Forms" and "Form 37s") at the NAI (for the south), PRONI and MMF (including a copy at SoG). The search forms asked for details of the person's parents, making them useful records now in their own right. They are online at www.pensear.org.

Directories

Directories are published lists of prominent residents, professionals and tradesmen that can be used to find addresses for people in censuses or as tools in their own right for learning about families and where they lived.

Dublin led the field in producing directories, starting in 1736 with *The Gentleman's and Citizen's Almanack*. Peter Wilson's *Directory* for Dublin City (1751–1837, except 1754–9) listed merchants and traders with addresses and occupations, and later increasing numbers of others — officers, clergymen, guildsmen, officials at Trinity College and so on. Between 1787 and

804   DUBLIN STREET DIRECTORY.

113 Jameson, T. solicitor
   ,, Fuller, T. solicitor
   ,, Hallenan, J. solicitor
   ,, Fitzmaurice, Francis, solicitor
114 Jackson, Mrs.   50*l.*
115 Lawless, Mr. Patrick,   50*l.*
116 Peebles, William, esq. and 4
      Usher's-quay,   45*l.*
.here Gloucester-place, Upper, intersects.
117 Morgan, Mrs.   41*l.*
   ,, Morgan, Robt. civil engineer
   ,, Morgan, Anthony, civil engineer &
      architect
118 Walsh, Miss,   41*l.*
   ,, Ince, Rd. Cunningham, barrister
119 Ryan, Samuel, M.D. apothecary
      and accoucheur,   36*l.*
120 Eagar, Frederick J. printer, stamp
      seller, stationery and account-book
      warehouse,   27*l.*
121 Brady, Ter. grocer, & 1 Summer-
      hill

———

Gardiner-street, Middle.

From Britain-st. Gt. to Mountjoy-sq. W.
P. St. George.—Mountjoy W.—City.
1 Grove, Miss, haberdasher, and
      trimming warehouse,   26*l.*
   ,, Grove, The Misses, milliners, dress-
      makers, and trimming warehouse
   ,, Kelly, Ellen, fruiterer
2 Vacant,   14*l.*

27 Russell, The Misses, board. schl. 22*l.*
......*here Gardiner's-lane intersects......*
28 Bowen, Johanna, spirit dealer,   13*l.*
29 Poole, Chas. house painter, paper
      hanger, and glazier,   13*l.*
30 M'Keon, Edw. groc. & spirit mer. 16*l.*
.....*here Belmont-place intersects......*
31 Ward, Thomas, tailor,   17*l.*
32 Tenements,   17*l.*
33 Dargan, Pat. scrivener & statr. 18*l.*
   ,, Collis, Maurice J. solicitor, master
      extraor. for the Court of Chancery,
      Com. for taking affidavits and
      acknowledgments of married wo-
      men, and Nelson-street, Tralee
   ,, Connor, James, solicitor, & Denny-
      street, Tralee
   ,, M'Swiney, Daniel O'Connell, solr.
      and Kenmare
   ,, M'Carthy, Charles Aylmer, solr. &
      Limerick
   ,, Mayberry, Richard, solicitor, and
      New-street, Killarney
   ,, O'Riordan, Joseph, and Killarney
   ,, Stack, Patrick, solicitor, & Nelson-
      street, Tralee
34 Lube, Jos. plumb. & bras found. 9*l.*
35 Brady, Ter. smith & bellhanger, 9*l.*
36 Vacant,   16*l.*
37 M'Cann, Mr. James,   16*l.*
38 Faucett, John, veteri. forge, 4*l.*10*s.*
39 Monks, Michael, provision deal. 9*l.*
40 Maguire, Hubert, painter & glaz. 9*l.*

64 Te
65 Lys
   ,, O'F
66 Fol
67 Ma
68 Fa
69 Wil
70 Kif
   —
   ex
   co
   co
   Pl
71 Ry
72 Nu
73 Ste
74 La
....*h*
Socie
St. F
Pre
   S
   C
   H
   E
   K
   D
   R
   M
   S
   M
   G
   Sis

Part of a page from Thom's *Irish Almanac*, 1852, showing residents of Gardiner Street, Dublin (courtesy of SoG).

1837, these and the *English Court Registry* were bound together in a single volume, *The Treble Almanack*. From 1834 to 1849, Pettigrew and Oulton's *Dublin Almanac and General Register of Ireland* appeared, providing street-by-street listings of an ever-increasing number of people in Dublin and its suburbs, from tradesmen upwards. This was superseded by Thom's *Irish Almanac and Official Directory* from 1844. As the 19th century progressed, the number of directories proliferated.

Other cities and larger towns acquired their own directories, starting with Ferrar's *Directory of Limerick* (1769). Directories covering all Ireland start from the 18th century: G. Taylor and A. Skinner, *Road Maps of Ireland* (1778), now on CD from **www.archivecdbooks.ie**, is one of several map books that double-up as pseudo-directories of landed estate-owners. Nationwide directories properly took off in the mid-19th century; the earliest, such as Pigot's 1820 *Commercial Directory of Ireland*, usually just listed the main towns and ignored smaller towns and villages.

Directories are cataloged in Ryan and Grenham. Substantial holdings are at the NLI, NAI, and Dublin City Archive and Library, and some are now available on Eneclann CD. Some CD copies have even been given away free by *Your Family Tree* magazine. Many are now online — see the excellent website **www.censusfinder.com/ ireland.htm**.

Thackeray's Irish Sketchbook

In 1842, William Makepeace Thackeray traveled through Ireland, zigzagging from Dublin to Bantry and Waterford to the Giant's Causeway, and compiled his *Irish Sketchbook*, under the nom-de-plume of M.A. Titmarsh. Copies of the first (1843), second (1863) or subsequent editions sometimes turn up at antiquarian booksellers, or are accessible in good libraries. Thackeray names many people, and it would be good luck for you if an ancestor appears among them. But what makes his book invaluable for any Irish family historian are his vivid word portraits of the places and characters he met on his journey. For example, at Glengariff, Co. Cork, he wrote evocatively of sketching a blacksmith:

"The scene was exceedingly wild and picturesque, and I took out a sketch-book and began to draw. The black-smith was at first very suspicious of the operation which I had commenced, nor did the poor fellow's sternness at all yield until I made him a present of a shilling to buy tobacco, when he, his friend, and his son became good-humoured, and said their little say. This was the first shilling he had earned these three years: he was a small farmer, but was starved out, and had set up a forge here, and was trying to get a few pence. What struck me was the great number of people about the place. We had at least twenty visits while the sketch was being made; cars, and single and double horsemen, were continually passing; between the intervals of the shower a couple of ragged old women would creep out from some hole, and display baskets of green apples for sale: wet or not, men and women were lounging up and down the road. You would have thought it was a fair, and yet there was not even a village at this place, only the inn and post-house, by which the cars to Tralee pass thrice a-week..."

CHAPTER 15

Religious registers

Registers of baptisms, marriages and burials have been kept in Ireland since at least the 17th century. Many Protestant ones were destroyed in 1922, and few Catholic ones pre-date the 1820s. Despite these shortcomings, much remains and forms an essential part of any Irish family tree.

Religious registers, of all denominations

Most religious registers for all of Ireland have been transcribed and indexed by the CHCs (see p. 77). They can only be searched by the centers' staff for a fee, and usually involve quite a long wait.

Surviving registers are cataloged meticulously (though new material may yet come to light), parish-by-parish, in Ryan and Grenham, the latter online at **www.ireland. com/ancestor/browse/counties/ index.htm**. Grenham provides exact dates for the start of registers and any gaps, whereas Ryan just gives the month and year. Some material is coming online, as detailed at **www.censusfinder.com/ ireland.htm** and **www.ireland.com/ancestor/ browse/links/counties/**. Of note are the Ulster Historical Foundation's database for Antrim and Down at **www.ancestryireland. co.uk**, and **www.cmcrp.net**, which has transcripts of various baptisms, marriages and

"Going to Mass from Mountain District," an Irish postcard from about 1905 (mind you, they won't get to Mass very quickly with their horse standing still like that!).

Going to Mass from Mountain District.

gravestones for counties mainly Clare, Cork, Dublin, Kerry, Limerick, Mayo, Tipperary, Waterford, Wexford and Wicklow.

A small proportion of Irish registers for all denominations is indexed — but not fully transcribed — at **www.familysearch.org**. Coverage of Catholic registers here is poor, confined to a few parishes in north Cork, Galway, Kerry, Roscommon and Sligo, not all from reliable transcripts. Once an entry is found, always check the original register, as the amount of detail in the latter will usually be greater.

Catholics

Under the Penal Laws (see p. 80) new Catholic parishes evolved and priests, theoretically deprived of their bishops, ministered to the peasantry and the dwindling ranks of the Catholic gentry. Deprived of money and status, standards declined. Some registers were kept and survive — the earliest fragmentary Catholic register is for Wexford town from 1671, followed by some information from towns in Counties Galway and Wexford. Registers seldom survive, though, until the mid-18th century. Those that do are usually for the better-off towns on the East Coast, or areas in the west where, as Grenham puts it, "pockets of Gaelic scholarship survived." The rest, especially the poorer areas of the north and west, don't start until the early 19th century.

Generally, parish registers are with the churches where they were made. Out of 1,153 known Catholic registers in all Ireland, 1,066 were successfully microfilmed up to the 1880s and are at the NLI. Grenham notes that a few of the films — such as St. John's, Sligo Town; Cappawhite, Co. Tipperary; and Waterford City — are not as comprehensive as the registers still in the parishes. Of those filmed, you must obtain written permission to inspect those for Cloyne (telephone Mgr O'Callaghan [022] 50302), Kerry (write to The Bishop of Kerry, Bishop's House, Killarney, Co. Kerry, [064] 31168) and Cashel and Emly (write to the Archbishop of Cashel and Emly, Archbishop's House, Thurles, Co. Tipperary [0504] 21512). Printed copies for Cashel and Emly are on free access at the NLI in Albert O'Casey (ed.), *O'Kief Coshe Mang, Slieve Lougher and Upper Blackwater in Ireland: Historical and Genealogical Items Relating to North Cork and East Kerry* (Knockagree Historical Fund, Birmingham, Alabama, 1952–68). The PRONI has microfilms of the Catholic registers of Northern Ireland; the Mormons have 398 sets of registers on film, some being copies of NLI films. Catholic registers were in simple Latin or occasionally in English. See p. 146 for interpreting Latinized names. Until the 19th or 20th centuries there was seldom money for a church, so baptisms, marriages and the "waking and keening" of the dead took place at home, at the priest's house or in the fields.

Baptisms usually state the date, child's name, parents' names including mother's maiden name, names of godparents, often with place of residence for parents and, less often, godparents.

The baptism of my 2 x great-uncle James Denning (see p. 50 and 106), son of "James Dening and Rose Magahan," took place the day he was born, June 15, 1863, at Drumgoon, the Catholic parish covering Cootehill, Co. Cavan. The godparents were Terence Connolly and Eliza Magahan (i.e. Mac Gahan).

January 1055

31 Thos Gillan Biddy M'Cann 99 John Bell & Margret M'Cann

February 55

Wm James Dennan & Ros M'Gahan 99 Alfrec Kinedy & Ros M' Cal...

...nard Hughes & Mary Brady 99 Michl M' Grath & Mary M' Gra...

...M'Cabe & Katharine Mullen 99 Peter Dichy & Ann Higgins

March — April — May 55 — June — July —

The marriage of James Dennan (Denning) and Rose M'Gahan. What looks like a reverse "PP" before the name of the witnesses is actually "TS," an abbreviation for the Latin for "witnesses," *testes*.

A 19th-century Irish wake (or funeral) in Co. Kerry. The body has been laid out and the priest summoned to say mass for the repose of the departed soul. The body is covered with white linen; tobacco, snuff and lighted candles are close by. The women of the household have begun their heart-rending cry, the dirge.

Ego baptizavi, *bapt* or *b* means "I baptized"; *filius*, *fil* or *f* means "son" and *filia*, *fil* or *f* is "daughter." *Legitium* means "legitimate," i.e. born of married parents. Often, "legitimate son/daughter" is abbreviated "*f.l.*" *Sponsoribus* or *sps* means "sponsors," i.e. godparents, who were often close relatives. *Gemini* means "twins."

Marriages: usually in the bride's parish, in late afternoon or evening, many just before Christmas or between the Epiphany (January 6) and Shrove Tuesday, for sex was forbidden during Lent. The donations made at weddings were often the cash-strapped priests' main income. Records usually give date, names of both parties, witnesses (who were often siblings of the bride and groom — relationships are stated very rarely,); sometimes residences of all four, ages, occupations and father's names are given. From the mid-19th century in Dublin, you'll find the names of the parties' mothers too, and where the bride and groom's parents lived. *In matrimonium*, *coniuxi* or *conj* means "joined in marriage," *testimonii* or *test* indicates witnesses. *Consanguinati* means the couple were related, followed by the degree. *In tertio gradio consanguineo* or *consanguinati in tertio grado* meant second cousins, i.e. sharing the same great-grandparent, while *In tertio et quattuor gradior* would indicate second cousins once removed. *Affinitatus* tells us the couples' families were somehow connected by a previous marriage, which was very common in smaller parishes.

Burials: the dead were usually laid out at home for two days. Mourners would pay their respects and have something to eat and drink with the family. There were few Catholic burial grounds: although the Church of Ireland had "stolen" the parish churches and graveyards, these were still consecrated places, and technically, in Catholic eyes, Catholic — one day, indeed, they longed to take them back. Catholic burials are often found in CoI burial registers, though not identified as such. Some priests, mainly in the northern areas, kept registers of their flock who died. Once Catholic churches were built and burial grounds established, of course, Catholic churches kept their own burial registers.

Extra information: Catholic records can include details of Poor Relief, dispensations for marriages between closely related people, local censuses, details of famine relief and even some personal letters.

Search tips: if the surname is relatively unusual, note everyone with it, including godparents and witnesses. It may be hard work, but you can then have many enjoyable hours piecing together the greater tree of your extended family from your notes. Always note the exact periods you have searched, too.

Catholic clergy: until they were legalized in 1782, and for some time after, Catholic priests were trained in Europe, especially at the Irish Colleges in Rome, Louvain, Lisbon, Salamanca and France. For the latter, see P. Boyle, *The Irish College in Paris from 1578 to 1901, with a Brief Account of the other Irish Colleges in France: viz., Bordeaux, Toulouse, Nantes, Poitiers, Douai, and Lille* (Art and Book Co., 1901). After the Relief Acts, three seminaries were established and these have printed alumni lists:

- St. Patrick's, Carlow: J. McEvoy, *Carlow College 1793–1993, the Ordained Students and the Teaching Staff of St. Patrick's College, Carlow* (St. Patrick's College, Carlow, 1993).
- St. Patrick's, Maynooth: Patrick J. Hammell, *Maynooth Students and Ordinations Index 1795–1895* (P.J. Hammell, Co. Offaly, 1992), which covers ordinations to 1902, and Patrick J. Hammell, *Maynooth Students and Ordinations 1895–1984* (Maynooth, 1984), which covers ordinations from 1903.
- All Hallows, run by the Vincentians, to train student priests for the missions: Kevin Condon, C.M., *The Missionary College of All Hallows, 1842–91* (All Hallow's College, 1986), which usefully includes students who did not complete the training.

From 1836 the *Irish Catholic Directory* had appeared annually, listing priests by their parishes. Priests could not marry, of course (though that didn't always stop them having children!). Records of their education are very useful, as they often name at least one parent. Frequently, vocations ran in families, and it is sometimes possible to reconstruct an entire family tree from the records of the priests it produced, not least because obituaries of priests often mention relatives — especially if they were other priests.

The Collegio Beda (www.bedacollege.com) was founded in Rome in 1852 to provide postgraduate education to British and Irish clergymen. Through its doors passed many a future parish priest, including my great-uncle William Denning, who is standing in the dead centre of the group.

The Dennings of Cootehill

My grandmother Maureen Denning and her brother William, who became a Catholic Monsignor, were born in Battle, Sussex, in 1910 and 1907 respectively. Their father William Denning (1856–1927) was head gardener at Battle Abbey, but before then had worked for M.P. Grace & Co., a shipping company based in the United States — work that had brought him to England, where he married Mary Barry in 1905.

William's grandchildren knew the Dennings were from Ireland, but that was all. But in family papers, William's brother's newspaper obituary (see p. 50) identified their place of birth as Cootehill, Co. Cavan. There was a further clue — when William's widow Mary moved to Ruislip, she called her house "Knockatane."

Cavan Genealogy, Cavan's heritage centre, searched their databases of religious registers for me and found William and his siblings' baptisms at Drumgoon, the Catholic parish covering Cootehill. I knew this was the right family, because William's London marriage certificate named his father as James.

William baptized 17 October 1855 son of James Denen and Rose McGahan Sp: Phill Dennen & Sally Mc Gahan

Mary baptized 2 January 1859 daughter of James Denen and Rose McGahan Sp: Henery & Lisy Mc Gahan

Michael baptized 19 September 1860 son of James Denen and Rose McGahan Sp: Edward Mc Kitrick & Ellen M. [No surname recorded, probably McKitrick.]

James baptized 15 June 1863 son of James Dening and Rose Magahan Sp: Terence Connolly & Elisa Magahan

After civil registration started in 1864, Cavan Genealogy switched to searching birth records instead, finding three more:

Catharine born 5 December 1865 daughter of James Dinning, farmer, Knocatane, and Rose Dinning formerly Mc Gahan

Anne born 30 September 1868 daughter of James Dinning, farmer, Knocatane, and Rose Dinning formerly Mc Gahan. [The corresponding baptism, for the same day, gives her godparents William Denning & Sarah Mc Donald.]

John born 18 November 1871 son of James Dinning, farmer, Knocatane, and Rose Dinning formerly Mc Gahan

This was the first time I had seen "Knockatane" in Irish records: it was an extra confirmation that this was my family — and quite an emotional experience to see it there.

James and Rose married on 8 February 1855 at Drumgoon. Their deaths appear in civil registration: Rose Dinnen died on January 25, 1878, aged 48, of "serious apoplexy, one day, certified," with the informant as James Dinnen, occupier of Knockatane, where the death took place. James Denning himself died on August 21, 1880, a widowered farmer, aged 68, of "gastritis, six weeks, uncertified, no medical attendant." The informant was "Michael Denning, Knockatane," presumably his son.

None of the children appear in the later Cootehill registers. They were orphaned in a decade when heavy rains and crop failures threatened a repeat of the Great Famine, so they all migrated to the United States, first the eldest, William, who found work with Grace & Co. — he even became a U.S. citizen — and then his siblings. They did well: Catherine, for example, married Hugh M. Battersby, a jeweller of the firm of Parker and Battersby, with a shop in the Rockefeller Centre, New York.

The names of the children's godparents indicate the wider relations of James and Rose, while the registers also show a William Dinnan and Mary McCabe having children baptized from when the registers start to 1843 — William could well have been a brother of James.

Griffith's Valuation, made in 1856–7 (see p. 84), shows no Dennings in the townland of Knockatane, but in nearby Drumgoonhill (owned, like Knockatane, by Richard Coote) were three: James Dinning, with "house, offices and land" of 5 acres, and 2 rods; the land was worth £3-15-0 and the buildings 10s. Next door was Phillip Dinning renting "house, office [i.e. sheds] and land of 13 acres, 3 rods and no perches"; the land was worth £9 and the buildings 15s. A few doors away was William Dinning, with "house, offices and land" of 8 acres, 2 rods and 38 perches; the land worth £5-15-0 and the buildings 10s. James and William were probably brothers Phillip may have been one too, or a member of an older generation. But judging from the size of the holding, James was the poor relation!

The Catholic registers there don't begin until 1829, and James was born about 1812, so that's about as far back as the line will go. But what more can the surname tell us?

There were 17th-century English immigrants called Denning (an English surname of rather uncertain origin) and the name Denin appears in O'Hart's list (see p. 158) of Huguenot immigrants, but there were also Gaelic names Anglicized to Dinning: Cavan Genealogy have noted 32 spellings of the name in their own records, including Dening, Dennan, Dennen, Dennin, Denning, Dennings, Dennon, Dinheen, Dinning. MacLysaght (see p. 155) states that Dina,

Dinane and *Denning* were considered synonyms of each other in a list compiled by the Cunard Company. This list carries no authority in determining surname origins as such, but I know William and his siblings sailed to America, quite possibly on a Cunard ship, and this could well explain why they ended up fixing their spelling as 'Denning'.

MacLysaght derives Dinan or Dinneen from Ó Duinnín, but this name was found mainly in Co. Cork. He refers to O Duig(e)nan, derived from O Duibhgeannáin, a family strongly associated with Counties Leitrim and Roscommon, from where they are known to have spread to Cavan, as Deignan and Dignam, etc. O'Hart equates the surname Dinan (hence Denning) with Dignum and O'Dugenan, descended from Doighnan of the southern Uí Neill, son of Tagan, a 7 x great-grandson of Main, a son of Niall of the Nine Hostages (see p. 165) himself.

MacLysaght also relates that they were bards and *ollamhs* (court poets) to the MacDermots, MacRannells and O'Farrells, and had a bardic school at Castle Fore, Co. Leitrim. My grandmother certainly had a good ear for music, for she trained as a concert pianist at the Royal School of Music. Maybe my passion for genealogy stems from them too, if you believe such things are hereditary, for the family included Magnus O'Duigenan, the chief compiler of the *Book of Ballymote* in about 1415, and Peregrine O' Duigenan (d. 1664), one of the eponymous writers of the *Annals of the Four Masters* (see p. 156), one of the greatest of Irish genealogical works.

My grandmother and her brother "Willie" as children in England.

This tiny, blurred picture shows "Knockatane," Ruislip, with my grandmother and great-grandmother standing outside.

A venerable old Irish relative of mine. Sadly, besides the fact that he looks very similar to my great-grandfather, I have absolutely no idea who he was, for nobody wrote on the back of the picture!

The local newspaper report of Maureen Denning's wedding states her deceased parents' names, and identifies their last home — "Knockatane," South Drive, Ruislip.

MARRIAGE OF MISS DENNING

RETINUE IN GREEN.

Considerable interest was evinced in the wedding of Mr. Jerome Collingwood Rietchel, son of Mr. and Mrs. J. Rietchel, of 10, Culverden Grange, Tunbridge Wells, and Miss Maureen Josephine Denning, daughter of the late Mr. and Mrs. W. Denning, of Knockatane, South-drive, Ruislip, which took place at the Church of the Sacred Heart, Ruislip, on Wednesday. The Rev. W. P. Denning, brother of the bride, came especially from Rome to conduct the service, and he was assisted by the Rev. A. E. S. Blount, and the Rev. J. J. Curtin.

THE ADVERTISER AND GAZETTE, FRIDA

Mr. Jerome Rietchel and Miss Maureen Denning leaving Ruislip Catholic Church after their marriage on Wednesday.

Church of Ireland

The Church of Ireland was disestablished on January 1, 1871. Its records became state property and many were deposited at the Public Record Office in the Four Courts, Dublin. The fire of 1922 destroyed nearly 1,000 Church of Ireland registers. Luckily, 637 other registers survived because they had yet to be deposited. The NAI's *Parish Register & Related Material Catalogue* indexes, by parish, extracts from now lost registers made between 1915 and 1922 as evidence of pension entitlements. This and other transcripts or extracts from registers mean that the total loss, though dreadful and in many cases irreversible, is far from complete.

Church of Ireland registers were kept systematically from 1634. Some surviving ones, especially for towns, start in the 17th century. Most, however, survive only from about 1770–1820; still, on average, somewhat earlier than their Catholic counterparts. A catalog, giving dates and locations, is in Ryan (but not Grenham) and another, *Church of Ireland Parish Registers*, is at the NAI. See also the slightly less comprehensive N. Reid, *Table of Church of Ireland Parochial Records and Copies* (IFHS, 2nd edn., 2002) at NAI and NLI. Most registers are at either the NLI (in original or microfilm form) or the CoI's Representative Church Body Library (RCBL), Dublin, which has various records from 830 parishes. For Northern Ireland, surviving registers are on microfilm at the PRONI; for specific coverage see *Guide to Church Records: Public Record of Northern Ireland* (PRONI, 1994). Copies of registers for Cavan, Donegal, Leitrim, Louth and Monaghan are at the PRONI and RCBL. In some cases, records are still with the parish, whose addresses are in the *Church of Ireland Directory* and in telephone directories.

Baptisms: recorded name, father's full name, mother's Christian name but not maiden name; sometimes the address was included and, usually from 1820, father's occupation.

Marriages: until 1845 recorded names of the parties marrying and the date, but seldom any more; an address may be given if one of the parties was from elsewhere. After this, they record the same details as civil marriage records (see p. 93).

Many pre-Civil Registration non-CoI marriages were recognized unofficially, but for full legal recognition couples had to marry in the CoI. The registers therefore contain many weddings for people of all denominations, though mainly those who were better off.

Some special records of Protestant marriages, including details of occupations and fathers' names, were sent between 1795–1862 to the Charleton Trust Fund, which offered money to Protestant laborers in return for perpetuating their religion by marrying Protestant women. These cover mainly Counties Meath and Longford, with some for Cavan, Offaly (King's), Louth, Westmeath and Dublin, and are in NLI Accessions vol. 37.

Raphoe Derry Connor
Armagh
Clogher Dromore
Down
Killala Kilmore
Achonry
Ardagh
Elphin
Tuam Meath
Kilmacduagh Clonfert Kildare
Dublin
Kilfenora Killaloe
Leighlin
Ossory
Cashel
Limerick Emly Ferns
Lismore Waterford
Ardfert & Cloyne
Aghadoe
Cork & Ross

——— Ecclesiastical provincial boundaries

Church of Ireland dioceses.

A devoted husband brings home his demure new bride, mounted on a white pony; a 19th-century wedding party witnessed in Co. Kerry.

Burials: usually just state name, age and townland. The registers often list people of other denominations, including Catholics, as the Church of Ireland burial ground was usually the only place available for burials.

Gravestones: most graves were marked with a wooden cross or unmarked stone. Those gravestones that were inscribed are worth tracking down. B. Mitchell's, *A New Genealogical Atlas of Ireland* (Baltimore, 1986), can help you find the graveyards nearest your ancestors' homes, but note that many burials were in old family home parishes, rather than newer places of settlement. Most Northern Ireland graveyards are listed at **www.historyfrom headstones.com**. Public cemeteries date mainly from the 20th century; their records, mainly listing sale of plots, are with the cemeteries.

Many gravestones, most of which no longer survive, were transcribed in the "Memorials of the Dead" — the *Journal of the Association for the Preservation of the Memorials of the Dead*

(1888-1937). This is fully indexed to 1910 and by volume thereafter, in the NLI and on Eneclann CD (see p. 75). Many more transcripts of

Banns or license?

Especially before 1820, it's worth seeing if banns or licenses survived. The reading or "calling" of banns was a means of preventing bigamy or clandestine marriages, dating back to the Middle Ages. They were either recorded in the same register or in a separate banns book. They should state the parishes of residence of both parties. Marriage licenses, originating in the 14th century, enabled marriages to take place immediately and were also seen as a status symbol. The local bishop would issue the license if both parties lived in his diocese or if not, the Archbishop of Armagh did so. The original bonds were destroyed in 1922, but information can still be gained from:

- the original indexes at the NAI and MMF, which at least tell you a marriage license had existed. Dublin's diocesan index is in the "Index to Dublin Wills and Grant Books" (*Report of the Deputy Keeper of the Public Records of Ireland*, 26, 1895) for 1270-1800 and vol.. 30, 1899, for 1800-58. These include, for example, the license for the marriage of Oscar Wilde's parents, William Robert Wilde and Jane Francesca Elgee, in 1851.
- Bonds issued through the Archbishop's Prerogative Court 1630-1858 are in the GO (ref. GO 605-7), which also has abstracts of some marriages recorded in Prerogative Court wills (GO 255-6).

The first burial?

Burial has a long history in Ireland. The first man to be buried there, according to the *Lebor Gabála* (see p. 172), was Ladra, pilot of the ship in which Cessair, granddaughter of Noah, sailed to Ireland just before the Great Flood. He was "the first dead man who went under the soil of Ireland," at Ard Ladrand, followed soon after by Bith, son of Noah, "in the great stone heap of Sliab Betha."

gravestones are online at **http:// interment.net**; **www.fermanagh.org.uk**; **www.webone.co.au/~sgrieves/cemeteries_ ireland.htm** (mainly for Tipperary) and **www.historyfromheadstones.com** (for Northern Ireland). Further transcripts are listed in Grenham and Ryan.

Vestry minutes: the "vestry" was a parish committee chaired by the resident clergyman. Minutes of their meetings can contain many details about the administration and maintenance of parish schools, almshouses, church, fire brigade, water supply and the care (or otherwise) of the poor. Most that survive are with the RCBL and the PRONI.

Church of Ireland clergy: most were educated at Trinity College Dublin (see p. 119) or Protestant universities overseas. Details of all CoI clergy are in Rev. J. Leslie's *Leslie Biographical Index*, at the RBCL Library, Dublin.

Presbyterians

During the 18th and 19th centuries, about 20 percent of Ireland's population was Protestant. Many of these were Presbyterian settlers in the north.

Presbyterianism (see p. 42) had become widespread in Scotland by the reign of James I (1603–25), when many were encouraged to settle in Ulster in the "Plantations" (see p. 201). Presbyterianism became quite popular in 17th-century England too, and in Cromwell's time congregations of English Presbyterian settlers were established, particularly at Athlone,

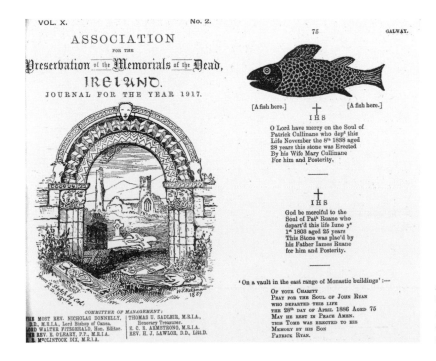

A page from the Clare-Galway Abbey section of *Memorials of the Dead* (courtesy of SoG).

Clonmel, Dublin, Limerick and Mullingar. Irish 18th-century Presbyterianism underwent several rifts, into Non-Subscribers, Seceders and Covenanters. In 1840, the Synod of Ulster and Secession Synod fused to form the General Assembly of the Presbyterian Church in Ireland.

Many Presbyterian events are in CoI registers (but these won't state that people *weren't* non-CoI). Presbyterians also kept their own registers, which are cataloged in Ryan. A few date back to the 17th century but most don't start until 1819. The PRONI's *Guide to Church Records* lists what has survived for Northern Ireland. The PRONI's copy also covers Éire, though in less detail. A rather incomplete list is in M. Falley, *Irish and Scotch-Irish Ancestral Research: A Guide to the Genealogical Records, Methods and Sources in Ireland, vol. I Repositories and Records, vol. II Bibliography and Family Index* (M.D. Falley, 1962, repr. GPC, 1998).

"Meeting the Ancestor: Encounter in a Country Churchyard." This painting, by leading Irish genealogist Justin Martin, shows his mentor the late Eric McAuliffe successfully uncovering a family's Irish origins.

Legacy of the workhouse

My great-great-grandfather Revd. Patrick Henry Kilduff was born in 1839 at Banagher, the beautiful village on the River Shannon in Co. Offaly, the place where Anthony Trollope wrote *The MacDermots of Ballycloran* (1843–7). Having gone to school in nearby Aughrim he entered Trinity College, Dublin, on April 26, 1870. Their records list him as a "pensioner" (someone paying a fixed annual sum for his education) and a "dissenter" (a Protestant who was not part of the Church of Ireland). Although baptized a Catholic, his family had probably been caught up in the tail-end of the Crotty Schism in Birr (see p. 113). After two years, Patrick was ordained a Church of Ireland deacon, and later became a priest. He worked all his life in London, as chaplain to the Edmonton Union Workhouse, but returned to Dublin between 1877 and 1878 to complete his B.A. course at Trinity. While researching this book I discovered why he has such a gaunt look: while he and two of his brothers, Michael (1840) and John (1844) were baptized in Banagher, where their father Michael was a farmer, the fourth, Thomas, was baptized in May 1845 in nearby Birr, because the family had been forced into the workhouse by the Famine, which struck in earnest that year, leaving 22,000 people in Co. Offaly dead by 1851. In fact, Patrick was probably lucky to have survived the Famine at all.

The registers are either with the congregations or (especially for defunct congregations from Éire) at the Presbyterian Historical Society. Belfast Presbyterian congregations tended not to be as stable as CoI parishes, and congregations could split and re-form at will, so a family's events may be found scattered through several registers. *The History of Congregations of the Presbyterian Church in Ireland* (PHS, 1982) is useful for background information, as is Lewis's *Topographical Dictionary of Ireland* (1837) — see p. 80 — and Thom's *Irish Almanac and Official Directory*, which included, from 1846, a full list of Presbyteries. B. Mitchell, *A New Geographical Atlas of Ireland* (GPC, 2nd edn., 2002) is excellent for the congregations of Ulster.

Presbyterian registers may include Stipend Rolls, Minute Books, Communicants' Roll Books and Session Minute Books, which sometimes provide extra information on ancestors. However, the main records are:

Baptisms: show the date, name and parents' names. In the 19th century they often include mother's maiden name, date of birth, godparents' names and parents' addresses too.

Francis Makemie (1658–1708) was born at Ramelton, Co. Donegal. He was a pioneer of Presbyterianism in America, establishing the first congregation there at Snow Hill, Virginia. He survived imprisonment by the governor of New York, and died at his farm in 1708.

Marriages: may include the bride's father. Presbyterian marriages were legally recognized from 1782 onwards, so some registers date from then. From 1819 they were supposed to show the date, names of parties, their congregation and at least two witnesses. People intending to marry had to inform their Session — the court that regulated their congregations' morals — so marriages can be traced through Session Minute Books too.

Burials: virtually all were in CoI cemeteries and will be in CoI registers.

Extra Presbyterian research: Belfast's Linen Hall Library was founded in 1788 by prominent local Presbyterians. Some families have been members ever since. Their collections include masses of family papers and books, Blackwood's 94 volumes of Ulster Presbyterian family pedigrees (and other miscellaneous material such as Belfast weather reports for 1796–1906!).

The Institute of Ulster Scots Studies at Ulster University is opening a Heritage Centre at Monreagh, Laggan, Co. Donegal, dedicated to Irish Presbyterianism, the main waves of Presbyterian migration to America (1717-20, 1725-9, 1767-76 and 1783) and the two most prominent Presbyterian pioneers in America, Francis Makemie and William Gregg.

Presbyterian ministers: the main sources in print are Revd. J. McConnell (et al), *Fasti of the Irish Presbyterian Church 1613–1840* (Belfast, 1938), including 156 ministers who went to America. The Secession Synod and Synod of Ulster fused to become the General Assembly, and for their ministers down to 1910 see J.M. Barkley, *Fasti of the General Assembly of the Presbyterian Church in Ireland 1840-1910* (3 vols., Presbyterian Historical Society, 1986-7).

Presbyterianism had a surprising local revival in Birr (Parsonstown), Co. Offaly, in the mid-19th century. Fr. Michael Crotty, the local Catholic priest, discovered that funds intended for building a Catholic church had been misappropriated. His protests led to a full-scale conflict with the local bishop and a massive increase in his local popularity. The furor culminated in 1836 with Crotty and his flock leaving Catholicism altogether and becoming Presbyterian. The Schism's tide ebbed in the 1840s but left a flotsam of Presbyterians behind at Birr, where one may not have expected any at all.

John Wesley, founder of Methodism, evangelized Ireland, but never made much of an inroad into traditional Catholic communities.

Methodists

Revd. John Wesley (1703–91), an Anglican clergyman, founded Methodism as an evangelical preaching movement within the Church of England in the late 1730s and did the same in Ireland in 1747, returning 20 times until his death in 1791 to found Methodist Societies within the CoI and Presbyterian churches. Initially, baptisms, marriages and burials were recorded in CoI registers. Methodism split from the Church of England in the 1770s and in 1816 Irish Methodism split over an argument as to whether their ministers could administer the sacraments. The Primitive Methodists remained with the CoI but the Wesleyan Methodist Connexion started holding their own services and registers. In 1878 the Primitive Methodists left the CoI to join the Wesleyans as the Methodist Church in Ireland.

Registers generally give similar information to CoI ones. They were the personal property of itinerant ministers who traveled in large circuits to visit their flocks so family events may be scattered through several sets of records without much clear geographical logic. Ryan catalogs surviving registers. Those for all Ulster are also traceable through the PRONI's list of Methodist registers, attached to its *Parish Register Index*. The PRONI also has an island-wide index, 1817–50. Those for Éire are best tracked through the CHCs, most of whom have included surviving Methodist registers in their databases. Some congregations also had registers of members and teaching classes.

The Wesley Historical Society's Irish Branch has the PRONI's microfilmed registers and much more material. Records of two offshoots, the Methodist New Connexion and Primitive Methodist Connexion, are at the John Rylands Library in England.

'M' for Methodist?

An unusual Irish Methodist connection is that of Dame Judi Dench, "M" in the recent James Bond films, whose parents married at Sandymount Methodist Church, Dublin, in 1924 and whose English-born grandmother Bessie Oak Dench is commemorated by a stained glass window there. Judi's mother Eleanora Jones's mother, meanwhile, was a Simons from Annaghcliffe, Co. Cavan.

For Methodist ministers, see C.H. Crookshank's *History of Methodism in Ireland*, which includes biographical notices for ministers and prominent laity to 1859. For the early-mid-19th century, see Revd. William Hill, *An Alphabetical Arrangement of all the Wesleyan Methodist Ministers, and Preachers on Trial, in connection with the British Conference* (1885). The Wesleyan Historical Society has *Minutes of Conference* from 1752, including brief obituaries of ministers.

Quakers

Sometimes mis-called Anabaptists, the Society of Friends was founded as a breakaway Protestant group in England during the English Civil War (1642–8) by George Fox and had reached Ireland by the 1650s. The Quakers' refusal to take oaths made them a particular subject of state hostility and many migrated to the Quaker colony of Pennsylvania. Most of those left behind eventually joined less demanding denominations, meaning that many people may have unsuspected lines of Quaker ancestry.

George Fox (1624–91), founder of the Quakers.

The Society of Friends was run by a hierarchy of meetings (one for men and another for women) starting with local "particular" meetings, several of which would congregate periodically at "preparative" meetings that sent representatives to "monthly" meetings in Antrim, Ballyhagan, Carlow, Cootehill, Cork, Dublin, Edenderry, Grange, Lisburn, Limerick, Lurgan, Moate, Mountmellick, Richhill, Tipperary, Waterford, Wexford and Wicklow. The Monthly Meetings kept records of births, marriages and deaths, and maintained a strictly observed system of settlement certificates and examinations.

The records are cataloged by Ryan and, in more detail, Grenham. They are divided between the Society of Friends Historical Library, Dublin, and Religious Society of Friends, Archives Committee, Lisburn, Northern Ireland. Copies of records are on MMF and at NAI, NLI and (for the north) PRONI. The Dublin and Lisburn libraries also have many other records and pedigrees of Irish Quakers. See O. Goodbody, *Guide to Irish Quaker Records 1654–1860* (Irish Manuscripts Commission, 1967), including many Quaker will abstracts.

Births: list name, place of birth, parents' names (though not mother's maiden name), residence and father's occupation.

Marriages: show parties' names, residences, date and place of marriage, parents' names and residence. Marriages are recorded under both bride and groom, with the parents of each in the respective entry only. Marriages could be witnessed by dozens of relatives.

Deaths: give name, age, occupation, residence, date and place of death, place of burial. From 1813, deaths recorded at Monthly Meetings were published in *The Annual Monitor*.

Baptists

Also called Antipaedobaptists, the movement started among English Puritan exiles in early 17th-century Amsterdam and held that only consenting adults should be baptized. It reached Ireland with soldiers of Cromwell's army but never numbered more than a few thousand. Records are with local congregations and cataloged by Ryan. Contact the Baptist Union of Ireland for more information.

Walloons and Huguenots

Walloons were Flemish Protestants fleeing Catholic persecution in the 16th century. Huguenots were Protestants fleeing France, especially after the St. Bartholomew's Day Massacre of 1572. Many went to England, from where some made it to Ireland, mostly between 1620 and 1641, though some came later, with Cromwell. A second major wave into England and Ireland followed the Revocation of the Edict of Nantes in 1685.

These asylum-seekers were generally welcomed, for they were mostly hard-working tradesmen, silk weavers, merchants or moneyed nobles who became valued taxpayers. They were encouraged to settle in certain towns and cities in mainland Britain and at Portarlington, Laois (Queen's Co.); Waterford City; Youghal, Co. Cork; Cork City; Lisburn, Co. Antrim; and Dublin City. Here they wove cloth of worstead and silk, famed as "Irish poplin."

Most conformed to the CoI, but some "non-Conformist Huguenots" remained completely independent. Dublin had two non-Conformist and two Conformist Huguenot chapels, one of the former being a chapel in St. Patrick's (CoI) Cathedral. Most surviving registers of both types have been published by the Huguenot Society with copies at the NLI and NAI.

The Irish Huguenot Archive housed at the RCBL includes much biographical material and records of Huguenot charities. Conformist Huguenot baptisms, marriages and burials are in CoI registers.

The St. Bartholomew's Day Massacre of 1572. Some of its survivors fled Paris to start a new life in England and, later, in Ireland.

Clandestine marriages

The "Schulze's Register" at the GRO, Dublin, is an unusual register of 55 baptisms and about 6,000 marriages conducted at the German Lutheran Church in Poolbeg Street, Dublin, by Revd. J.G.F. Schulze between 1806 and 1837 (mainly between 1825 and 1837). Schulze was one of 11 "couple-beggars" who held no-questions-asked weddings in Dublin, but only his have survived the 1922 fire at the Four Courts. Most weddings were for ordinary Irish people eloping, or where the bride was heavily pregnant.

Lines can often be traced back to France using naturalization records (see p. 136).

Congregationalists or Independents

Originally a Puritanical movement in England, and popular in Cromwell's army, this denomination had a small Irish following by the 18th century. Records for Belfast are detailed in the PRONI's *Guide to Church Records*. Those for the congregations at Dublin (Zion Chapel, King's Inn St.; York St.; Oriel St.; and Dún Laoghaire, formerly Kingstown) and Limerick are at the PRONI. The Salem Chapel, Kilmainham, still keeps its own records.

Palatines

In May 1709, war between England and France displaced many Protestants from the Rhine Palatine, particularly Mannheim, Hesse and Baden. They fled up the Rhine to London, but as there was no room for them, some 821 families (numbering about 3,000–6,000 people) were shipped to Ireland. They were given leases of land, but the venality of the commissioners responsible for them disheartened most so much that they migrated surreptitiously back to England. Those that remained were mainly on the Southwell estate at Rathkeale, Co. Limerick, and Abel Ramm's estate near Gorey, Co. Wexford, with smaller groups in Counties Cork and Dublin. They had distinctive German surnames, such as Switzer, Fitzell and Tesky. Most appear in normal CoI registers, though many in Limerick became Methodists. Their communities tended to stay culturally isolated, and many migrated to America in the 19th century. See H.Z. Jones, *The Palatine Families of Ireland* (Camden, Maine, 1990).

Jews

There were Sephardic Jews in Ireland in the Middle Ages, expelled officially (though probably not entirely) in 1290 and readmitted in the 1650s. There was a community with a rabbi in Dublin by 1700, with a cemetery established in 1718. By 1811, there were only two Jewish families there, but soon they were joined by many Ashkenazi Jews fleeing persecution in Eastern Europe. Communities sprung up in the other main towns and cities — Cork, Limerick, Waterford, Drogheda, Belfast and Derry — which offered scope for the main Jewish activities, banking and trade, while the poorer Jews working as gold- and silversmiths, tobacco and snuff dealers, and watchmakers. By 1911, there were some 5,000 Jews in Ireland. The Dublin Jews found unexpected fame through the character of Leopold Bloom, the Jewish-born advertising salesman and hero of James Joyce's *Ulysses*, which is set in Dublin on June 16, 1904. "The Jews were foreigners at that time," Joyce explained in a letter to Jacques Mercanton. "There was no hostility toward them, but contempt, yes the contempt people always show for the unknown."

Records are with local synagogues and the Irish Jewish Museum, Dublin. See also the genealogy section of the Irish Jewish Community website **www.jewishireland.org/ genealogy.html** and L. Hyman, *The Jews in Ireland from the Earliest Times to the Year 1910* (Irish University Press, 1972), which includes the Dublin community's 19th-century registry book of births and deaths.

Moravians

Founded in Bohemia and originally aimed at reforming the Lutheran church from within, the Moravian church became a denomination in its own right. It spread to Britain and Ireland in the 1730s, with Irish congregations at Corofin, Co. Clare (with no surviving records); Cootehill, Co. Cavan; Dublin; and Gracehill (Gracehill Moravian Church, Church Road, Gracehill, Co. Antrim: see **www.gracehillvillage.org/ index.asp?id=3**). The latter is the only one surviving and has the registers of the others, which are very detailed. Copies are on microfilm at the PRONI. Other sources for Moravian ancestry are congregation books, elders' minutes, memoirs and congregation diaries.

James Joyce (1882–1941), whose novel *Ulysses* aimed an unexpected spotlight on Dublin's Jewish community.

The Ulster Covenant

Among Ireland's many "census substitutes" is a list of under half a million signatures with addresses of men and women who signed the Ulster Covenant and parallel Declaration on September 28, 1912, hoping to block Home Rule for Ireland. It is at the PRONI and is now online at **www.proni.gov.uk/ ulster covenant/index.html**. As a "census substitute," it provides evidence of who was alive at the time, where they lived, and with whom.

— Ulster's —
Solemn League and Covenant.

Being convinced in our consciences that Home Rule would be disastrous to the material well-being of Ulster as well as of the whole of Ireland, subversive of our civil and religious freedom, destructive of our citizenship and perilous to the unity of the Empire, we, whose names are underwritten, men of Ulster, loyal subjects of His Gracious Majesty King George V., humbly relying on the God whom our fathers in days of stress and trial confidently trusted, do hereby pledge ourselves in solemn Covenant throughout this our time of threatened calamity to stand by one another in defending for ourselves and our children our cherished position of equal citizenship in the United Kingdom and in using all means which may be found necessary to defeat the present conspiracy to set up a Home Rule Parliament in Ireland. ¶ And in the event of such a Parliament being forced upon us we further solemnly and mutually pledge ourselves to refuse to recognise its authority. ¶ In sure confidence that God will defend the right we hereto subscribe our names. ¶ And further, we individually declare that we have not already signed this Covenant.

The above was signed by me at_____ "Ulster Day," Saturday, 28th September, 1912.

—— God Save the King. ——

CHAPTER 16

Occupational records

These record people in the context of what they did for a living. Most Irish people worked as small farmers and laborers and went almost completely unrecorded in this category of documentation. There are, however, plenty of exceptions.

A popular depiction of a late 19th-century Irish peasant farmer, enjoying his ubiquitous pipe.

Education

In the 18th century, itinerant teachers, impoverished heirs of the *aos dána*, the bards and druids of ancient Ireland, provided the peasantry with rudimentary education, teaching in rough shelters or actually in the shelter of hedges (explaining the name "hedge schools"). Despite this, the majority of Irish received little or no formal education until 1811, when the Society for Promoting the Education of the Poor of Ireland, also called the Kildare Place Society, was established. It aimed to provide primary education for the poor, regardless of denomination. Records of teachers to 1854 are at the Church of Ireland College of Education. D.R. Dingfelder and E. McAuliffe, *Schoolmasters and Schoolmistresses in Ireland, 1826-27* (California, 1982), based on the Irish Education Enquiry of 1826, is also useful. Teachers' salaries paid under the National School system for the mid-19th century are in NAI (references ED 4 and 5).

Primary education was established in 1831 under the Board of Commissioners for National Education. School records give the pupil's name and age, denomination, father's occupation and residence, along with miscellaneous notes. Most are still with the school or local church with some for the 1870s and 1880s at the NAI (ref. C.145). About 1,500 school records, mainly registers and inspectors' reports for Northern Ireland, 1832-89, are at the PRONI.

Thackeray's sketch of children in Dundalk's Infant School in 1842. Though run by the Church of Ireland, it was filled mostly by Catholic children: *"Eighty of these little people, healthy, clean and rosy, some in smart gowns and shoes and stockings, some with patched pinafores and little bare pink feet, sat upon a half a dozen low benches, and were singing at the top of their fourscore fresh voices."*

For details (for the period 1844–1926) of the Royal Hibernian School, Dublin, that cared for the sons of soldiers posted abroad, see **www.rhms-searcher.co.uk/**.

Universities

Until recent times, Ireland's only university was Trinity College, Dublin, whose registers have been published in G.D. Burtchaell and T.U. Sadlier (eds), *Alumni Dublinenses, a Register of the Students,*
Graduates, Professors, and Provosts of Trinity College, in the University of Dublin (Williams and Norgate, 1924). Records after that are with the university and can be accessed by postal enquiry.

Many Irishmen attended university abroad. Protestants went to Oxford and Cambridge or the Scottish Universities, all of which have published admission registers. Catholics had a wide choice of establishments in Europe, especially France, Spain and Portugal.

Education for the poorest children very often began with a village storyteller, such as the one shown here in Co. Kerry, c. 1934 (picture courtesy of National Folklore Collection, UCD).

The Queen's University opened its colleges in Belfast, Cork and Galway in 1849. Despite its name, women were not admitted until the 1870s. It became the Royal University of Ireland in 1880, splitting in 1908 to become Queen's University, Belfast and the National University of Ireland (based at Cork and Galway). The Catholic University of Ireland was founded by Cardinal Newman at St. Stephen's Green, Dublin, in 1854. It became University College, Dublin, in 1881 and was joined to the National University of Ireland in 1908. Graduates of these institutions appear in the *Royal University of Ireland Calendar* which, for 1909, provides an almost complete list of graduates to date, living and dead.

Many clergymen were university graduates; they are described in the chapter on religious registers (see p. 102).

Civil service

Applications for British Civil Service commissions from the mid-19th century included a birth or baptism certificate. Applicants came from all over the world, but many were actually Irish. The records are at the SoG.

Coastguards and revenue officers

To avoid corruption, coastguards were moved from station to station, sometimes leading to Irish officers leaving Ireland, and mainland British ones and their families arriving. Coastguards' records are TNA class ADM, dating from 1822, and described in TNA information leaflet 8. Mrs. E.R. Stage has an index to over 70,000 coastguards (see p. 216). For Irish Revenue Service officers from 1709 see **www.from-ireland.net/lists/revenue officers ireland 1709.htm**.

Doctors

T.P.C. Kirkpatrick, *Biographical File on Irish Medics* (National Library Office, n.d.) is virtually complete up to 1954; copies are at the NLI and The Royal College of Physicians of Ireland. Medics can also be traced through regular directories (see p. 100) and *Irish Medical Directories*, published from 1843.

Many medics trained at universities (see p. 119). Trinity College, Dublin, had a School of Physic from 1711. Many joined or were registered by medical bodies, particularly:

- **Dublin Guild of Barber-Surgeons** (from 1576), with records at Trinity College, Ms 1447.
- **Royal College of Physicians of Ireland** (from 1667) holds its own records.
- **Royal College of Surgeons in Ireland** (from 1784) holds its own records.
- **Apothecaries' Hall** (from 1747), with records from 1833 on microfilm at the NLI.

Flax spinners

Linen-making was a widespread occupation in Ulster and to a lesser extent in Dublin and Wicklow. In 1796 the Irish Linen Board

Occupational dictionaries

Ancestors with unusual or distinctive occupations may appear in occupational dictionaries at the NLI. For example:

- A. Crookshank and the Knight of Glin, *The Painters of Ireland*, c. 1660–1920 (Barrie and Jenkins, 1978).
- G. Fennell, *A List of Irish Watch- and Clockmakers* (Dublin: The Stationery Office, 1963).
- W. E. Hogg, *The Millers and Mills of Ireland of about 1859* (Dublin, 1997).
- R. Loeber, *A Biographical Dictionary of Architects in Ireland*, 1600–1720 (John Murray, 1891).
- W. Strickland, *A Dictionary of Irish Artists* (Irish University Press, 1969).

A handy online bibliography is at **www.ireland.com/ancestor/browse/records/occupation/**.

A stalwart female spinner posing with her spinning wheel in Letterbrone, Aclare, Co. Sligo: the pedal wheel was introduced to Ireland by the Huguenots and was most commonly used for spinning flax, which was then woven into linen. A larger wheel was used for spinning wool (picture courtesy of the National Folklore Collection, UCD).

published a list of some 60,000 people who had entitled themselves to free spinning wheels and looms by having planted flax. The list is at the NLI and searchable at **www.failteromhat.com** and, partially, through **www.censusfinder.com/ireland.htm**

Freemasons

Nobody knows when Irish Freemasonry started: the Scottish planters (see p. 201) may have been influential in bringing "The Craft" to Ireland, or at least popularizing it. Lodges proliferated in the army, and Freemasonry was endemic among the Jacobites and Wild Geese (see p. 207). The Grand Lodge of Ireland was established in 1723-4, with membership records from 1760 at Freemason's Hall, Dublin. However, as professional genealogist Paul Gorry points out, you need to know which Lodge to search under, and the records will do little more than confirm that the person was a member! The unindexed charity petitions,

however, give some interesting family history details.

Innkeepers

As Rosemary Ffolliott (see p. 143) observed, local newspaper announcements don't concern themselves "at all with medium to small farmers or cotters," but they're "one of the very few sources that give any information about those maddeningly mobile innkeepers."

Lawyers

Irish barristers and solicitors (the latter also called attorneys) between 1607 and 1867 had to register — and provide details of their origin — at King's Inn, Henrietta Street, Dublin 1. They are listed in E. Keane, P. B. Phair and T.U. Sadlier (eds), *King's Inn Admission Papers 1607-1868* (Stationery Office for the Irish Manuscripts Commission, 1982). After this date barristers' details can be found at King's Inn

Some strapping members of the 19th-century Royal Irish Constabulary in their fine new uniforms (picture courtesy of RUC Museum, Police Service of Northern Ireland).

Some strapping members of the 19th-century Royal Irish Constabulary in their fine new uniforms (picture courtesy of RUC Museum, Police Service of Northern Ireland).

1221–1921 (John Murray, 1926) covers judges: see also P.B. Phair, 'Early Genealogical Sources for Attorneys and Barristers', *Irish Genealogy: a Record Finder*, p. 181–194.

Nurses

The SoG has a *Register of Nurses, 1937* (Dublin, 1937) with entries such as

'*Sr M. Celestine Kilduff, Co. Home, Loughrea, qualifications Crumpsall Infirmary and City Fever Hospital, Manchester, April 1914–June 1921 (after exam), registration date 26 July 1926.*'

Policemen

Dublin (county and city) had a police force of sorts from 1786, later becoming the Dublin Metropolitan Police, with records on microfilm at the NAI. Elsewhere policemen (called "barony constables") were employed by local authorities. The Armed Peace Preservation Force was established in 1814, followed by full-time County Constabularies from 1822. These groups merged in 1836 to become the Irish ("Royal Irish" from 1867) Constabulary. In 1922, the RIC split into the Royal Ulster Constabulary for the north, and (after a year's hiatus) the *Garda Síochána* in the south.

Library, while attorneys belonged to the Incorporated Law Society of Ireland. Most are also listed in Dublin directories (see p. 100). Catholics were barred in theory (though not always in practice) from becoming lawyers between 1704 and 1794, and could not become judges until 1829. Records usually give fathers' names. Many also studied at one of the English Inns of Court in London — Lincoln's Inn, Gray's Inn Inner and Middle Temple, whose records are in London. F.E. Ball, *The Judges in Ireland*

Some police records before 1816 are in the

LEFT: **A rag man, Dublin, about 1937. Many occupations were** *ce hoc* **affairs: the rag man traveled around collecting rags and sometimes other "rubbish," such as tin foil, and sold it wherever he could. Rags were often sold to paper mills to make paper. Children sometimes brought him rags in return for small toys (courtesy of National Folklore Collection, UCD).**

RIGHT: **Fish and vegetable dealers (courtesy of the National Library of Ireland).**

(see p. 100)

Trade guilds

Many tradesmen are listed in directories (see p. 100). Town guild membership records state how the tradesman (or, rarely, tradeswoman) had qualified, whether by patrimony (as a child of a guildsman), purchase or apprenticeship. Though technically excluded under the Penal Laws until 1793, many Catholics actually joined as 'quarter-brothers,' paying their dues each quarter of the year. The guilds were abolished in 1846. Sadly, few records survive — those that do are best searched for locally. Dublin's, however, are excellent: see *Admissions to the Guilds of Dublin, 1792–1837, Reports from Committees, Parliamentary Papers*, 1837, vol.. 11 (ii), Freeman's *Rolls of the City of Dublin 1468–85 & 1575–1774* in GO 490-493 (Thrift Abstracts) and 'Dublin City Tradesmen employed by Board of Works', *Dún Laoghaire Genealogical Society Journal* (vol.. 4 [2], 1995). Associated with guild records are records of freemen of boroughs, whose main privilege was being able to vote. For these enquire locally or see M. Clark, 'Sources for Irish Freemen' in *Aspects of Irish Genealogy* (vol.. 1, n.d., Irish Genealogical Congress Committee).

Trades unions

Membership records may be found using S. Ward-Perkins, *Select Guide to Trade Union Records in Dublin* (Irish Manuscripts Commission, 1996).

Scott Crowley investigates an old whiskey still on Inishmore. In *The MacDermots of Ballycloran* (1843–7) Anthony Trollope writes, only somewhat ironically,

"*Every one knows that Ireland, for her sins, maintains two distinct, regularly organised bodies of police; the duties of the one being to prevent the distillation of potheen or illicit whiskey, those of the other to check the riots created by its consumption. These forces, for they are in fact military forces, have each their officers, sub-officers, and privates, as the army has; their dress, full dress, and half dress; their arms, field arms, and house arms; their barracks, stations, and military regulations; their captains, colonels, and commander-in-chief, but called by other names; and, in fact, each body is a regularly disciplined force, only differing from the standing army by being carried on in a more expensive manner.*"

House of Commons Sessional Papers (183102 XXVI). Police records from 1816 (to 1922, for Éire) are in TNA series HO 184, and on microfilm at the NAI, PRONI and MMF, indexed by J. Herlihy, *The Royal Irish Constabulary: a Complete Alphabetical List of Officers and Men, 1816–1922* (Dublin: Four Courts, 1999) and at **www.ancestry.co.uk/search/db.aspx?dbid= 6087**. The service records include details of wives, counties of origin and usually a character reference from someone from the applicant's place of origin. Pension records are in TNA series PMP 48. For recent records, next-of-kin may only contact the *Garda Síochána* or RUC direct.

Postmen

Service records from 1860 to 1922 are at the Post Office Archives, London, which also has Northern Irish postmen's pension records to 1940. For postmen and telegraph employees in Éire after 1922, contact the Department of Public Enterprise.

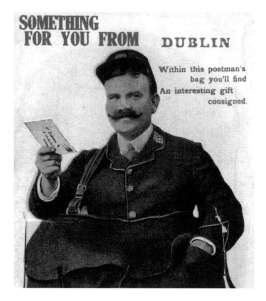

A jovial Dublin postman from an early 20th-century postcard. In his sack are tiny pictures of Dublin landmarks.

Militia

In times of emergency, able-bodied men were called up to local militias. These existed in Ireland from the 17th century onwards, though records are patchy. The GO has 1761 militia lists for Counties Cork, Derry, Donegal, Down, Dublin, Kerry, Limerick, Louth, Monaghan, Roscommon, Tyrone and Wicklow. Many militia brigades were formed in the period 1793–1816 because of the Napoleonic wars; for this see Sir H. McAnally, *The Irish Militia 1793–1816* (Dublin, 1949). Able-bodied men (of all denominations) were chosen by ballot, but could pay for others to serve instead. The muster rolls and pay books are in TNA series WO 13 and name men and officers, often including details of income and what weapons they had. Notable was the Irish Yeomanry, formed in November 1796 (their muster books to the 1830s are in WO 13/4059–4159. Some early lists are transcribed in Capt. G.S. Cary, *A Collection of Irish Lists* (typescript, 1944), a copy of which is at the SoG.

The militia was recalled for various emergencies during the 19th century. In 1881, it was attached to the Irish county army regiments. The Militia Attestations Index (1872–1915), covering 12,500 men in the Royal Garrison Artillery (the modern Royal Artillery), is at **www.irishorigins.com**, and includes marital status, next of kin, birthplace and employer. For an interesting list of Irishmen in English militia battalions see Jenifer A. Edmonds, *Ireland's Royal Garrison Artillery, 1872–1915*, on CD from **www.jenlibrary.u-net.com**.

The Army

For many poor Irishmen, the armed services offered attractive opportunities for employment and, especially, pensions. By the mid-19th century, an estimated 40 percent of the British Army was Irish. The army took men from Ireland all over the globe, and when their service was completed many chose to remain in the places where they were stationed, contributing greatly to the Irish Diaspora. Army records are in TNA department WO (War Office), though much extra information is in dedicated museums.

Early 20th-century postcard entitled "The girl I left behind me," illustrating the special affection felt by many soldiers and sailors for Irish girls.

Army sources

Officers

Until the 20th century, officers were almost entirely from the middle and upper classes, with ranks down from general to colonel, lieutenant colonel, major, captain, 1st lieutenant and 2nd lieutenant.

Medieval armies were *ce hoc* affairs, drawn from the land-holding aristocracy and their tenants. The standing army was first established in 1660 and initially you are only likely to find mention of officers. C. Dalton, *English Army Lists and Commission Registers 1661–1714* (Eyre & Spottiswoode, 6 vols., 1892–1904, repr. Francis Edwards, 1960) and *George the First's Army 1714–27* (Eyre & Spottiswoode, 2 vols., 1910–12) cover the period to 1727. From 1740 there have been regular *Army Lists*, including all officers and giving basic details about them, accessible in the TNA and SoG. TNA has much documentation on officers, the main being "services of officers on the active list" in series WO 25 and 76 (partially indexed), dating back to 1829 and in some cases to 1764, including age and place of birth. Records of World War I officers are indexed at **www.catalogue.nationalarchives.gov.uk**.

Regiments

The army was divided into regiments, and Irishmen served in most, not just the specifically Irish ones. Most have excellent museums and published histories that provide detailed background information and may have details or pictures of your ancestor. Enquiries can be made through the Army Museum Ogilby Trust and Imperial War Museum, and see the online guide **www.army.mod.uk/unitsandorgs**.

Other ranks

Non-officers' service records from 1760 to 1854 are indexed at **www.catalogue.nationalarchives.gov.uk**, through which the records themselves can be searched for. Because records are generally arranged by regiment, it is best, for soldiers after 1854, to try to discover their regiment from a mention elsewhere, such as the birth record of a child. Besides service records, you can also use muster rolls, pay lists — a few of which go back to 1708 — description books (some back to 1754) and records of casualty, desertion, attestation, discharge, prisoners of war and pensions. Pensions were paid through Kilmainham (Dublin) for all soldiers demobbed in Ireland, and through Chelsea for those discharged in the mainland, but also from Chelsea for all not actually resident at Kilmainham from 1822. Pension records can also be a short-cut to learning a soldier's regiment after 1854.

Medals

Medal rolls, which tell you by implication the campaigns in which men served, are in TNA series WO 372. Those for World War I, which partially substitute those service records that are lost, are online at **www.documentsonline. nationalarchives.gov.uk**. Also contact the Army Medals Office (see p. 216).

Officers of the Royal Irish Rifles stationed at Belfast, 1892.

Twentieth-century army sources

World Wars I and II

Many other ranks' service papers were blown up, but some 2 million are still extant (called "burned documents"), so it's always worth searching for an ancestor here. The medal rolls (see p. 125) are a partial substitute for destroyed papers. The many published memorials include the *National Roll of the Great War 1914–18* (National Publishing Company, 14 vols., 1918–21), containing information on about 150,000 men, alive or dead. The Dublin Royal Fusiliers Association (**www.greatwar.ie**) and The Somme Heritage Centre (**www.irishsoldier.org**) have much on Irish soldiers who died in World War I. All British Army World Wars I and II armed forces deaths are indexed by the GRO, London, online at **www.1837online.com** (Irish soldiers dying 1914–18 are also indexed at the GRO, Dublin). Deaths, war graves and war memorials are indexed by the Commonwealth War Graves Commission at **www.cwgc.org**. *Ireland's Memorial Records* (Dublin, 1923), lists Irish people killed in World War I and also foreigners killed serving in Irish regiments are on an Eneclann CD (see p. 75).

Post-partition

Records, including pensions and medals, of members of the Republican Army between c. 1913 and 1921, including participants in the 1916 Rising and War of Independence, are available to next-of-kin only at The Veterans Section, Department of Defence, Renmore, Galway. The Irish Army was formed in 1922. Records are available for next-of-kin up to the 1940s only, from Defence Force Headquarters and the Military Archives for officers.

The GRONI holds returns of births, marriages and deaths for Northern Irish servicemen in the British Army from January 1, 1927, and a separate index of World War II deaths of Northern Irish service people (1939–48).

The Irish Soldiers' and Sailors' Trust

Various trusts were established to provide affordable homes for servicemen who had survived World War I. One was established in 1924 for Irish soldiers and sailors. Records are in TNA series AP 1–8, including details and photographs of the cottages themselves. Related records are in T 233/145, 146 (sales to tenants); HO 351/199; CAB 27/85; and papers on allocation of houses in Northern Ireland 1921–24 in HO 45/11708. The Northern Irish fund ran to 1952.

Many Irishmen were killed fighting for Britain in World War I. Some are commemorated in *Ireland's Memorial Records, 1914–18; being the names of Irishmen who fell in the Great European War 1914–18*, Dublin, 1923 (picture courtesy of SoG).

Army births, marriages and deaths

The English Registrar General has returns of armed forces births, baptisms, marriages and deaths from 1761. From 1879, under the Births, Deaths and Marriages (Army) Act, events concerning Irish soldiers were registered with the Registrar General in Dublin. These were indexed separately until 1888 and later dates were added separately to the end of the regular indexes. Note that some events for soldiers taking place within the British Isles can appear in *either* civil or army registers, so it is always sensible to look in both until you find what you want. Irish soldiers dying in the Boer War between 1898 and 1902 are in a special index appended to the regular Irish death volume for 1902.

Royal Marines

Established in 1665 to serve as soldiers on navy ships, they fall into three divisions: Chatham, Plymouth and Portsmouth. Records are in department ADM at TNA, in whose Research Enquiries Room is (in particular) a card index to most attestation forms (ADM 157/1–659). See G. Thomas, *Records of Royal Marines* (PRO Publications, 1994). Also useful is the Royal Marines Museum.

The Royal Navy

This was established by Henry VIII in 1546 with records (mainly for the 18th century onwards) at TNA in department ADM (Admiralty). See B. Pappalardo, *Tracing Your Naval Ancestors* (TNA, 2003) and N.A.M. Rodger, *Naval Records for Genealogists* (PRO Publications, 3rd edn., 1998), and if possible visit the National Maritime Museum, London.

The Royal Air Force

This was formed in 1918 by amalgamating the army's Royal Flying Corps and the navy's Royal Naval Air Service, founded in 1912 and 1914 respectively, all with records in TNA. See W. Spencer, *Air Force Records for Family Historians* (PRO, 2002) and the RAF Museum for more information.

Royal Navy sources

Officers

There were commissioned officers (admiral, rear admiral, commodore, commander, captain and lieutenant) and warrant officers, who were in charge of functional aspects of the ship, such as master, engineer, sailmaker, gunner, boatswain, surgeon and carpenter. Commissioned officers between 1660 to 1845 are outlined in:

- J. Charnock, *Biographia Navalis, or Impartial Memoirs of the Lives and Characters of Officers of the Navy of Great Britain* (vols. 1–4 and supplemental vols. 1–2 by R. Faulder 1794-98).
- J. Marshall, *Royal Naval Biography* (Longman, Hurst, Rees, Orme & Brown, 4 vols. & supplements, 1823-35).
- W.R. O'Byrne, *A Naval Biographical Dictionary* (John Murray, 1849, repr. 1861).
- *Navy Lists*, published from 1782.
- *The Naval Who's Who 1917*, covering many World War I officers.

Officers' service papers and other records are at TNA.

Ratings

Until 1853, non-officers were only employed — sometimes against their will — per voyage, so can be very hard to locate in ships' musters. If you can't guess the ship, you might never find them. From 1853 to 1923 they appear in "continuous service engagement books," fully indexed in ADM 188/245-267 and now indexed on **www.national archives. gov.uk/documentsonline**, which give dates and places of birth. Muster rolls in ADM 36-39 (1740-1808, with a few back to 1688) can lead you from ship to ship, and will tell you age and place of birth from 1764, together with other details such as tobacco and clothing allowances. Pay books, seamen's effects papers, medal rolls, description books and pension records can also be consulted at TNA. Pensions were paid through the Chatham Chest (records from 1653-7 and 1675-1799) and then through the Royal Naval Hospital, Greenwich.

British armed forces records for the last 80 years

Service records less than 80 years old are only released to next-of-kin. Apply to the Army Records Centre, Royal Marines Historical Records and Medals, RAF Personnel and Training Command, and Royal Naval Personnel website.

The Merchant Navy

The "merchant navy" is the term given to all the British ships not in the Royal Navy. The best guide is C. and M. Watts, *My Ancestor was a Merchant Seaman* (3rd edn., SoG, 2004). Records are in TNA department BT (Board of Trade). There are some muster rolls from 1747, but most are from the mid-19th century. Records are generally arranged by port, making them very hard to search except between 1835 and 1857, which are indexed in the "registers of seamen" (BT 120, 112, 119 and 114). These lead straight to crew lists (BT 98), which give age and place of birth. BT 114 can also be used to look up "seamen's tickets" (1845–53), which include

date and place of birth. After 1857, searching becomes very hard, until 1913–41, which is covered by a Central Index Register of Seamen at TNA.

A lot of merchant naval material, including many post-1861 crew lists, are now at the Maritime History Archive (Newfoundland), which offers an online search service. Those who died at sea between 1852 and 1889 are indexed in BT 154. Further records that you can search include ships' log books. Many boys and men were trained for the merchant navy by the Marine Society whose indexed registers (1772–1950) are at the National Maritime Museum. Medals awarded to merchant seamen who served in World War II — some 100,000 of them — are now searchable online at **www.documentsonline.nationalarchives.gov.uk**.

Merchant navy captains were called "master mariners," and second-in-commands were "mates." From 1845 (and compulsorily from 1850), new masters and mates could obtain a "certificate of competency." Including year and place of birth, their records are indexed in BT 127.

"The Coffin-Ships," 1873. Many merchant vessels were sent to sea in an unworthy state, and losses were often due to overloading ships and other poor practices. Here, a sailor sets off to sea, clearly more optimistic about his chances of survival than the wife he is leaving behind.

A flour mill stands incongruously in the rural lanscape of Milford, Co. Carlow. Mills in the district exported flour through the towns of New Ross and Waterford to London and Liverpool, while the local Irish had to make do with potatoes.

Other records of them include a list covering 1868 to 1947, which gives date and place of birth, in Lloyd's Marine Collection at Guildhall Library, London.

Trinity House Petitions

A.J. Camp, *The Trinity House Petitions: A Calendar of the Records of the Corporation of Trinity House, London, in the Library of the SoG* (SoG, 1987) details applications made to the Trinity House charity from 1787 to 1854 by needy ex-sailors and their families from both the Royal and Merchant Navies.

further reading

■ S. Fowler, *Army Records for Family Historians* (PRO Publications, 2nd edn. 1998, rev. W. Spencer).

■ S. Fowler, *Tracing your First World War Ancestor* (Countryside Books, 2003).

■ S. Fowler, *Tracing your Second World War Ancestor* (Countryside Books, 2005).

■ M.J. and C. Watts, *My Ancestor was in the British Army: How can I find out more about him?* (SoG 1992, repr. 1995).

Irish industry

Largely because of its lack of substantial mineral resources, Ireland was relatively untouched by the Industrial Revolution. In Belfast, however, the Harland and Wolff Shipyard employed tens of thousands from the mid-19th century onwards. Localized industry included china-making in Fermanagh and rope-making and iron founding in Drogheda. Dublin had a fair share of factories, including Goodbody's Cigarette Manufactory, Jacob's Biscuit Factory, the Hosiery Factory at nearby Ballybriggan, and of course, the Guinness Brewery. A visit to the latter is highly worthwhile: you can see a reconstruction of the factory as it was, and have a pint of Guinness in the circular glass bar at the top of the building, with grand views across the city to the Wicklow Mountains. It was outside the brewery that I encountered a traditional drayman (pictured below).

CHAPTER 17

Dictionary of Irish sources

There are many more records you can use for tracing your Irish roots, including deeds, wills and "census substitutes" that list people in the context of where they lived.

A 19th-century sketch from Mr. & Mrs. S.C. Hall's *Ireland, its Scenery and Character* (1841–3) showing a "hereditary dispute" between what appears to be an extended Irish family and a couple of rather defensive bailiffs, over land or rent — a typical sight in Ireland at the time.

Catholic Qualification Rolls

These list some 1,500 prominent Catholics who, as a step towards religious emancipation, took oaths of loyalty to the Crown in 1775–6. A copy survives, made by Ignatius Jennings, showing names, occupations and addresses, published as an appendix to the *59th Deputy Keeper's Report*. The *First Catholic Relief Act* (1778) and subsequent acts bestowed benefits on better-off Catholics who took further oaths of loyalty at the Four Courts or at Quarter Sessions. Many did so, in 1778, 1782, 1792 and 1793. Indexes (probably no less detailed than the originals, which were destroyed in 1922) survive at the NAI, one for 1778-90 and the other for 1793.

Deeds Registry

In the 17th century, most Irish land was confiscated from its indigenous people — and from many older Cambro-Norman families — and regranted to the new Protestant settlers from Britain. Considerable confusion soon arose over precisely who owned what. This, coupled with a desire to ensure that land remained in Protestant hands, led to the founding of the Deeds Registry in Dublin in 1708.

The records are ledger copies of copies ("memorials") of the originals that had been sworn before Justices of the Peace. The ledgers are indexed by townland and by grantor — the person

parting with the land, money or goods — but not, sadly, by the grantees (recipients), until 1833. Copies of the indexes and records are on film at the NLI, PRONI, and on MMF, so it's seldom necessary to visit the Deeds Registry in person.

All parties concerned had to be 21; guardians had to act for "minors" who were under age. Most records concern Protestants. In the 18th century, Catholics could only hold leases of up to 31 years. From 1772 they could have up to 61-year leases on bogs. The 1778 Catholic Relief Act removed many restrictions on leases, and allowed Catholics to bequeath their land like anyone else (before, it could only descend to the eldest son, but if a younger son became CoI he could claim the lot). From 1782, Catholics could also buy land, except in Parliamentary boroughs. These matters had no effect on most Catholics, who were too poor to buy or lease anyway, but it does lead to better-off Catholics appearing in Deeds Registry records. However, poorer people do sometimes appear in these records.

Before the Relief Acts, Catholics were only allowed to own limited amounts of land. If a Protestant "discovered" a Catholic owning more than his quota, he could submit a "Bill of Discovery" and claim it. Most Bills of Discovery, however, were actually registered by Protestants acting for Catholic friends, to prevent hostile parties doing so and to enable them to keep their land. In such cases, the Protestant "discoverer" would register a further deed stating that they were holding the land in trust for the Catholic. This device was opted for in particular by Catholics who had decided to convert to the CoI, to cover the interim between admitting to being Catholic, and actually becoming Protestant, during which they were vulnerable to "discovery" by unscrupulous parties.

The records usually start with date, type of deed, and names and addresses of the parties involved. The main types of deed are:

Bringing home turf from a bog in Connemara. From 1772, Catholics could hold 61-year leases on bogs, that could not be cultivated to produce food.

Leases were set to run for a period of years. The registry recorded any running between three and 999 years. Some were "for lives," i.e. set to last as long as a number of named individuals (usually three) were living (a new name could often be added each time someone died, for a renewal fee). These usually identify several generations of the same family.

Sales were usually clearly labelled as such, but the "lease and release" was actually a device to facilitate the sale of land too.

Mortgages were loans secured by land and rent charges (fixed sums paid out of pieces of land) and were often made to pay off debts.

Marriage settlements were agreements made prior to a wedding settling some money or land on the wife in the event of the husband's death and protecting the rest of the husband's estate for his heirs. They were common among landowners but also used sometimes among the middling sort, and often mention the parties' fathers, and other relatives acting as trustees.

Wills were registered when some legal dispute was likely (see p. 141 on wills in the Deeds Registry).

Contracts were made especially between merchants, Protestant and Catholic alike.

Convert Rolls

While poor Catholics had nothing to lose, the pressure of the Penal Laws, especially from the 1703 *Act to Prevent the further Growth of Popery*, caused many wealthier Catholics to convert, at least nominally, to the CoI. E. O'Byrne, *The Convert Rolls* (Irish Manuscripts Commission, 1981) lists converts 1703–1838. It's worth noting that if someone wanted to hold public office both he *and his wife* needed to be CoI. Hence entries such as this:
'*Crowly, Catherine, certificate 18 September 1736, enrolled 26 September 1736, p[arish of] Traction, Co. Cork, conformity 4 April 1736.*'

Elections

As voting rights were determined by landholding, various freeholders' lists from the 17th century onwards survive to show who held freehold land and to what value. Valuations of land (for the same purpose) were made from the late 18th century, some recording householders. Poll books recorded who voted, and how. Grenham catalogs what survives. When the Secret Ballot was introduced in 1872, electoral lists just recording who could vote were compiled. There are modest collections of these in local archives and at the NAI and PRONI (as cataloged in the 'Crown & Peace' calendars).

Elphin census, 1749

Compiled by John Synge, Bishop of Elphin (explaining its alternative name, the "Synge census"), this listed some 20,000 householders, stating their gender, religion and the numbers of children and servants they had, for parts of Galway, Roscommon and Sligo. It is at the NAI and published as M.-L. Legg (ed.), *The Census of Elphin* (2004). It can be seen for a fee at **www.irishorigins.com**, with parts free at **www.leitrim-roscommon.com**.

Estate records

Estate records are well worth searching if your family owned one. Many list tenants, so they can be useful for some of the many families who spent their lives paying rent for their homes.

From the 17th century onwards, much of Ireland was owned by a relatively small number of English or Anglo-Irish landlords, from whom

Members of the Royal Ulster Constabulary guard a polling station in Derry during a by-election, 1913.

most of the smaller gentry leased their lands. Estate records usually concern themselves only with direct tenants. The poor were usually subtenants of tenants, so you may have to search down several layers of tenancies before seeing their names mentioned. Frankly, however, relatively few poor people will appear in these records, many being "tenants at will," with no signed legal agreement with their landlord. When exceptions to this rule occur, of

Elphin census

The Elphin (or Synge) Census, 1749. Jane Hemsworth (1787-1860) was wife of Richard Charles Brown (1776-1837), publisher of the *Laity's Directory*, which she continued publishing after his death. Her father was described in the directory as "John Hemsworth Esq. of Strokestown, Co. Roscommon," and his will was proved in 1803, though it has not survived. As parish registers have not survived either, the Elphin Census was an obvious place to look for earlier generations. Strokestown was in the Church of Ireland parish of Bumblin, where two Hemsworths are listed: Henry, a Protestant tanner, and William James Hemsworth, shown here, a Protestant farmer of Upper Ballyfeeny, with three children under 14 and one over. One (or perhaps a further child, still to come) was probably Jane's father John (who, one can only assume, became a Catholic). William and Henry's surname was very rare in Ireland, and they probably descend by an unrecorded younger branch, from Revd. Henry Hemsworth from Yorkshire, Rector of St. Anne's, Dublin, whose son Revd. Thomas settled at Abbeville, Co. Tipperary, only 40 miles south of Strokestown. I hope so, as Jane was my 4 x great-grandmother, and in 1716 Thomas married Lucy, daughter of Godfrey Boate, one of the Justices of the King's Bench in Ireland, son of Godfrey de Boot, a natural historian and physician, who was born the son of a soldier and author in Gorinchem, The Netherlands, in 1604 — not the sort of "Irish ancestor" one would expect! Note that this can rely only on conjecture and is not a proven line of descent.

HEMSWORTH *formerly* OF SHROPHAM

CANON NOEL EDWARD CAMPBELL HEMSWORTH, F.R.G.S. (1934), Vicar of Sompting, Sussex, since 1936, Vicar of Portslade, nr. Brighton, Sussex, 1928–33, Canon Residentiary of Bermuda Cathedral from 1933, Grand Chaplain Royal Ancient Order of Buffaloes, 1929, late Capt. Indian Army, *b.* 8 Aug. 1894 ; *educ.* Forest Sch. and Selwyn Coll. Camb., M.A. (1925) ; *s.* his uncle as representative of the family, 1931.

Lineage.—REV. HENRY HEMSWORTH left Yorks about 1650, became Rector of St. Anne's, Dublin, and had two sons. Mr. Hemsworth, whose will dated 19 Feb. 1696, was *pr.* 9 May following, was *s.* by his eldest son,

REV. THOMAS HEMSWORTH, of Abbeville, co. Tipperary, Rector of the parishes of Birr, Kinnety, St. Clerens, and Lockeen, *m.* 1716, Lucy, dau. of Godfrey Boate, one of the Justices of the King's Bench in Ireland, and by her (*d.* 10 April, 1753) had

1. THOMAS, his heir.
2. John, M.D., *b.* 1703 ; *m.* Mary, dau. of Humphrey Minchin.
3. Godfrey, *b.* 1704 ; *m.* Mabel, dau. of Lancelot Gubbins, of Kilbreedy, and was father of
  Godfrey, of Donass, co. Clare, who *m.* 14 Sept. 1802, Eliza Fitzgibbon.
4. Denton Boate, *m.* Miss Greenshields, and had three sons. The eldest son, Denton Boate Hemsworth, *b.* 1772 ; *m.* Agnes Macartney, *b.* 1779, who *d.* 1812. He *d.* 1814, having had issue, a 2nd son, William Henry Hemsworth, *b.* 14 Dec. 1797 ; *m.* Marianne Smith, dau. of William Steele, son of Sir Richard Steele, 1st Bt., and Angelina, his wife, only dau. of the Rt. Hon. Sir Michael Smith, 1st Bt. She *d.* 11 March, 1884. He *d.* 11 May, 1871, leaving issue. His 3rd son, Thomas Arthur Hemsworth, *b.* 1842, *m.* Charlotte Methley, and *d.* 15 June, 1900, having had issue, Harry Denton, Sub-Native Commissioner, Zoutpansberg, Transvaal, *b.* 8 July, 1877 ; *k.* as the result of an accident, 24 Aug. 1927, and Kathleen Marianne, *b.* 22 Jan. 1879.
1. Jane, *m.* George Minchin.

The eldest son,

REV. THOMAS HEMSWORTH, of Abbeville, *b.* 1699 ; *m.* 1st, Mary, dau. of Edward Eyre, by whom he had an only dau., Lucy, *d. unm.* ; and 2ndly, Elizabeth, dau. of Lucius Wilson, of Deer Park, co. Clare, and by her had (with two daus., Ellen, wife of William Newstead, of Derrignaston, co. Tipperary, and Mary) three sons. Mr. Hemsworth, whose will dated 24 Nov. 1768, was *pr.* 15 April, 1779, was *s.* by his eldest son,

THOMAS HEMSWORTH, of Abbeville, *m.* 8 Jan. 1782, Mary, eldest dau. of Henry D'Esterre, of Rosmanagher, co. Clare, and by her (*d.* 1837) had issue,

1. THOMAS, of Abbeville, J.P., *b.* 24 Oct. 1783 ; *m.* 4 March, 1808, Jane, eldest dau. of Gerard Irvine, of Rockfield, co. Fermanagh, and *d.* 1 Sept. 1856, having by her (*d.* 22 May, 1868) had issue,
  1. THOMAS GERARD, of Abbeville, *b.* May, 1809 ; *m.* 22 Feb. 1868, Charlotte, eldest dau. of John Hubert Moore, of Cherry Hill, Cheshire, eldest son of Garrett Moore, and grandson of John Hubert Moore, of Shannon Grove, co. Galway, and *d.* 1883, leaving issue,
    (1) THOMAS GERALD, of Abbeville, *b.* 22 May, 1869.
    (2) John Hubert Moore, *b.* 12 April, 1876.
    (1) Alice Emily, *b.* 15 Dec. 1870.
    (2) Charlotte Jane, *b.* 1 and *d.* 31 July, 1872.
  2. John, *d.* 7 Nov. 1861.
  3. Henry.
  4. William, Barrister-at-Law, *m.* Jan. 1850, Frances Delap, 2nd dau. of Nathaniel Robbins, of Hymenstown, co. Tipperary,

The Hemsworth's pedigree from
***Burke's Landed Gentry* (1937).**
(Courtesy of Burke's Peerage.)

Address of Owner.	Extent. (A. R. P.)			Valuation. (£ s.)	
98, Lower Gardiner-street, Dublin.	1,623	2	8	590	5
Mohill, co. Leitrim,	23	3	20	9	5
Lismoy, Newtownforbes.	135	1	25	64	10
Dublin,	773	3	5	3,246	8
Aghakine, Arvagh,	46	3	2	18	5
Annaghdaniel, Arvagh,	199	0	8	31	0
Dooling, Longford,	79	1	30	39	10
Ballinalee,	96	2	33	128	0
Ballinalee,	47	2	35	33	15
Rockfield House, Dalystown, Granard.	936	1	36	646	10
Ballygarane, Longford,	146	2	18	96	5
—	78	2	31	56	5
Edgeworthstown, co. Longford.	611	3	36	432	15
70, Lower Baggot-st., Dublin.	311	1	24	262	0
Richfort, Ardagh,	289	2	38	191	5
—	547	3	30	262	10
Ratharney, Colehill,	74	1	16	71	10
Wales,	692	2	5	315	5
Lissglassick, Keuagh,	890	0	35	291	10
Riversdale, Borrisokane,	262	1	18	221	5
Castlepollard,	62	0	16	37	15
Benison Lodge, Castlepollard.	150	3	30	106	15
Lissaniskey,	372	1	22	266	0
Lissanode, Moate, co. Westmeath.	740	3	38	393	5
1, Lower Leeson-st., Dublin.	342	0	32	185	2
Achil, co. Mayo,	786	1	30	654	5
Bunnyfield, Abbyshrule, Ballymahon.	79	2	9	68	5
Farrageens, Lennamore,	33	3	9	63	0
Abbeyshrule,	183	3	39	67	15
Ballymahon,	270	3	27	208	5
Rathmore, Ballymahon,	275	0	33	214	11
Mortmore, Ballybrocke,	2,571	3	10	2,681	5
Clinan, Colehill,	1,016	3	29	710	12
Ballymahon,	70	2	29	169	5
Portarlington,	659	3	26	135	3
Middle Abbey-st., Dublin.	56	1	18	28	15
Bellewstown House, Drogheda.	5	3	36	213	15
Bruming, Ardagh,	21	0	33	18	10
Ballinrobe, co. Mayo,	50	3	13	19	15

Name of Owner.	Address of Owner.	Extent. (A. R. P.)			Valuation. (£ s.)	
Stewart, James R.,	Leinster street, Dublin,	802	0	4	470	0
Straine, Rev. H.,	Delgany,	44	1	35	33	10
Synge, Francis H.,	—	1,664	0	7	600	10
Tandy, Mary,	Everton, Carlow,	746	2	26	331	9
Thompson, Henry B.,	Hollywood, co. Dublin,	169	3	10	172	0
Thompson, John E.,	Cloonfin, Granard,	1,662	3	39	1,036	4
Topham, Rev. J.,	Shrule, Ballymahon,	56	0	4	55	5
Tresham, Mrs. Jane,	Tipperary,	47	1	34	30	15
Trustees of Convent,	Longford,	3	1	0	5	0
Trustees of Roman Catholic College.	Longford,	24	0	7	108	15
Trustees of Wilson's Hospital.	Multyfarnham, co. Westmeath.	231	3	21	146	5
Tuite Joseph,	Sonna, Mullingar,	2,307	0	1	1,424	1
Tuite, Thomas,	Granard,	198	1	37	115	5
Twaddle, Charles,	Trillickacurry, Longford.	43	3	36	26	0
Twaddle, Edward,	Nappagh, Moydow,	122	0	10	77	0
Twaddle, James,	Trillickacurry, do.,	42	3	35	26	0
Tyrrell, James,	2, Kildare-st., Dublin,	1,145	2	15	477	0
Walsh, Mrs.,	Enniskillen,	9	2	20	9	5
Walsh, Thomas,	Dublin,	195	3	27	139	7
Ward, Mary,	Forgney, Moyvore,	4	3	9	4	10
Whelan, James,	47, Smithfield, Dublin,	154	0	22	120	5
White, Henry W.,	United Service Club, Dublin.	3,197	0	25	1,627	19
White, Luke,	Eversham, Blackrock,	1,394	1	38	850	5
White, Peter,	Clonwheelan, Edgeworthstown.	369	0	33	149	0
Whitney, Edmd. W. T.,	Newpass, Rathowen,	121	3	21	90	15
Wilson, James,	Currygrane, Edgeworthstown.	1,158	2	31	835	15
Wilson, William,	Street, Rathowen, co. Westmeath.	2,432	0	5	839	5
Wilson-Slator, G. W.,	Cartron, Edgeworthstown.	1,300	3	10	934	0
Woodward, Very Rev. Thomas.	Downpatrick,	1,222	3	30	489	0
Wright, Thomas S. B.,	Cartrons, Ballymahon,	245	2	20	170	0
Total for 372 Owners of Land, of One Acre and upwards,		256,648	0	0	149,677	0
Add for 64 Owners of Land, of less than One Acre in extent		20	0	0	2,062	10
GRAND TOTAL, 436 Owners in the County,		256,668	0	0	151,739	10
ESTIMATED EXTENT of Waste Lands in						

A section of the 1876 Returns of Owners of Land for Co. Longford (courtesy of SoG).

course, the records can be marvelous. For example, the Kenmare Manuscripts, published by the Irish Manuscripts Commission in 1942, include many details of poor tenants, including comments on their competency — "he instantly took to drunkenness...," or "a most unpunctual wrangling tenant..."

Some estates had "ejectment books." Some record mere threats of eviction, made to warn unruly tenants. In the 1850s though, speculators bought up some 5 million acres (over 2 million hectares) of land affected by the Famine and evicted many survivors in order to "improve" their new estates. The worst instances of this were in Counties Clare, Galway, Kerry and Mayo. Some landlords, such as Lord Lansdowne in Co. Kerry, paid for evicted tenants to emigrate, this being cheaper than them becoming a burden on the poor rates.

Sometimes, an obscure place of origin recalled in the family may turn out to be the name of the estate from which they once rented. Otherwise, you can work out the likely landlords from:

- Griffith's Valuation (p. 84), though this only names the person to whom rent was paid, who may themselves have been leasing from the ultimate estate owner.
- Lewis's *Topographical Dictionary* (see p. 80) names the main landowner(s) in each parish.
- The 1876 *Landowners in Ireland: Return of Owners of Land of One Acre and Upwards* (HMSO, 1876, repr. GPC, 1988) lists 32,614 landowners, county-by-county, giving address, size and value of property.
- O.H. Hussey de Burgh, *The Landowners of Ireland* (1878) states the size and location of estates.
- John O'Donovan's *Ordnance Survey Name Books*, which began in the 1830s, list names and addresses of landowners for each place, arranged by civil parish within counties. They are at the NLI and Ordnance Survey Office, Dublin.
- "Form B" of the 1911 census states the landholder's name.

Many estate records are at the NAI and NLI, and PRONI, as cataloged in Hayes (see p. 74). Grenham lists collections of estate papers in his county sections.

Irish estate records are cataloged in M.D. Falley, *Irish and Scots-Irish Ancestral Research* (repr. GPC, 1998). Some have been published: for example, C. McNeill and A.J. Otway-Ruthven, *Dowdall Deeds* (Irish Manuscripts Commission) prints documents concerning Co. Louth and parts of Meath back to the 12th century.

Remember that as many estate owners were English or Scottish, many estate records are now in mainland Britain. The best places to search for English and Scottish estate records are **www.a2a. org.uk** and **www.scan.org.uk** respectively.

Fiants

These are *Fiant litterae patentes*, or Warrants to Chancery for issue of Letters Patent under the Great Seal. The records were destroyed in 1922, but calendars summarizing those of 1531–1603 were published as *The 7th–21st Reports of the Deputy Keeper of the Public Records*, and also as *The Irish Fiants of the Tudor Sovereigns During the Reigns of Henry VIII, Edward VI, Philip & Mary, and Elizabeth I* (4 vols., Burke, 1994). Those for James I and Charles I (1603–49) were calendared by the Irish Record Commissioners. Details of many originals are found in the work of pre-1922 genealogists.

The most useful fiants are the many pardons granted to Irish chieftains who submitted to the Tudors in return for their land being regranted under the Crown. These list not just chiefs, but their spouses, extended families and tenants, and are the last major source for the old Gaelic order in the process of its collapse.

Irish Land Commission

In 1870, only 3 percent of people in Ireland owned any land. Gladstone's first *Irish Land Act* of that year aimed to enable normal Irish people to buy their own land. Despite this, conditions of tenure for most were so awful that in 1879 the Irish National Land League was founded, with Charles Stewart Parnell as its president, to fight "landlordism." It was funded by contributions from peasants and generous donations from America and helped rehouse evicted tenants in temporary cabins. Gladstone's second *Land Act* of 1881 established the Irish Land Commission partly to take the wind out of Parnell's sails: its aim was to establish fairer rents and further facilitate peasant land ownership. From 1923 it also incorporated the similar Congested Districts Board. Records are cataloged at the NLI.

> KEEPER OF THE PUBLIC RECORDS IN IRELAND. 213
>
> 1601. FIANTS.—ELIZABETH.
>
> Provisions *as in* 6497.—14 May, xliii. (Cal. P. R., p. 576).
> **6516** (5231.) Pardon to Donnel M'Carty, alias M'Carty Reogh, of Kilbrittaine, Margaret fitz Tho. Gerald, his wife, Donogh M'Cartie, of the Fiale, Fynen M'Cartie, of Gortnecloghe, Ellinor ny Gibbon, his wife, Teige oge m'Teige O Crowly, of Lishleavane, Ellen ny Donnell Murhelly, his wife, Donell m'Owen M'Callaghane, of Garrifiasog, Katherine ny Morhelly, his wife, Ranell oge beg Murhelly, of Ballenecarrigie, Ellen ny Teige Cartie, his wife, Owen bwoy m'Deirmodie Y dolee, of same, More ny Sawny, his wife, Shane m'Fynen m'Donell O Donogh, Ellen ny Teige, his wife, Fynen m'Shane m'Fynen, of Ballenecarrigye, Donogh and Conoghor m'Shane m'Fynen, Diermody m'Shane M'Deirmody, Donell, Teige, and Shane m'Deirmody M'Shane, Donell m'Donogh O Morhelly, Teige row O Morhellie, Deirmod m'Conoghor riough O Crowly, and Conoghor oge M'Enestlis, of same, Neavan m'Dermody O Hangelen, of Ballincoursie, Donell m'Shane M'Conoghor, of same, Philip O Riegan, of Lishane, Katherine ny Ryegane, his wife, Donogh bowy O Morroghow, of same, Margaret ny Horagh, his wife, Donell O Moynig, of same, Katherine ny Whody, his wife, Fynen O Driscolle, of Rynkollusky, Joan ny Donell M'Cartie, his wife, Wm. oge Riough, of Burren, Honora ny Edm. O Morogh, his wife, Deirmod m'Conoghor Croane, of same, Deirmod m'Wm. riogh O Riegan, of same, Ellis Mallifont, his wife, Wm. reogh O Riegan, senior, of same, Teige m'Rickard M'Melaghlin, of same, Katherine ny Callaghan, his wife, Conoghor m'Teige M'Rickard, of same,

This translated abstract of a fiant dated 1601 appeared in the Appendix to the *17th Report of the Deputy Keeper of the Public Records in Ireland*, published in 1885 and held at the NAI, Dublin. It shows a long list of Irish men and women pardoned during the reign of Elizabeth I. Here you can learn what the Elizabethan government knew of men's wives and where they held land. Most importantly, it shows the family and clan ties that still bound Gaelic Ireland together (picture courtesy of National Archives, Ireland).

Charles Stewart Parnell (1846–91) giving a rousing speech to a meeting of the Irish Land League, of which he was president.

Landed Estates Court

These records, not cataloged by Hayes, cover roughly 3,000 estates sold between 1849 and 1875 by the Landed Estates Court. Also called the Encumbered Estates Court and Land Judges Court, it was established in the aftermath of the Great Famine to deal with land whose owners had gone bankrupt. Records name small tenants and include maps. They are at the NAI in two sets (called "Green" and "Library"). The NAI has an index to the townlands covered by these — though, as Grenham points out, they are contemporary with Griffiths (see p. 84), thus making their use somewhat limited (unless, of course, you're researching the landowner's family).

Loan funds

Some 20 percent of Irish households took out loans from between 1822 and 1854 (mainly in the 1840s) from funds established to help the "distressed poor" during the famine years by lending people money to buy the means to make an income. Records of most funds have not survived, but the original Reproductive Loan Fund's records, running up to 1848, are at TNA (T/91). Records include details of borrowers, the security put up, repayments, defaulters and miscellaneous notes on individual circumstances, health, migration and so on. They are mainly for parts of Clare, Cork, Galway, Limerick, Roscommon, Sligo and Tipperary. They are unindexed but the Returns to the Clerk of the Peace for each of these counties except Clare and Sligo are indexed in **www.movinghere.org.uk**. These show accounts from 1846–8, giving names and addresses, sureties and amounts outstanding, and subsequent townland-by-townland listings made by the police in 1853–4, showing what had happened to people who had had loans — including death and migration.

Naturalizations

Few people who migrated into Ireland left a discernible papertrail. Naturalization by Act of Parliament (or from 1844, by a certificate from the Home Secretary), or Denization by a Crown grant was desired by some to remove the status of being a foreign-born "alien" and to acquire the right to bequeath property. The records are published by the Huguenot Society from 1603 to 1800:

- Vol.. 18, W.A. Shaw (ed.), *Letters of Denization and Acts of Naturalization in England and Ireland 1603–1700* (1911).
- Vol.. 27, W.A. Shaw (ed.), *Letters of Denization and Acts of Naturalization in England and Ireland 1701–1800* (1923).
- For families that came to Ireland via England 1509–1603, such as early Walloon and Huguenot families, see also Huguenot Society vol.. 8, W. Page (ed.), vol.. VIII, *Letters of Denization and Acts of Naturalization for Aliens in England, 1509–1603* (1893).

From 1800 to 1922, records are at TNA, mostly indexed in HO 1. As crown subjects, of course, the Irish entering mainland Britain needed no naturalization.

Newspapers

Dublin had its own newspapers from the late 17th century which started containing genealogically useful information from the mid-18th century. You may find reports of trials and oddities, such as this, from the *Limerick Chronicle* (6 July 1772): "I caution the public from crediting my wife Catherine Connor as she has turned out contrary to my expectations. Michael Connor, Glinn."

The most prominent 18th-century newspapers were *The Dublin Evening Post* (1719), *Faulkner's Dublin Journal* (1725), *The Freeman's Journal* (1763) and *Dublin Hibernian Journal*

(1771), based in Dublin but which also covered many birth, marriage and death notices from provincial papers. Outside Dublin, the *Corke Journal* (1753) covered much of Munster. For the north, the most important was the *Belfast Newsletter* (1737), covering much of eastern Ulster (indexed for 1737-1800 at **www.ucs. louisiana.ed/bnl/**). Most local newspapers date from the 1830s onwards.

Some CHCs have indexes to local newspaper collections. Ryan provides an outline of coverage. The *Irish Genealogist* has published many genealogically useful extracts. All historically useful Irish newspapers are cataloged at **www.nli.ie/new_cat.htm**, which includes the substantial Irish holdings of the NLI, Belfast Central Library and Belfast's Linen Hall Library (which has much partially indexed for the north) and the British Library. Irish Newspaper Archives

Ltd aims to index and produce online all Irish newspapers at its site **www.irishnews paperarchives.com** and currently has:

- *The Irish Independent*
- *The Freeman's Journal*
- *The Anglo-Celt*
- *The Leitrim Observer*
- *The Meath Chronicle*
- *The Sunday Independent*
- *The Connaught Telegraph*
- *The Tuam Herald*

It will soon include:

- *Irish Farmers Journal*
- *Nation*
- *Munster Express*
- *Irish News*
- *Connacht Tribune*
- *Galway City Tribune*
- *Connacht Sentinel*

DEN 10, 1854.

KERRYMEN IN THE CRIMEA.
(From the Tralee Chronicle.)

The following documents show, if proof were needed, how gallantly the men of Tralee bore themselves :—

"Crimea, September 10th, 1854.

"DEAR MOTHER—I am now going to state to you how I and my comrades are situated on board ship on the Black Sea, bound for Sebastopol or Odessa. We don't know which place we are going to attack, but the troops are dying with the cholera to a great pitch, and especially on board the ship that I am in. Generally one or two are thrown overboard every day, but it is not so bad now, thanks be to God for his goodness towards us. I am happy to tell you, dear mother, that I or my townsmen did not get one hour's sickness, thanks be to God for his goodness to us all. Let ——'s (a brother soldier) parents know that he wrote two letters and never got an answer, which grieves him very much, and I suppose he nor I will hear the answers of the letter to this unless God spares us our lives and drives us out of harm's way of our enemy. Dear mother, the last letter you wrote to me you mentioned to go to confession, but I did so myself, and Cain Reidy and myself paid great attention to our duties towards the Almighty. Our expeditionary army is composed of English, French, and Turks, about 70,000, and with that much men and our fleet, that none can compare to them on the sea, we are sure to beat the enemy. * * * No more at present from your loving son,
"PATRICK LYONS,
"Grenadier Company, 88th Regt."

Little knew the brave grenadier when writing the foregoing letter that he had written the last page of earthly communication—had given the last adieu to his mother.

"Scutari Barracks, Constantinople,
October 8th, 1854.

"MY DEAR MOTHER.—I now take the opportunity of writing these few lines to you, hoping to find you and all the family well, as this leaves me only poorly. I was sent down from Russia on the 27th of last month, and, thanks be to God, I am for the next draft that is going up again to join our regiment. Dear mother, I must inform you that Johanna's husband got wounded in the first day's squib. He got the ball through the collar bone, but, thank God, it was the left shoulder, and no way dangerous. I was three days engaged, and never got the slightest injury. Dear mother, tell Pat Lyons's mother that I am sorry to inform her that her son Patrick Lyons was shot dead through the

DIED,

On the 12th of March, of a broken heart, shortly after being ejected from his ground, Mr. Thomas Greany, Ballynagrane, Craughwell, county Galway, a small farmer. He was born on the lands from which he was evicted, and there his forefathers lived from time immemorial. His wife and family, his brothers and their children, are now as human wrecks on that desolate sea where home is not.
He fears no more the enormous social wrong
That leaves the peasant, willing, bold and strong,
Without employ : fixes as fate the rent of land—
The price of crops—less sure than marks on changing sand.

BIRTHS.

At Dromoland, on Thursday, the Lady of Captain O'Brien, Royal Navy, of a daughter.
At Kilworth, the Lady of James Morrogh, Esq. of a son.
In Waterford, the Lady of William M. Ardagh, Esq. of a son.
The Lady of the Rev. Robert Synge, M. A. Chaplain to the British residents at Bahia, of a son, in that city.
At Tamar Terrace, Portsmouth, the Lady of Lieut. J. Mould, R. N. of a daughter.
In London, the Lady of Lieut.-Colonel Sir Grey Campbell, Bart. of a daughter.
At Strabane, the Lady of James Hamilton, Esq. of a daughter.

MARRIAGES.

At Morelands, near this City, Lieutenant O'Dwyer, of the 97th Regiment, to Miss Doras, daughter of Lieutenant Doras, half-pay 27th Regiment.
Rice Hussy, Esq. of Upper Fitzwilliam-street, Dublin, to Miss Grace, daughter of John Grace, of Mantua, in the County Roscommon; Esq.
At Cannan Grove, Scotland, Captain A. Fullarton, late of the 38th Regiment, to Janet, youngest daughter of Mr. John Robertson.
James Major, Esq. of Foyle View, County Londonderry, Barrister at Law, to Catherine, eldest daughter of William Miller, Esq. of Bellemonte, in the same County, and niece of John Wilson Croker, Esq. and of the Dean of Rosse.
At Carrickfergus, Henry Fitz-Gibbon, Esq. of Dublin, to

Extracts from:
The Freeman's Journal, **November 10, 1854** (LEFT); *The Freeman's Journal*, **March 20, 1843** (TOP RIGHT); and the *Limerick Chronicle*, **August 23, 1821** (BOTTOM RIGHT).

Protestant householders, 1740

Returns of Protestant Householders, listed by parish and barony and giving names only, survive for parts of Antrim, Armagh, Derry, Donegal and Tyrone in copies made by Arthur Tenison Groves. Relevant sections are at the PRONI, NLI and GO.

Religious census, 1766

A census was made in spring 1766, parish-by-parish, of all householders and their denominations. Lists vary from detailed lists to numerical summaries. Only later transcripts, mainly by A.T. Groves, survive (and these only for some areas) at the NLI. See M.T. Medlycott, *1766 Religious Census of Ireland* (survey: typescript at SoG, 1992): Grenham's county section lists those that provide names.

Tax lists, 17th century

Subsidy Rolls for 1662-6 listed taxpayers' names and occupations by parish. Only those with movable goods worth more than £2 were taxed. They survive mainly for Ulster, at the PRONI and NLI as appropriate.

A Hearth Tax was raised between 1662 to the 18th century. This was payable on the number of hearths in your home. The returns, made by parish, list all but the poor (and those such as bakers and brickmakers, who used hearths for their work) who were exempt. The records survive mainly for the 17th century as Hearth Money Rolls, at the PRONI and NLI. Those for Dublin are at **www.irishfamilyresearch.co.uk**.

These and other tax lists, often called "cess" lists ("cess" is short for "assessments"), are listed by county in Ryan and Grenham.

Shipping lists

Because of worries of Fenians coming home to ferment rebellion, between 1858 and 1870, passenger lists of arrivals in major British and Irish ports from North America were recorded at Dublin Castle. The records are on an Eneclann CD, *Returning Home: Transatlantic Migration from North America to Britain & Ireland 1858-70.*

Wills

The vast majority of wills were made by people from the level of tradesmen and relatively comfortable farmers upwards. The great majority of peasants left no wills, for they had virtually nothing to bequeath. The Land Purchase Acts of the late 19th and early 20th century, however, encouraged tenant farmers to buy their land, prompting many families to start making wills for the first time.

Wills after 1858

From 1858, the work for proving wills — making them legally valid — and granting authority to people to administer the estate of those who died without a will (intestate) has been done by District Registries, under a Principal Registry in Dublin. The Dublin Registry, which covered a wide area encompassing Counties Dublin, Meath, Kildare, Wicklow and part of Offaly (King's Co.) also had jurisdiction over all estates that lay in more than one registry's district.

The registries made copies of their wills and administrations and sent the originals to the Principal Registry (which also kept copies of its own documentation), all of which were deposited ultimately at the Four Courts. These records were

Registries

The District Probate Registries from 1858:
South:
Ballina, Cavan, Cork, Kilkenny, Limerick, Mullingar, Tuam, Waterford.
North:
Armagh, Belfast, Derry.

destroyed in 1922. Almost all local copies survive, however; those for Éire are at the NAI and for the North at PRONI (which also has original wills for Belfast, Londonderry and Armagh that had not yet been forwarded to the Four Courts by 1922). In fact, because of the time-delay entailed in actually sending wills to Dublin, most originals from around 1900 onwards survive, as do those proved at Dublin from 1904. On the flip side, not all of the local copies were complete — sometimes, documents appearing in the indexes turn out not to be available.

The Principal Registry's annual nationwide indexes are easily searched and provide the deceased's name, residence, occupation, date and place of death, value of the estate, names and addresses of executors or administrators, and often their relationship to the deceased. A consolidated index covers 1858-77. Copies of the indexes are at NAI and PRONI. The PRONI is scanning its wills for 1858-1900 and plans to make them available on its website.

Wills from 1922 onwards (currently to 1994) are at the PRONI for Northern Ireland and the NAI for Éire, up to 1986, after which they must be searched for at the registries. Lists for the latest years of deposit for the NAI are at **www.nationalarchives.ie/research/probate.html**.

Wills before 1858

Before 1858, power to prove wills and grant administrations lay with the CoI. Each diocese had a Consistory Court, proving wills for people whose estates (whether in land, goods or money) lay within their jurisdiction. If the person's estate was mainly in one diocese, but with a small part, worth more than £5, in another, then the will had to be taken to the Prerogative Court of the Archbishop of Armagh, the supreme Church of Ireland authority in Ireland. The Prerogative Court moved about quite a bit, but from 1816 it was housed at the King's Inns in Henrietta Street, Dublin. People with property in Ireland and on the mainland had their wills proved at the Prerogative Court of Canterbury, whose wills are at TNA, fully indexed and downloadable at **www.nationalarchives.gov.uk/documentsonline**.

From 1858, all probate material from the dioceses was gathered together at the Four Courts. Virtually all was destroyed in 1922, except:

- **Will books:** these survive for the dioceses of Connor (1853–58) and Down (1850–58).
- **Grant books**, recording grants of probate, survive for Cashel (1840–45), Derry and Raphoe (1818–21) and Ossory (1848–58).

The former home of the Heraldic Office in part of Dublin Castle, where Sir William Betham created his invaluable will abstracts.

- **Prerogative Court of Ireland wills** (and a few administrations) survived the flames for small periods, 1664–84; 1706–8 A–W; 1726–28 A–W, 1728–29 A–W; 1777 A–L; 1813 K–Z; 1834 A–E. However, many wills had been copied completely or as abstracts (partial transcripts, showing only the genealogical details and not the legal verbiage), so sometimes, with enough searching, details of what a lost will contained can be recovered.

Manuscript indexes to the Consistory and Prerogative Courts are at the NAI. Some are published, especially Sir A. Vicars', *Index to the Prerogative Wills of Ireland 1536–1810* (1897). Especially for the 17th and 18th centuries, there are plenty of cases where a reference in a will index is the only realistically accessible record of someone's existence. The indexes state the name of the deceased, where they lived and when the will was proved or administration granted — this is usually the year of death, though sometimes the executors or administrators were slower to act. The associated administration bond indexes sometimes give occupations. They also indicate what may survive in the following collections. Until such time as a consolidated index appears, how far you persist in searching these sources is, I'm afraid, a judgment call based largely on how desperate you are to find a particular document. However, you can hone your search using the excellent table given at **www.irishgenealogical.org/meetings/o6may2.html** that indicates, broadly, which collections are covered by which archives.

These are the main collections:

- **Bank of England:** will abstracts for estates including government stocks, 1717–1845, are held in the Bank of England Archives and indexed in **www.englishorigins.net**.
- **Betham's abstracts:** in the early 19th century, Sir William Betham, Ulster King of Arms (1779–1853), was commissioned by the

68 BLOOD, THOMAS, senr., Bohersalta, Co. Clare, gent. 14 April 1713. Précis, ¾ p., 22 June 1713.

Son Thomas Blood of Cahirnemohir, Co. Clare, gent. Son Neptune Blood of Bohersalta, Co. Clare, gent.

Bohersalta, Cahurgrenane, Cahunemohir [? Cahirmohir], and Dorode, all in parish of Rathon, B. Inshign [Rath, B. Inchíquin], Co. Clare.

Witnesses : Edmond O'Hogan, John Hogan and Thomas Wise.

Memorial witnessed by : Edm. O'Hogane, Thos. Wise.

9, 396, 4031   Nept. Blood (seal)

This is an example of an Irish will abstract, taken from P.B. Eustace's book, *Registry of Deeds, Dublin, Abstracts of Wills*. "Senr" is an abbreviation for "senior" and "gent" for "gentleman."

Irish Record Commission to find the scattered records of the Prerogative Court wills and create an index. While doing so, Betham personally made abstracts of most of around 37,000 wills up to 1800, and of many probate grants up to 1802. They are at the NAI, with a fully alphabetical copy of the latter at the GO. See GO 223-6 (wills pre-1700), and GO 227-54 (1700-1800).

- **Betham's pedigrees:** Betham also made many sketch pedigrees from these wills, which are at the GO together with additions made by his successor Sir John Burke. GO 203-14 is an incomplete rearrangement of the resulting sketch pedigrees into alphabetical order. All are included in McAnlis's index (see p. 158).

- **Deeds Registry:** copies of some 2,100 wills were registered between 1708 and 1832 as part of evidence of land transfer and inheritance at the Deeds Registry. Many concern people being disinherited. These are abstracted in P.B. Eustace, *Registry of Deeds, Dublin, Abstracts of Wills* (3 vols., Irish Manuscripts Commission, 1954-84).

- **Estate Duty wills:** Copies from 1812 to 1857 of some 3,000 Irish wills liable for Estate Duty were sent to London and are in TNA series IR 27. There is a rather complicated index online at **www.nationalarchivist.com**. Copies of material for 1821-57 are at the PRONI.

- **Genealogical Office abstracts:** most of the GO's other will abstract collections are indexed there and a published index to them (but not to the Betham collection) is in *Analecta Hibernica*, vol.. 17.

- **Inland Revenue wills:** from 1828 (to 1879), the Inland Revenue compiled their own annual indexes to Irish wills and administrations. These are at the NAI and state the name of the deceased and their executors or administrators. Between 1828 and December 1833 and July 1834-9, there are also Will Registers giving the exact date of death, summaries of the estates and their distribution to beneficiaries, stating how much everyone received, and somewhat less detailed but still very useful Administration Registers covering 1828-39.

- **Irish Genealogical Research Society** has a card index of wills and abstracts held, and its journal the *Irish Genealogist* has published abstracts from its inception in 1937.

- **Land Commission wills:** copies of about 10,000 wills, mainly 19th century but with some going back earlier, are at the Land Commission on closed access. An index to them is at the NAI and PRONI.

- **NAI Collection:** since 1922 the NAI has collected copies of lost probate material, including many original wills found in family

A seal of approval

The English descendants of Dominic French (1750–1825) always knew there was something unusual about his origins, not least because of the unusual seal he passed down to his descendants. A boy from Co. Roscommon, Dominic joined the East India Company navy aged 14, and worked his way up to become a 1st Mate, surviving fevers, storms and perennial on-board violence: the ships' logs show him once being walloped while trying to break up a brawl in the hold. Like many sailors, he amassed savings by buying tea, spices and silks in the East and selling them on his own account in London. By 1784, however, he had surpassed most other ships' mates by setting himself up as a ship insurer for Lloyd's of London, living at India House in Margate, Kent. It is said that he would sit at the window there, watching out for the safe return of vessels he had insured.

The Frenches of Frenchpark, Co. Roscommon, claim descent from Sir Theophilus French, a French knight who fought at the Battle of Hastings and who was a close relation of William the Conqueror. This is probably pure fantasy. We do know for sure, however, that the Frenches were well established in Co. Wexford by the 15th century and a branch of them were in Galway by 1425. They were one of the "Tribes of Galway," an (originally) derisory term coined by Cromwell for the merchant families of Galway Town who extended their control across the county, and amassed great fortunes. Francis French, who died in 1624, married the daughter the Chief of the O'Connors of Sligo and their grandson Patrick was to establish a great estate at Dungar.

Patrick renamed the estate Frenchpark, building a magnificent mansion near the old Dominican abbey there — and from then on Dominic became a family name. Patrick's grandson John owned so much land that the Irish called him *Tierna More*, "the great landowner." In 1691, he fought in William of Orange's Protestant army at the Battle of Aughrim. This John married Ann, daughter of Sir Arthur Gore, 1st baronet of Newtown Gore, Co. Mayo, whose Villiers cousins were ancestors of both Prince Charles and Princess Diana.

The family's history is outlined in *Burke's Peerage*, and this confirms that their arms were identical with those shown on Dominic's seal. But just how did our seafaring lad fit in?

Although most of Ireland's pre-1858 wills were destroyed in the bombing of the Four Courts in 1922, abstracts of many survive. When undertaking research for the pilot of my Channel 4 series, *Extraordinary Ancestors*, back in 1999, I found Dominic named clearly in the will of Arthur French of Frenchpark, grandson of John and Ann. It was written on April 24, 1799 and proved on May 24 that year, and survives in volume 26 of Sir William Betham's will abstracts at the NAI. In this extraordinary document Arthur listed his legitimate children — whose descendants include the present Baron De Freyne — and also his "bastard children by Margaret Daly — Patrick; Dominick; Thomas; Emilia; Louisa." Illegitimate, but not denied by his natural father, this explains Dominic's unusual start in life that enabled him eventually to achieve prosperity in England.

papers, and abstracts and copies from the records of genealogists and solicitors. The index is at the NAI and on CD from Eneclann (see p. 75). It also holds collections of will abstracts assembled by genealogists including Philip Crossle, Ignatius Jennings, Gertrude Thrift, A.T. Groves and Edmund Walsh Kelly. The NAI's collections include abstracts of wills making "Charitable Donations and Bequests" 1800-58, including

the testator's name, details of executor and probate. The PRONI has a collection too, indexed in the *Pre-1858 Wills Index*. The site **www.irishorigins.com** has a partially complete master-index to all the will abstracts (1484-1858) at the NAI.

- **Royal Irish Academy** has some copies for the 17th and 18th century; the Upton Papers (will abstracts for Cavan, Longford and Westmeath, also on film at NLI); the

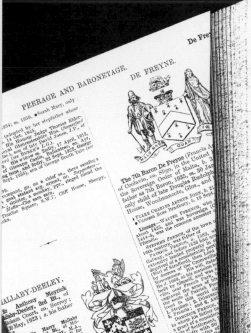

MacSwiney Papers (Cork and Kerry); and the
Westropp Manuscripts (Clare and Limerick).

- **Trinity College** has some abstracts, which
  are now on film at the NLI.
- **Wallace Clare** edited *A Guide to Copies and
  Abstracts of Irish Wills*, reprinted in 1972.
  This includes lists of Irish will copies and
  abstracts at the SoG in London, some that
  were deposited in England, and abstracts he
  had found in journals.

further reading

- Rosemary Ffolliott, 'Newspapers as a
  genealogical source' in *Irish Genealogy: A
  Record Finder*, p. 117-38.
- Rosemary Ffolliott, 'The Deeds Registry
  for Genealogical Purposes' in *Irish
  Genealogy: A Record Finder*, p. 139-56.
- Ian Maxwell, 'Turned out of House and
  Home', *Ancestors*, August 2006.

PART 4

Tracing ancient Irish roots

This part of the book is designed to help you trace back your family line as far as it will go. With the fantastic repositories of traditional Irish genealogy available, you may reach as far as the ancient and legendary figures associated with Ireland's very first recorded history by linking them with your name or DNA make-up.

A Celtic cross and round tower at Clonmacnoise, Co. Offaly, a center of early Irish Christianity founded by St. Ciaran, c. 545 CE.

CHAPTER 18

Irish names

The more you know about Irish names, the more fascinating they become because of the amount of coded information they contain on family histories.

Christian names

Most Irish first names are either ancient Gaelic ones, those of saints, Biblical ones — or a combination of both.

Gaelic first names may be recorded either in their original Gaelic form, such as *Conchobhair*, or an Anglicized form, such as Connor. They are usually formed from Gaelic words that mean something. *Conchobhair* (Connor), for example, means "lover of hounds" and *Maedhbh* (Maeve)

means "intoxicating." Gaelic names were used extensively until the 16th century. After then, the clergy often substituted them with Christian names that did not mean the same thing at all, but simply sounded quite similar, for example:

- *Conchobhair* and *Niall* (Anglicized to Connor and Neil respectively) = Cornelius (a name very popular in south Munster)
- *Diarmaid* (Anglicized to Dermot/Darby) = Demetrius, Jeremiah or Jerome
- *Eóghan* (Anglicized to Owen or Hugh) = Eugene (though in Britain, some Owens were native renderings of the Roman name Eugenius)
- *Aonghas* (Anglicized to Angus) = Aeneas
- *Briain* (Anglicized to Brian) = Bernard

The Iron Age fort of Dún Eochla on Inishmore. Though much rebuilt in the 19th century, it has lost none of its air of mystery and remains a potent symbol of Ireland's ancient past.

- *Callagh* = Charles
- *Tadhg* = Thaddeus (giving us "Thaddy")

Once these substitutions had become well-known, they became "Irish" names that passed down in families in their own right. So when a peasant had his son baptized Cornelius in 1800, he may have chosen the name because:

1. earlier generations had been called Cornelius.
2. it was a familiar local name.
3. he wanted his son to be called Connor, but the priest rendered this "Cornelius."
4. he may have wanted "Connor," but mistakenly thought Cornelius was the "correct" version, so chose this instead.

By the same token, a child officially called "Cornelius" may always have been known as Connor in daily life. Or vice versa.

With the Gaelic revival of the late 19th century, Gaelic names resurfaced and are now very popular again. Many Irish people with "translated" Christian names have reversed the process, so someone christened Charles might decide to "Gaelicize" himself to *Callagh*, despite the two names not originally having been the same. Equally, various names, such as *Liam* and *Sean*, never existed in ancient Ireland but are Medieval Gaelic forms of foreign names (William and John). However, modern Irish people now revert to these names in place of the equivalent "foreign" one. My grandmother was christened Mary Josephine but was always called Maureen — not because it sounded similar to both her Christian names combined, as I used to think, but because Maureen is a recognized Anglicization of *Máirín*, a pet-form of *Máire*, itself a Gaelicization of Mary.

By 1650, most people were baptized with Christian saints' names. These were either from the *New Testament* or from subsequent Catholic history. John, Patrick, William and Thomas were the most popular for boys (Joseph and Michael, later very popular, were rare then but

William remained popular, despite William of Orange). Later, many explicitly Catholic saints' names (like Ignatius, the beatified founder of the Jesuits) were chosen in defiance of the new Protestant régime. Some (but not all) patron saints of dioceses had a strong effect on the choice of boys' names, making the following Christian names popular in these dioceses:

- *Brendan* = Kerry and Clonfert
- *Colman* = Cloyne
- *Eugene* = Derry
- *Finbar* = Cork
- *Kevin* = Dublin
- *Kieran* = Clonmacnoise and Ossory
- *Lawrence* = Dublin
- *Malachy* = Down and Armagh
- *Nicholas* = Galway
- *Phelim* = Kilmore

When priests wrote their registers in Latin, they created a further layer of complication, by Latinising names. Some names, like Cornelius and Demetrius, already were Latin but others were Latinized, such as:

Ignatius Loyola (1491–1556), Spanish soldier and founder of the Society of Jesus, the Jesuits. The Jesuits' work in Ireland popularized names such as Ignatius and Aloysius and also ones associated with Polish Catholicism, including Stanislaus and Anastasia.

An excellent online guide to pronouncing Gaelic, "A Beginner's Guide to Irish Gaelic Pronunciation," is at **www.standing stones.com/gaelpron.html**, but I often find myself referring to the two-page guide given in the front of Randy Lee Eikhoff's electrifying translation of *The Cattle-Raid of Cooley* (Tom Dohert Associates, New York, 1997), which nobody interested in Irish ancestry should miss reading. Consonants at the start of words are usually pronounced as they are in English. When they come in the middle, they can be very different: *ch*, as in loch (which the English seldom pronounce properly) is the same as the *ch* of Bach, which they often do. The letter *b* is pronounced "v," *d* as "j," *s* as "sh" and *t* as "ch." Of the four provinces of Ireland, the only difficult one to pronounce is Connacht, for which Eikhoff suggests "KON-NAXt." The name of *The Raid*'s feisty heroine, *Maedhbh*, is pronounced "MAYv," while its hero *Cúchulainn* is "koo-HOOL-in." *Cnoc*, the word for a hill, is (confusingly) pronounced "crock." For the Gaelic language in general, see **www.ibiblio.org/gaelic/gaelic.html**.

- Charles = *Carolus*
- William = *Gulielmus*
- James or Jacob = *Jacobus*
- John = *Ionannes*, *Joannes* or *Johannes*
- Margaret = *Margarita*
- Mary = *Maria*
- Neil = *Nigelus*
- Timothy = *Timotheus* or *Thaddeus*
- Joan or Jane = *Joanna*

Some translations created new names. Bridget (and its short-form Biddy) was Latinised to Bidelia, which people then shortened to create the name Delia. Thus, Delia and Bridget could be used interchangeably. Equally, shortening "Margarita" created the name Rita. Joanna was often used interchangeably with Julia, Judith, Jane, Joan and even Hannah, and Honoria was also interchangeable with Hannah, as well as Anne, Nora and Norry.

Don't be misled by Latin declension endings, which cause changes to names according to tense, etc.: the accusative of Maria is *Mariam* (the form used to describe her doing something), and the dative is *Marie* (the form identifying her as the recipient of something), but these versions reflect Latin usage, not the name of the Irish person themselves — "Mariam" in the register was still plain old Mary in real life!

Presbyterians and, somewhat less commonly, Catholics, used naming patterns — the eldest son was often named after the father's father, second son after mother's father and third after the father; daughters were named likewise after both grandmothers and mother.

Middle names were rare, though in villages people with common names had nicknames ("Black Tom," for example). Middle initials often appear in passenger lists of ships to America, most likely representing the initial of the father's name, as a means of distinguishing different men of the same name on board. As the 19th century went on it became customary to use the additional name taken at Confirmation (the Catholic rite admitting a baptized person to full participation in the church) as a middle name.

Irish surnames

Unlike most of Europe, Ireland's surnames arose at a time when the ancient tribal system was still functioning. Many Irish surnames therefore indicate the original bearers' membership of a clan or *sept*. Because Ireland's ancient genealogical material was preserved and recorded assiduously in the Middle Ages, your Irish surname can connect you into Ireland's ancient web of tribal genealogies.

Irish surname distribution is a useful and often reliable means of finding where your family came from. But Irish surnames tell us a great deal more than that: unlike most mainland British ones, they often unlock your earlier ancestry, from the early Middle Ages back, if you believe the pedigrees, to Milesius himself. And because families tended not to move about much, and had surnames that identified their kindred in terms of their common ancestry, there is every reason to believe that, right back into the Middle Ages at least, they are remarkably reliable indicators of ancestry.

The earliest Irish hereditary surnames were patronymics or papponymics, taking the name of the father or grandfather respectively. *Mac*, "son [of]," is one of a handful of words common to languages worldwide that might have been part of the original tongue ("Proto-world") of our earliest human ancestors. It appears, for example, in native American tongues as *make* ("son"), in New Guinea as *mak* ("child"), Tamil as *maka* ("child") and Gaelic as *mac* "son." So when you address someone as "Mac," you're using a word that, in all probability, your 180,000 x great-grandparents would have understood! M' and Mc are contractions of Mac, found in both Ireland and Scotland — it is a myth that Scots used only Mc and the Irish Mac; the spellings are completely interchangeable in both countries.

Papponymics are more common than people realize, for, as the Irish historian Francis J. Byrne points out, some "Mac" surnames, especially those arising before the 11th century, often started as *mac meic*, meaning "son of the son of." MacLochlainn, for example, was originally *Mac meic Lochlainn*. It arose with Domnall Mac meic Lochlainn and stuck, more because of Domnall's importance than anything his rather dull grandfather Lochlainn accomplished. The more usual type of papponymic, which became hereditary (including all male-line descendants of the ancestor so-named) was *Ua*, also spelled *Uí*, *O'* or *O*. In Irish society, the individual or his sons was not as formidable a social unit as a *fine* (see p. 190) of interrelated first cousins: identifying yourself by who your grandfather was made a lot of sense.

Other types of surname

Most Gaelic surnames are patronymics or papponymics, but a small proportion arose differently. Some are from nicknames or

Hereditary surnames

In the first millennia CE, before the Irish adopted hereditary surnames, people were defined both by their membership of a family group descended from a common ancestor, and also by non-hereditary surnames; that is, ones used for one person but which were not passed on to their children. Such surnames were chiefly nicknames and patronymics — the ancient Irish King Brian Boru's "surname," which was actually *Bóruma*, meant "of the tributes," while his patronymic was Brian *Mac Cennétig*, "son of Cennétig," for that was his father's name.

The first truly hereditary surnames emerged in the 8th and 9th centuries, among certain dynasties of abbots, such as the Uí Shuanaig in Rahen and Uí Búirecháin in Cloyne. The practice then spread into noble and royal families: Tigherneach Ua Cléirigh (O'Clery) Lord of Aidhne, Co. Galway, appears in the *Annals* (see p. 157) in 916 CE: his descendants claim to have the oldest surname still in existence in Western Europe. Among royalty, High King Domnall of the Uí Néill called himself *Domnall Ua Néill*, not

after his 5th century ancestor Niall of the Nine Hostages, High King of Ireland, but after his grandfather Niall Glúndub (d. 919), though the coincidence probably helped make it stick. Domnall's son was called Áed Ua Néill and his great-nephew was Flaithbertach Ua Néill — the surname, later Anglicized as O'Neill, had become truly hereditary.

Tadhg Mac Dáire's 17th-century poem *Contention of the Bards* maintains that Brian Boru (d. 1014) invented hereditary surnames, the better to preserve people's knowledge of their ancestry. This is clearly wrong, not least because the surname Ua Briain (O'Brien) only appears when his great-grandsons Conchobar (d. 1078) and Cennétig (d. 1084) were exiled in the north, while the grandchildren of High King Muirchertach Ua Briain (d. 1119) called themselves not Ua Briain, as you'd expect, but MacMathgamna, after Muirchertach's son Mathgamain (d. 1129). It was from this time, however, that hereditary surnames started becoming widespread and they clearly predate their general appearance on the British mainland and in Europe.

occupations, such as McNulty (*Mac an Ultaigh*, "son of the Ulsterman"), Ward (*Mac an Bháird*, "son of the bard"), Hickey (*O hÍceadha*, "descendant of the doctor or healer" and MacDowell (*Mac Dubhghaill*, "son of the black stranger"). Many use *Mac* or *O* followed by *Giolla*, "servant," either a literal servant, or the religious devotee of a saint. Kilduff (*Mac Giolla Dhuibh*) means "son of the servant of Dhuibh" (a Gaelic personal name meaning "black") and McElhaw (*Mac Giolla Chathair*) means "son of the servant of [St.] Cathair." The word *Maol* (from *mul*, "bald") referred to the tonsured (shaved) heads of monks, hence Malone (*O Maoileoin*, "descendant of the devotee of St. John"). Sometimes, "Giolla" might have a third meaning, "fellow/lad," as in MacGilreevy (*Mac Giolla Riabhaigh* "son of the grey lad").

All Gaelic surnames starting "Mac" or "O" define the original bearer and their descendants in terms of an ancestor's name. Yet the rhyme "and if he lacks both O and Mac, no Irishman is he" is an exaggeration, for there are a handful of Gaelic names with neither. Some were nicknames of the original bearers, such as Bain (*Bán*, "white"), Roe (*Ruadh*, "red") and Gall (*Ghaill*, "foreigner") — perhaps all were "fatherless" in the sense of being immigrants. A few others are locative, denoting places of origin, such as Galbally, Finglas, Santry and Yourell (*de Orighiall*, "from Oriel"), or even wider areas — Desmond "from Desmond"; Lynagh, "Leinsterman"; Meade, "Meathman"; Minnagh, "Munsterman"; and Dease or Deasy "from the Decies": it is likely that most in this category arose as "English" surnames for Irishmen living within the Pale.

Anglicization

Ireland's surnames have been brutalized by foreign influence and, as the surname historian MacLysaght puts it, they have become "hidden under alien guise." English-speaking clerks recorded Gaelic surnames with English spellings, often choosing English words that sounded similar. Thus *O Chruadhlaoich*, "descendant of Chruadhlaoich," from *chruadh* and *laoich*, "hard hero," became "O'Crowley" (thus sounding and spelled like the English surname Crowley, from the Saxon *leah* and *cawes*, "wood of crows"). *O Troighthigh*, from *trioght* and *heach*, "foot soldier," became O'Trohy. Similar changes took place when the Irish Wild Geese (see p. 207) went abroad: Sheas in France became Chaix and O'Donoghues in Spain O Donoju. Beware, too, a similar phenomena, whereby unusual Gaelic surnames were recorded as if they were more familiar ones. Kelly is a well known surname, so many Keallys, Khillys and Kilkellys have been rendered "Kelly": their descendants may now be unaware that their ancestors were not originally Kellys at all.

The English conquerors pruned most "O"s and "Mac"s away. The 1367 Statute of Kilkenny, intended to stop the English in the Pale from becoming Gaelicized, banned the use there of Gaelic speech and Gaelic prefixes. It's a myth that this rule was imposed outside the Pale or that it became part of the Penal Laws, but it was occasionally enforced elsewhere in Ireland, such as by the Anglicized O'Conor Roe in 1637, who ordered his people to "forego the customs and usages of their Brehon Law… and give up prefixes to their surnames." While the peasantry never lost their "O"s in spoken Gaelic, most vanished from written records: O'Crowley became Crowley; O'Trohy became Troy. By the 19th century, Irish nationalist Daniel O'Connell's family is said to have been virtually unique among the Irish middle class in keeping their "O," yet even his uncle Maurice O'Connell signed himself "Maurice Connell," a symptom,

MacLysaght suggests, of the demoralisation of a thoroughly subjugated race.

More "Mac" surnames survived intact, because "Mac" was also used by Scottish settlers in Ulster and also, MacLysaght suggests, because dropping "Mac" can change a surname far more than losing the "O": O'Crowley and Crowley are clearly very similar, but the change from MacEnroe to Enroe or Ma[c]guire to Guire is too much.

The Anglicization of surnames means that you cannot always be sure what the original surname was. Several different Gaelic surnames could be Anglicized to one English spelling, such as O Duinnin and O Daghnáin both becoming Denning, a problem made much worse when people bearing the English surname also settled in Ireland (see p. 106). Some surname dictionaries (see p. 155), such as MacLysaght's, alert readers to this issue, while others, such as Revd. Patrick Woulfe's, do not. Equally, non-Irish surname dictionaries, even the otherwise wonderful Reaney and Wilson's *Oxford Dictionary of English Surnames*, often provide the origin of English surnames without mentioning that Irish surnames have also been Anglicized to resemble them, a factor that is relevant considering the number of people of Irish origin now living in England. A Crowley in London now is as likely to be an O'Crowley as a Saxon "crow-wood" Crowley. MacLysaght's *Irish Families* (p. 199-201) gives a helpful list of English names used as Anglicizations in Ireland to help avoid potential pitfalls.

Anglicization sometimes caused massive distortion of names. *Mac Oisdealbha* didn't become Ostello because the "c" of Mac was retained, first in speech and then in writing, to create the surname Costello. Similarly, *Mac Eochaidh* became not Eogh, but Keogh. Another factor was direct translation: the Gaelic surname *Bán* is sometimes Anglicized as Bain, but because it means "white" its bearers sometimes ended up being called White. *Mac Giolla Phádraig* means "son of the devotee of St. Patrick" and was badly translated into the "Cambro-Norman" FitzPatrick. Because the end of *Mac Giolla Eoin* sounds like the Gaelic *Luain*, meaning Monday, this surname, meaning "son of the servant of Eoin" was mistranslated as Monday. Marginally worse still for its complete lack of effort was *O Draighneán*, "descendant of Draighneán," a Gaelic name meaning "blackthorn," which was mistranslated not into Blackthorn, but Thornton! Similarly, in Spain Keating, on the misapprehension that it was from *céad tiene* ("a hundred fires"), was rendered in Spanish *cien-fuegos*, meaning the same thing: it's actually far more likely to be from the Welsh personal name, Cethyn! Remember, though: once the error was established, your ancestors could be recorded either way.

Irish villagers dancing a traditional Irish jig. The accompanying song in the original publication illustrates the revival of Irish culture from the end of the 19th century: "Then a fig for the new fashioned waltzes imported from Spain and from France, And a fig for the thing called the polka, Our own Irish jig we will dance."

De-Anglicization

With the revival of Irish culture, especially after the Gaelic League was founded in 1893, many Irish families started adopting Gaelic spellings for their surnames. Some were returned accurately to what they had been, but many were retranslated incorrectly or simply translated for the first time (I *could* Gaelicize Adolph [a German patronymic meaning "noble wolf"] into *Mac Uasalmactír*, which may sound great, but it isn't an authentic Gaelic name!). Many also restored their lost "O"s and "Macs": in the 1861 census, for example, only 4 percent of Sullivans had an "O." By 1914, 20 percent had it, and by 1972 it had spread to nearly 70 percent of all Sullivans in Ireland. Unfortunately, some made mistakes: John Aloysius Costelloe (1891–1976), *Taoiseach* of Éire, was Gaelicized in official records as *O Coisdealbha*, despite his surname having been *Mac Oisdeabh* in the Middle Ages.

This peasant girl, Bridget, photographed c. 1865, was one of the many Irish people to have the surname O'Sullivan.

Additional surnames

Surnames could become so widespread in an area that it was common for individual family units to add additional unofficial ones to distinguish between themselves. Researching her family in Co. Waterford, my friend Alison Weaver encountered O'Sullivans who added their mother's maiden names to their own, thus enabling her to find her people descended from the marriage of an O'Sullivan to a Joy identified as O'Sullivan Joys. Bill Crowley, similarly, tells me of the Crowley Klondikes of Co. Cork, descended from a Crowley who returned home rich from the Klondike gold rush. Sometimes, the original surname might be lost: the Crowley Keohanes' second surname is *ceocháin*, "in the fog" because, it is said, a party of Crowleys were late for the battle of Kinsale (1601) when a thick fog descended on them; however, some people in that part of Cork now just have the surname Keohane, having dropped Crowley altogether. Keohane's true status as a nickname must have been known in the 19th century, for there are tales of famine migrants who "got on a ship in Ireland as Keohane and got off the other end as Crowleys."

Foreign surnames

Many foreign surnames have entered Ireland. The Viking invasions brought in Harold, Trant (*Treamht*, the Gaelic form of the Old Norse name Tramant), McAuliff (*Mac Amlaoimh*, "son of Olaf") and the more obvious McIvor. The Normans used Fitz for "son of," hence Fitzgerald, "son of Gerald" and FitzMaurice, "son of Maurice." Some of these surnames have become so widespread in Ireland that they are rightly regarded as Irish, though not of course native Gaelic. Some incoming names changed once in Ireland. The surname *Le Poer*, "the poor man," is now the widespread Waterford surname Power (sometimes re-Frenchified

The quay at Waterford, c. 1860. This fine harbor distinguishes Waterford from its neighbor, Cork: the river Suir is navigable for very large ships, having sufficient depth of water to allow large trading vessels to discharge their cargoes at the quay which was unrivaled in Ireland and brought many foreigners to the area, with their associated impact on local culture and, in particular, names.

incorrectly as the rather grand-sounding De La Poer!). The De Burghs who invaded Connacht, and whose name means literally "of the borough," became De Burca and Burke, the surname made famous through the family of 19th-century genealogists. Bunyan (Old French *bugne*, "a swelling") became Banane or even Bennett. More extremely, Jocelin de Nangle, a Cambro-Norman invader, had children surnamed FitzJocelin (i.e. "son of Joscelin"), Gaelicized to *Mac Goisdealbha*, hence *Mac Oisdealbha* (these two names being Gaelic versions of Joscelin) — the ancestors (as explained on p. 151) of the Costellos!

The implications for genealogy

The free Anglicization, de-Anglicization, translation and mistranslation of surnames in Ireland means that while researching, whatever your surname *should* have been, it *might* appear without any prefix or with "Mac," "Mc" *or* "O." Equally, you can't rely on consistent spelling *under any circumstances*. Studying the origin or several

possible origins of a surname will, however, alert you to the main spellings you can expect.

While many Irish surnames denote a specific ancestor, you need to make sure there was only one person of that name. Some very common surnames, such as Murphy and Kelly, are widespread because a number of *Murchadhas* and *Ceallaighs* became the eponymous founders

Swans on Claddagh Quay, Galway. The old fishing port existed long before the bustling city grew up under the guiding hand of the Burkes.

This pedigree from the ancient Milesian collection at the GO in Dublin is of Grace O'Malley, the infamous "Pirate Queen of Connacht," who ruled the western seas and was the focus of much local resistance to the Tudors (GO Ms. 222, courtesy of National Library of Ireland).

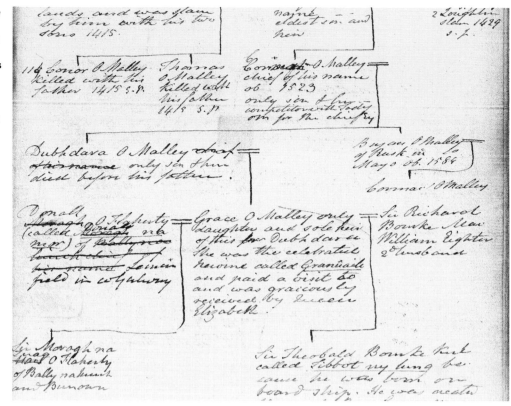

of completely different families. A further complication arises when peasants assumed the surname of their lords. We know this happened but MacLysaght for one thought that overall "the consensus of opinion is that such assumption [of surnames] was not at all widespread."

These massive cautions aside, Ireland's surnames are immensely helpful for us genealogists, as they often indicate very specific family origins. This is not the same in most other countries: someone called Baker may be descended from a baker, but that's all you know. I know I had a German ancestor with the first name Adolph, but I don't know when or where he lived, as no traditions survive about him. In Ireland, immigrant surnames can often be traced back to a specific person, even if their origins outside Ireland are uncertain. More importantly, Gaelic surnames generally point

back to an ancestor whose position in the corpus of ancient Milesian genealogies is known (for more on the descendants of Milesius, see p. 172). Using the O'Briens as an example, MacLysaght wrote "I think it can be accepted that, even though the surname was undoubtedly assumed at some period in the middle ages by families not of Dalcassian O'Brien stock, the great majority of people so called are of that descent."

In all cases, DNA tests (see p. 212) performed on groups of people with the same surname are starting to show how true or false such assumptions are.

Surname dictionaries

Although the Anglicization and Gaelicization of surnames in Ireland has clouded the waters considerably, a great deal of unraveling has been undertaken by surname historians, of

Surname sources

MacLysaght's books include:

- *Irish Families: Their Names, Arms & Origins* (4th edn., Irish Academic Press, 1991). Note: editions from 1985 incorporate the important corrections and additions printed in his earlier *Supplement to Irish Families*).
- *More Irish Families* (1970, repr., incorporating his *Supplement to Irish Families*: Irish Academic Press, 1982).
- *The Surnames of Ireland*, Irish Academic Press (1985, 6th edn., 2001).

Dr. Edward MacLysaght (pictured left), as newly-appointed Chief Herald.

whom the undoubted prince was the late Edward MacLysaght.

Edward MacLysaght (1887–1986), on whose writings I have drawn heavily, though certainly not exclusively for this chapter, spent his early career in politics, business and farming. In his 30s he wrote an MA thesis on his own family, later published as *Short Study of a Transplanted Family*. In 1938, he became an inspector for the Irish Manuscripts Commission, which began his long career in Irish genealogy, during which he served as Chairman of the Irish Manuscripts Commission, Keeper of Manuscripts at the National Library (NLI) and Genealogical Officer at the Irish Office of Arms. He was the first Chief Herald of Ireland, appointed in 1943, three years after the death of the last Ulster Herald of Arms.

MacLysaght's works developed those of contemporaries, such as Dr. John Ryan, S.J., and predecessors, such as the *Sloinnte Gaedhael is Gall (Irish Names and Surnames)* of Revd. Patrick Woulfe (1923). He was able to correct many past mistakes (many of Woulfe's derivations were guesses and some have been overturned by scholars of Middle Irish, to whom — and often only to whom — his errors are transparent). MacLysaght added the results of years of his own research among the Irish records, to which he had unparaleled access,

acknowledging traditional Irish genealogies and also incorporating modern scientific approaches to surname origins and distribution.

No surname dictionary will ever be fully accurate. New research into the linguistics behind names and discoveries of ancient examples add constantly to our knowledge. Your own research into a surname may throw up important new evidence. If MacLysaght had lived to see the arrival of DNA technology in genealogy, he would have reveled in the new light it is already shedding on many old mysteries.

further reading

■ R. Bell, *The Book of Ulster Surnames* (Blackstaff Press, 1988).

■ G.F. Black, *The Surnames of Scotland, Their Origin, Meaning, and History* (New York Public Library, 1946) — excellent for Scottish surnames, but poor for Irish ones.

■ I. Grehan, *Irish Family Histories* (Roberts Rinehart, 1993).

■ J. Grenham, *Irish Family Names* (HarperCollins, 1997).

■ P. Hanks, F. Hodges, A.D. Mills and A. Room, *The Oxford Names Companion: The Definitive Guide to Surnames, First Names, and Place Names of the British Isles* (OUP, 2002).

■ L. Quilliam, *Surnames of the Manks* [sic] (Cashtal, 1989).

■ P.H. Reaney and R.M. Wilson (eds.), *A Dictionary of English Surnames* (OUP, 2005 [Routledge, 1958]).

■ http://nualeargais.ie/gnag/ainm.htm, "The Noun" section of the *New Insights* website contains fascinating material on Gaelic names.

CHAPTER 19

Recorded pedigrees

As you trace your Irish roots back, you may be lucky enough to find a link into a pre-recorded family tree, possibly Gaelic, Cambro-Norman or Anglo-Irish. Equally, while you may not be able to trace back step-by-step beyond about 1800, your surname may indicate your place in an ancient Gaelic pedigree. But where can you find such pedigrees, how did they come to be and how accurate are they?

You will seldom be able to prove a genealogical link in the form preferred by British genealogists —

an unbroken pedigree showing each generation carefully chronicled. In some cases, especially if the family kept its land or is exceptionally well documented in fiants (see p. 135) and surviving deeds and wills, you can. In most cases, the overthrow of the Gaelic order combined with chronic shortage and destruction of records makes this simply impossible. Therefore, once you have traced your family line as far back and as honestly as you can, to the point where records cease, it is perfectly acceptable to add — with a suitable dotted line and clear explanation of all uncertainties and lack of proof — the

Annals of the Four Masters

A page from the *Annals of the Four Masters* (see p. 157). The entry for the year 3500 (i.e. 3,500 years since the creation of the world as described in the Bible) reads:

"The fleet of the son of Milidh came to Ireland at the end of this year, to take it from the Tuatha De Dananns; and they fought the battle of Sliabh Mis with them on the third day after landing. In this battle fell Scota, the daughter of Pharaoh, wife of Milidh; and the grave of Scota is to be seen between Sliabh Mis and the sea. Therein also fell Fas, the wife of Un, son of Uige, from whom is named Gleann Faisi. After this the sons of Milidh fought a battle at Tailtinn, against the three kinge of the Tuatha De Dananns, Mac Cuill, Mac Ceacht, and Mac Greine. The battle lasted for a long time, until Mac Ceacht fell by Eiremhon, Mac Cuill by Eimhear, and Mac Greine by Amhergin."

(Courtesy of Irish Script on Screen, a project of the School of Celtic Studies, Dublin Institute for Advanced Studies; and Seamus Helferty, James Joyce Library, Dublin.)

UCD Franciscan MS A 13, f. 24 r © OFM-UCD Partnership, 2004

pedigree of the known originator of your family name — all the way back, if applicable, to Milesius himself!

The Irish historian Byrne has written, *"Many Irishmen boast descent from kings. The claim is not always justified, but it is not altogether preposterous, for Ireland had redundance [i.e. an excess] of royal blood. In many parts of the country tribal sub-kings and provincial over-kings remained in power until the end of the sixteenth century, and by virtue of the Irish system of succession and of marriage laws, which approximated to polygamy, dynastic families proliferated at the expense of the commoner sort, so that Elizabethan officials complained that most Irishmen were bastards and claimed to be gentlemen."*

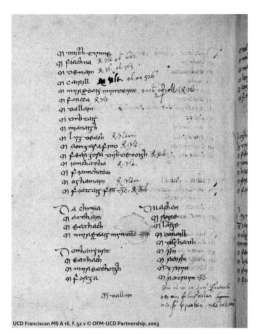

UCD Franciscan MS A 16, f. 52 v © OFM-UCD Partnership, 2003

This page from the *Genealogiae Regum et Sanctorum Hiberniae* shows part of a genealogy of the kings and saints of Ireland in the hand of Brother Mícheál Ó Cléirigh (courtesy of Irish Script on Screen and Seamus Helferty, James Joyce Library, Dublin).

Sources for ancient genealogy

The fire at the Four Courts in 1922 destroyed much genealogical material for recent centuries. Let it not be forgotten, however, that in terms of Medieval and ancient genealogy, Ireland's records are second to none.

We know about ancient, orally-transmitted Irish genealogies because they were eventually written down. The earliest written material probably took the form of historical annals created when Christianity came in the 5th century CE. These do not survive, but 7th or 8th century copies do.

Notable among the annals that contain much genealogical material are the *Annála Ríoghachta Éireann* — the *Annals of the Kingdom of Ireland*, now commonly known as the *Annals of the Four Masters* (see p. 156). Michael O'Clery and his companions, Peregrine O'Clery, Farfassa O'Mulconry and Peregrine O'Duigenan, compiled these at the Convent of Donegal between 1632 and 1636 under the patronage of Fergal O'Gara basing their work on "the most authentic annals I [Michael] could

find in my travels from CE 1616 to CE 1632 through the kingdom…" Following these come two other compilations, *The Great Book of Genealogy* of Dubhaltach Óg Mac Firbhisigh (MacFirbis), the 17th-century genealogist (1666), and Roger O'Ferrall's *Linea Antiqua* (1709).

Sir William Betham, Ulster King of Arms, made substantial collections of Irish pedigree material. At the GO are his pedigrees of Milesian Families (GO 220-2) and Ancient Irish Families (GO 215-19). His transcript of O'Ferrall's *Linea Antiqua* (GO 145-7, indexed in GO 147) includes his own notes. His addition of coats of arms to this manuscript, though sadly without stated sources, is the basis for those in MacLysaght's *Irish Families*. Betham further collected genealogical extracts from plea and patent rolls from the reigns of Henry III to Edward VI (GO 189-93), and created two series of miscellaneous pedigrees (1st series, GO 261-76, 2nd series, GO 292-8). All his sketch pedigrees are indexed by McAnlis in GO 470. Finally, Betham's collections of received correspondence (GO 580-604 and NAI

M.744-51 contain much useful material. Many of these records, of course, contain much on Cambro-Normans (see p. 195) and later incoming families as well. For more on the GO's records, see p. 169.

Also at the GO are records of Irish lords and baronets, largely but not always entirely duplicated by printed sources such as *Burke's Peerage*. Letter Books (GO 361-78) cover the period 1789-1853. Genealogical research papers include those of Sir Edmund Bewley, T.U. Sadlier and Revd. H.B. Swanzy. Material after 1943 includes much research on Gaelic family origins of migrant families as well as the more traditional subject of the Anglo-Irish. Most GO records are on Mormon microfilm. Many of the families and arms are indexed in Hayes's *Manuscript Sources for the Study of Irish Civilisation* and a consolidated index to most of the GO's indexes has been made by Virginia Wade McAnlis (NLI Ir.9291 C 11/1).

There are many genealogical details in Irish topographical poems and annals, such as those of Innisfallen and Loch Cé, and helpful information in the Irish Archaeological Society publications (especially John O'Donovan's notes) and the *Journal of the Royal Society of Antiquaries Ireland*. The Irish Manuscripts Commission's *Analecta Hibernica* has published much useful material and criticism over the years, especially 'A Guide to Irish Genealogical Collections, 700-c. 1850' (no. 7, p. 1-167); 'Treatise on the O'Donnells of Tirconnell...' (no. 8, p. 375-418); 'Description and Composition of Roger O'Ferrall's *Linea Antiqua*, 1709' (no. 10, p. 289-99); and 'The O'Clery Book of Genealogies...' (no. 18, p. 1-194).

Several modern attempts have been made to combine these older sources. John O'Hart, *Irish Pedigrees* (Dublin 1892: GPC, 1999) is a two-volume work, the first cataloging Milesian families, and the second concerned with the Cambro-Normans and later incomers. O'Hart's laudable aim was to show that the "mere Irishe" had a considerably more noble history and civilization than their English oppressors and also, incidentally, to prove to the world that his own family were the rightful Princes of Tara. He drew heavily on *The Four Masters*, MacFirbis, O'Ferrall and other native sources, and also English-generated material such as the fiants (see p. 135). "The serious genealogist," wrote MacLysaght, "uses O'Hart with caution, if at all, for he is far from a reliable authority except for the quite modern period. John O'Hart, however, undoubtedly did a vast amount of research, no matter how he used the information he acquired..." The SoG has an interesting alternative collation of the main pedigrees, *Ancient Irish Pedigrees, from Japhet Mac Noah to CE 1265* (anon mss., 1908).

A page from O'Ferrall's *Linea Antiqua II*. This chart shows the royal descent of families from Luy, Monarch of Ireland (GO Ms. 146, courtesy of the National Library of Ireland).

Much more reliable than O'Hart is M.A. O'Brien, *Corpus Genealogiarum Hiberniae* (Institute for Advanced Studies, Dublin 1962). This names some 13,000 people alive before the 12th century. It is a secondary source, drawing heavily on M.S. Rawlinson B.502 (the earliest, dating from the 12th century), the *Book of Leinster Genealogies*, the *Great Book of Lecan* and *Book of Ballymote*. Useful too is T. O'Raithbheartaig, *Genealogical Tracts 1: A. The Introduction to the Book of Genealogies; B. The Ancient Tract on the Distribution of the Aithechthuatha; C. The Lecan Miscellany* (Irish Manuscripts Commission, 1932).

M. Archdall (ed.), *The Peerage of Ireland by John Lodge (1750)* (7 vols., Dublin, 1789) is important for ennobled Irish families to 1750. Since 1826, the family of John Burke (1786–1848) from Co. Tipperary (and later the Burke's publishing house in its different incarnations) have been publishing pedigrees of the peerage and gentry for the whole British Isles, including many Irish families, Gaelic and non-Gaelic alike. Because so many intermarriages have taken place over the centuries, very few Irish families — perhaps none — are really pure-bred Gaelic, Cambro-Norman or Anglo-Irish anyway. The latest *Burke's Peerage*, and *Landed Gentry of Ireland* are online at **www.burkes-peerage .net**, but examine earlier volumes as well, using *Burke's Family Index* (Burke's Peerage, 1976) to discover all the families covered in different editions. Specifically Irish publications are B. Burke, *Burke's Irish Family Records* (Burke's Peerage, 5th edn., 1976), (previously *Burke's Landed Gentry of Ireland* [1899, 1904, 1912 and 1958]), and M. Bence-Jones, *Burke's Guide to Country Houses* vol.1, "Ireland" (Burke's Peerage, 1978). Notable too is a non-Burke's publication, J.J. Howard and F.A. Crisp, *Visitation of Ireland* (6 vols., London, 1897–1918).

Burke's Peerage, available in book form and online, contains many pedigrees of Irish nobles of mainland British origin and also a handful of Gaelic origin too, such as the Barons of Inchiquin, who survived despite the odds and continue Brian Boru's line unbroken to this very day (courtesy of Burke's Peerage).

Other published sources

The NLI, Trinity College Dublin, SoG and the Mormons' Family History Library have huge collections of published family histories, of wildly varying quality and usefulness. Their catalogs, such as the SoG's online at **www.sog.org.uk/ sogcat/access/**, act as bibliographies. Many published sources are listed on the *Irish Ancestors* website **www.ireland.com/ ancestor/**. Older guides to published sources are:

- G.B. Barrow, *The Genealogists' Guide, an Index to Printed British Pedigrees and Family Histories 1950–75* (Research Publishing Co., 1977).
- B. de Breffny, *Bibliography of Irish Genealogy and Family History* (Golden Eagle Books, 1964).
- M.D. Falley, *Irish and Scotch-Irish Ancestral Research* (repr. GPC, 1998). This includes several bibliographies.
- G.V. Fleming-Haigh, *Ireland: the Albert E. Casey Collection and Other Irish Materials in the Samford University Library: An Annotated Bibliography* (Birmingham, Alabama, 1976).
- E. MacLysaght, *Bibliography of Irish Family History* (Irish Academic Press, 1982).
- G.W. Marshall, *The Genealogists' Guide* (4th edn., 1903, repr. GPC, 1973).
- T.R. Thompson, *A Catalogue of British Family Histories* (Research Publishing Co. and SoG, 3rd edn., 1980).
- J.B. Whitmore, *A Genealogical Guide, an Index to British Pedigrees in Continuation of Marshall's Genealogist's Guide* (repr. J.B. Whitmore, 1953).

The Crowleys' ancient roots

The Crowleys of Glasgow can be traced back for certain (see p. 86) to William Crowley, born about 1800, who farmed in the parish of Annaduff, Co. Leitrim. Michael-Patrick Crowley's book *Uí Chruadhlaoich, Clann O'Mhac Diarmada: The Origins and History of the Crowleys, an Irish Clan* (privately published by Michael-Patrick Crowley, 25 avenue de l'Europe, 92310 Sévres, France, mcrowley@ businessobjects.com, 2001) provides a scholarly account of the origins of the Crowleys' claimed descent from Dermot Chruadhlaoich (d. 1218). *Chruadhlaoich* means "hard warrior": it arose originally as a nickname, but stuck as a surname, later becoming Anglicized to Crowley. When Prince John was in Ireland in 1201, he took many hostages from among the noble Gaelic families: Dermot Crowley was one, though he managed to return home a year later. His descendants in 16th-century Cork are recorded in the *Lebor Muihneach (Book of Munster)* as *Uí Chruadhlaoich o'Mhac Diarmada*. The pedigree claims that this Dermot was son of Connor, son of Dermot (1124–59), King of Moylurg, the ancestor of the MacDermots.

It's instructional to see how the pedigree in the *Book of Munster* was actually recorded. They did not use easy-to-understand charts then but rather lists of names, X *mic* (i.e. Mac, "son of") Y, etc. It starts with Dermot O'Crowley, chief of the O'Crowleys at Kilshallow Co. Cork, about 1550, and works back:

CXXXIII

Geinalach I Chruadhlaoich annso :

Diamaid: mac Amhlaoibh, mic Cormaic, mic Taidhg Mhailighigh, mic Amhlaoibh, mic Daibhith, mic Conchubhair, mic Raghnaill, mic Lochlainn Mhoir, mic Aodha, mic Ruaidhri, mic Diarmada, mic MeicRaith, mic Donnchadha, mic Diarmada (darbha ainm an Cruadhlaoch), mic Conchubhair, mic Diarmada (o raidhtear Mac Diarmada), mic MaoilRuanadha, mic Taidhg mic Cathail, mic Conchubhair, mic Taidhg Mhoir, mic Muirgheasa, mic Tomaltaigh, etc ., ut supra i ngeinelach I Chonchubhair Ruaidh.

M.-P. Crowley compared the Crowley pedigree with the relevant sections of Keating's genealogies and also the MacDermots' own family pedigrees, as recorded at the GO and in their own possession, with the aid of the chief of the clan, The MacDermot, Prince of Coolavin. He found some discrepancies, but none that were altogether surprizing considering the amount of time that had elapsed between events taking place and their being recorded. The discrepancies actually show that several independent

Brian Boru (926-1014), King of Ireland, who defeated Danish invaders at the Battle of Clontarf, 1014, where he died. He became an Irish national hero.

traditions (as opposed to just one copied several times over) were at play, and this lends much greater weight to the overall descent (discrepancies aside) being true. Little doubt exists that the Crowleys were, as they claimed, a younger branch of the MacDermots.

Yet their pedigree on its own looks rather doubtful — how could an obscure family have such illustrious ancestors? M.-P. Crowley's book explains exactly how and it is a very similar story to many other offshoots of the old Irish royal families.

Maelruanadha (Mulrooney) Mor, younger son of Tadhg of the Three Towers (d. 956), King of Connacht, was given the sub-kingdom of Moylurg and Artech with the hereditary role of commanding the King of Connacht's army in war. They were initially known as *Uí Maelruanadh*, but after Dermot, King of Moylurg (d. 1159), they became known as MacDermot.

Tradition preserved by the Crowleys of West Clare tells of Muirchetach, a son of Mulrooney Mor who led his *sept* into battle under Brian Boru at Clontarf on Good Friday 1014, helping defeat the Vikings. Before the battle, Brian Boru himself told Muirchetach *Anois than, a chruadh laoich teaspeian dom am meid neart ata ido laimh* — "Now, hard warrior, show me the strength of your hand." Muirchetach didn't acquire the nickname *chruadh laoich* himself, but six generations later King Dermot (d. 1159)'s grandson Dermot evidently did.

In 1177, Connacht was invaded by the Burkes, aided by the O'Briens. The ancient kingdom was greatly reduced, but it survived with the sub-kingdom Moylurg as part of it, though substantially reduced in size and power. In the south, meanwhile, the MacCarthys were engaged in a bitter war with the O'Briens in Munster. The MacCarthys were old allies of the O'Connor kings of Connacht, and in 1283, two Crowleys — who were of course junior cousins of the Connacht dynasty — appear in Munster, fighting on the side of the MacCarthys. One, Ragnall Ua Chruadhlaoich, was slain, but Dermot Ua Chruadhlaoich married the heiress of Kilshallow (Co. Cork) and settled there. After that, Dermot's family, Anglicized as O'Crowley, grew into a *sept* at Kilshallow, serving for generations as Galloglasses (see p. 200) or mercenaries for the MacCarthys, right down to the wars with the Tudors, after which they lost their lands. The last Irish-born chief, Miles O'Crowley, was one of the Wild Geese (see p. 207), settling in James II's court-in-exile at Saint-Germain-en-Laye, where his noble ancestry was recorded and confirmed. Most remained behind, however, and the name Crowley is now very common in Co. Cork.

It is clear, however, that not all of Dermot Chruadhlaoich's descendants went to Cork; presumably those inclined to fighting went, and those who preferred a quieter life remained behind. Moylurg lies in the north-western corner of Co. Roscommon, its western border being the River Shannon, as it flows south from Lough Allen. Annaduff, where the Glasgow Crowleys came from, is barely five miles from the southeastern corner of Moylurg, on the opposite bank of the Shannon. The 19th-century Crowleys of Annaduff lived within a stone's throw of where, 700 years earlier, the surname Crowley is known to have arisen. Barring an extraordinary coincidence, the Annaduff Crowleys seem highly likely to be descended from Dermot Chruadhlaoich (d. 1218), son of Conor MacDermot, King of Moylurg, and to be lineal descendants of the O'Connor kings of Connacht (though it must be admitted that their DNA seems now to be distinct from the Crowleys of Co. Cork. See p. 152.).

Genealogically, however, the Crowleys can trace their Irish roots even further back to Muiredhach Muilleathan, King of Connacht (697–702). They and all his male-lineal descendants are known as the Silmurray (or "Clan Murray"). Before him, the line of kings of Connacht go right back to Dauní Tenga Uma, King of Connacht (d. 502), son of Brión, progenitor of the Uí Bríóin. He is said (and here DNA does support the genealogy) to have been a son of Eochu Mugmedón and thus a brother of Niall Noígiallach — Niall

of the Nine Hostages (see p. 165), whose family extended their rule from Connacht into the north when they conquered Ulster from the Ulaid.

Scholars accept that the ancient pedigrees stretching back before Eochu Mugmedón are partly fables, though with some elements of genuine tradition thrown in. Six generations back from Eochu appears Conn of the Hundred Battles — probably in origin an ancient Irish god, from whom the pagan Connachta had claimed descent. Two generations before him in the pedigree appears the legendary Tuathal Teachtmar, said to have conquered his kingdom back from invaders with Roman help, and probably a genuine ancestor who did indeed carve out the ancient realm of Connacht. From Tuathal, a further 41 generations takes us back to Heremon (see p. 174), the original Gaelic conqueror of the northern half of Ireland, elder son of Milesius himself, and 37th in descent from Adam and Eve.

Fiction? Maybe. But it is a fable that was recorded in the Middle Ages and that dates back over one-and-a-half millennia, incorporating traditions that go back long before the time of Christ. It's a fable with a long pedigree, then, and one of which its descendants can justifiably feel proud.

Carrick MacDermot, in Loch Cé, in the heart of ancient Moylurg, where the unfortunate Cormac MacDermot (1218–44), King of Moylurg, was forced to surrender to the de Burghs in 1235. Legend has it that the unfortunate King Cormac was forced to entertain the fearsome Hag of Loch Cé there for a year too. Despite all this, it remained the family home until 1592.

The ancient pedigrees

Ultimately, Ireland owes its ancient pedigrees to its rich oral history. Gaelic Ireland had an *aos dána* or "mantic class" of professional bards, genealogists, poets, musicians and druids. Such a group is found in most native cultures that have not been crushed by invaders, for such were Homer and his contemporary poets, and the

Jewish genealogists who remembered the ancient genealogies that were later recorded in the Bible.

Ireland certainly compares very favorably with other countries with ancient genealogical traditions. On the opposite end of the Eurasian landmass, China has an almost identical system of genealogies, each identifying the founder of one family with the younger son of someone on a yet older stem. Eventually all go back, one way or another, to Huangdi (2697–2597 BCE), the "Yellow Emperor," the legendary founder of the Chinese nation. Because of the remarkable way that genealogies in different areas match up — in most cases, the founder of a family in one place will indeed appear independently as a younger son in the records of the supposed ancestral family — the accuracy of these Chinese genealogies is widely accepted back to at least the 5th century BCE. DNA, moreover, has shown that vast swathes of the Han Chinese actually do have a common male-lineal ancestor, perhaps even Huangdi himself!

Unlike the Chinese, however, the Irish seem never to have been ancestor worshippers. The Irish of several thousand years ago probably claimed descent from totemic ancestors — fish, wolves and so on, echoes of whom still linger on, perhaps, in the animal charges of Irish heraldry. Later, under Brehon Law that persisted until the 17th century, ancestry underpinned the tribal system, which determined land holding, political allegiance and clan chieftainship. Ancestors certainly counted, but it was not so much your ancestors as to whom you were related on account of your ancestry that really mattered. As O'Donovan wrote in 1849,

"those of the lowest rank among a great tribe traced and retained the whole line of their descent with the same care which in other nations was peculiar to the rich and great; for, it was from his own genealogy each man of the tribe, poor as well as rich, held the charter of his civil state."

The Croly (Crowley) pedigree from vol. 1 of O'Hart's *Irish Pedigrees*. It shows the origin of the surname and a line coming down from it — no collateral branches are shown. To trace the line further back, O'Hart refers to the MacDermot pedigree, which in turn traces the line back to the O'Connor kings of Connacht, ultimately derived from the line of Heremon, son of Milesius. The numbering follows the system used in the 17th-century genealogies, whereby Adam is 1, Noah 10 and their descendant Milesius 36.

Maintaining this system of the *aos dána* were the *brithem* (law-giver); the *filid* ("poet-seer"), to whom the *bard* was an attendant composer, usually of satires and panegyrics; and the *seanchaidhe* ("genealogist/storyteller/historian"), particularly concerned with preserved oral genealogies. Their accuracy was astonishing: Irish poet W.B.Yeats once compared the *Tale of Dierdre* as recited by an illiterate storyteller with a "very ancient manuscript" at the Dublin Royal Society, and found the two compared "almost word for word."

The oral *seanchaidhe* or "shanachie" (sometimes miscalled "*filid*") tradition was severely disrupted by the English invasions of the 16th and 17th centuries, not least because the tie between genealogy and landholding that had made their work so important was broken. Some *shanachies* remained, however, though much reduced in prosperity. One of the last was Mrs Bridget Fitzgerald of Barrymore (1728–1808), called *Brighid na Senchas* or "Bridget of the Histories." She would go about the gentry's

Brehon Law

This system was named from the Irish *breitheamhan*, meaning "that given by lawgivers or judges." The lawgivers were hereditary: the MacClancys were lawgivers to the O'Brien Dynasty, for example, and the O'Dorans to the Kings of Leinster.

houses with her gold-handled walking stick, constantly updating her oral history, a practice perpetuated by at least two more generations of her family, probably with considerable accuracy. In her day, Bridget was a rarity, but by then many oral genealogies had been recorded.

How accurate are they?

Some pedigrees, such as the O'Neills' (on p. 166), are considered accurate back to the 5th century CE, but genealogies stretch much further back. "Cuchulain, Fionn, Oisin, St. Patrick, the whole ancient world of Erin," as Yeats wrote rhetorically, "may well have been

BELOW LEFT:
This page from a *Book of* (heraldic) *Visitations*, begun in 1568, shows a visitation dated May 4, 1570 with brief pedigree descriptions.

BELOW RIGHT:
Early pedigree of the Fitzgerald family, descended from Otho, "a nobleman in Italy." (Both images courtesy of the National Library of Ireland.)

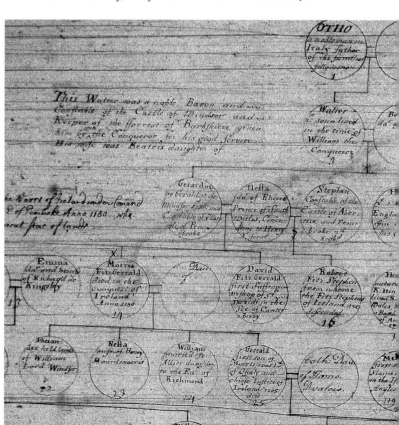

sung out of the void by the harps of the great bardic order." They were more likely based in accurate oral traditions, but there is simply no way of proving this by cross-checking them against any other sources — there are none. Professor H.M. Chadwick considered there was "no adequate reason for doubting that the genuine native proportions [of the genealogies] may go back — I will not say without change," to the 1st century CE, "or even one or two centuries earlier." While some scholars are less generous, even the sceptical 20th-century scholar Thomas F. O'Rahilly accepted that Tuathal, who lived about 150–50 BCE, was probably a real person.

It must be admitted that if you look at ancient genealogies not so much as stores of ancient folk-memories than as charters to certain privileges and rights subject to change according to the will of rulers and as political necessity demanded, it is easier to see why unhistorical features may have crept in. Ancient Irish genealogies tend to be divergent, tracing many lines back to common ancestors. This gives royal ancestry to a vast number of people with Irish roots. While many pedigrees are undoubtedly accurate, some links may have been forged to flatter genealogists' patrons, to lend historical weight to contemporary alliances or to legitimize usurpations or invasions. By showing ultimately that all Irish lords and princes were related, the ancient genealogists may also have been trying to impose a sense of unity on Ireland's disparate, warring tribes, in the hope of fostering a more peaceful society. Yeats wrote of the ancient bards, *"riding hither and thither gathering up the dim feelings of the time, and making them conscious. In the history one sees Ireland ever struggling vainly to attain some kind of unity. In the bardic tales it is ever one, warring within itself, indeed, but always obedient, unless under some great provocation, to its high king."*

The more prominent the king, the more lines were traced back to him. Often, early versions of royal pedigrees show far fewer offshoots than later ones, enabling us to see which may have been added falsely. The way to get the closest you can to the truth, therefore, is to work back to the earliest extant versions of the pedigree, and see what they have in common. Frustrating though the consequent lack of certainty may be, let's remember that very few countries have anything approaching Ireland's wealth of early genealogical material — at least the different pedigrees that can be argued over exist at all!

It's worth noting, too, that Gaelic oral tradition has recently undergone a considerable vindication thanks to archaeology. For example, a wooden trackway or *togher* found stretching across the bog of Corlea, Co. Longford, dated to 148 BCE, seemed too impractical to serve any useful purpose. *The Wooing of Étaíne*, part of the Ulster Cycle, however, describes the heroic tasks given to the hero Midhir by the king at Tara, including building a causeway over a marsh called Móin Lámhraighe. It was a purely symbolic effort, therefore — and perhaps identical to the one at Corlea that had puzzled archaeologists.

further reading

■ F.J. Byrne, *Irish Kings and High-Kings* (Four Courts Press, 1973, 2001).

■ H.M. Chadwick, *Early Scotland: The Picts the Scots and the Welsh of Southern Scotland* (C.U.P., 1949).

■ J. Morris, *Arthurian Sources*, vol.5, 'Genealogies and Texts' (Phillimore, Chichester, 1995).

■ T.F. O'Rahilly, *Early Irish History and Mythology* (School of Celtic Studies, Dublin Institute for Advanced Studies, 1999).

The O'Neills

The O'Neill (Uí Néill) pedigree (see the next two pages) back to the High King *Niall Noígiallach*, Niall of the Nine Hostages, in the early 5th century CE, is generally considered the oldest proven one in Europe and one of the longest in the world. *Burke's Peerage* acknowledges that while "the early [i.e. pre-5th-century] part of this family's genealogy in Ireland is largely legendary in detail… it does seem to be based on a solid stratum of truth."

In 431 CE the Christian missionary Palladius arrived in Ireland and wrote of King Laogaire, son of *Niall Noígiallach mac Echach*, i.e. son of Eochu: thus, argues O'Rahilly (see p. 164), we can accept that Eochu existed too. Gaelic tradition makes Niall's mother Cairenn, whom Eochu had captured on a raid in Britain. Eochu was indeed nicknamed "Mugmedon," "lord of slaves" and Cairenn seems to be a Gaelic version of the Roman name, Carina, so O'Rahilly felt she was likely to be real as well. Not so plausible, he felt, were Niall's half-brothers Fiachra, Brión and Aillil, ancestors of the kings of Connacht. They could have been grafted onto the pedigree later (that they were Niall's *half*-brothers indicates some uncertainty on the pedigree-makers' behalf), as could the "three Collas" (princes), the ancestors of the kings of Orgiall, whom later pedigrees make sons of Niall's (supposed) great-uncle Eochu Domlén.

The ancient pedigrees take Niall's ancestry right back to Milesius (for more on Milesius himself, see p. 172). O'Rahilly was cautious of believing any pedigrees that went back much before the arrival of Christianity, and hence contemporary records. Others argued that because instances were known of people "who could repeat their pedigree back for seven generations," the pedigree of King Loegaire (d. 463) must be trustworthy for at least a couple of centuries previous to his time. But O'Rahilly's response was,

"Unfortunately the cases are not parallel. The record that we possess of the ancestors of Loegaire was not derived from Loegaire himself or from any contemporary of his, but from part of a lengthy pedigree, invented several centuries after his death, in which his descent is traced back to the fabulous Míl[esius]. Moreover, as we have seen, the inventors of this and similar pedigrees were very far indeed from being animated by a desire for historical truth and accuracy; indeed one need not hesitate to say that their object was rather to disguise the truth."

We can accept the main lines down from Niall's sons to the Uí Néill of the north and the Uí Néill of the south, from which the High Kings were chosen until 1002, though the lines of kings of Meath and Brega from his great-grandson Diarmait mac Cerbaill (d. 565) could be later fabrications. According to the scholar John Morris, some two dozen names were "tacked on" to the descendants of Niall's grandson Enda mac Loegairi in the mid-17th century alone. The reliable main line, O'Neill of Clannaboy, Chief of that Name, descends from Shane ("Joao") O'Neill, an 18th-century Wild Goose (see p. 207), who settled in Portugal. His descendant Hugo O'Neill, a lieutenant in the Portuguese navy, married Dona Julia de Serpa Pimentel, a great-great- granddaughter of Joao VI, King of Portugal and Emperor of Brazil. Hugh's son Jorge O'Neill was recognized by the Chief Herald of Ireland as The O'Neill, a title now borne by his son Dom Hugo O'Neill, born in 1939, who lives in Setubal, Portugal. Another branch of the family descends from Arthur O'Neill (1736–1814), who served in the Spanish army and became 1st Marques del Norte. His descendant Carlos O'Neill (b. 1927) is 12th Marques de la Granja and 5th Marques del Norte in Seville.

The latest DNA results have had surprising implications for O'Neill's genealogy, as you will see on p. 213.

St. Patrick (Patricus) sleeping, watched over by Christ. According to tradition, Patricus, the patron Saint of Ireland, was stolen from Britain as a child by Irish coastal raiders. Some suggest that early Irish law allowed the taking of "hostages," and as Niall of the Nine Hostages was King of Ireland at this time, he has been held responsible for the enslavement of Patricus. Another story holds that Niall gained his epithet when he took hostages from each of the five provinces of Ireland (Ulster, Connacht, Leinster Munster and Meath) and one from the Scots, Saxons, Britons and French).

The Uí Néill pedigree

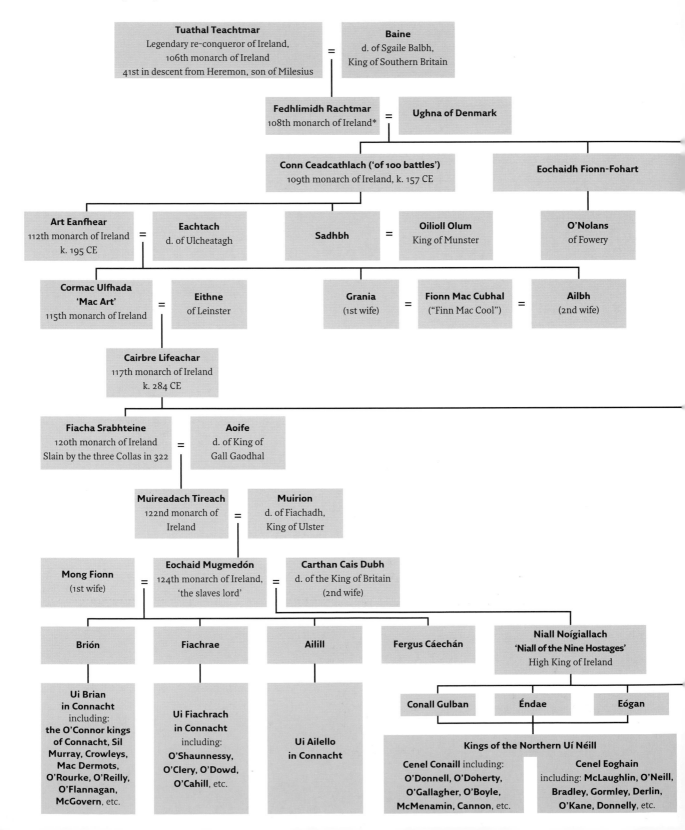

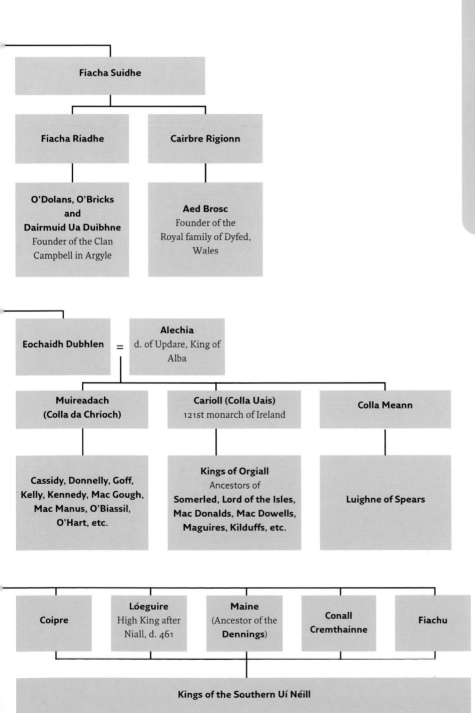

Fiacha Suidhe

Fiacha Riadhe

Cairbre Rigionn

O'Dolans, O'Bricks and Dairmuid Ua Duibhne
Founder of the Clan Campbell in Argyle

Aed Brosc
Founder of the Royal family of Dyfed, Wales

Eochaidh Dubhlen = **Alechia**
d. of Updare, King of Alba

Muireadach (Colla da Chrioch)

Carioll (Colla Uais)
121st monarch of Ireland

Colla Meann

Cassidy, Donnelly, Goff, Kelly, Kennedy, Mac Gough, Mac Manus, O'Biassil, O'Hart, etc.

Kings of Orgiall
Ancestors of
Somerled, Lord of the Isles, Mac Donalds, Mac Dowells, Maguires, Kilduffs, etc.

Luighne of Spears

Coipre

Lóeguire
High King after Niall, d. 461

Maine
(Ancestor of the **Dennings**)

Conall Cremthainne

Fiachu

Kings of the Southern Uí Néill

CHAPTER 20

Heraldry

Researching your Irish roots may reveal a coat of arms in your family. But what does this mean, and are you allowed to use it?

Tribal societies the world over define themselves by animal totems. Over and above family membership, Australian Aborigines belong to clans defined *not* by blood, but by those who dream of a particular animal ancestor. In North America, tribes connected by blood identify with an animal totem and the same applied in ancient Ireland. In the epic Irish legend *The Cattle-Raid of Cooley*, for example, we hear of the *Partraighi*, "the people of the stag." Further south, many Munster families revered the stag, defining borders by the routes of stag hunts and choosing rulers from among the ruling house, the Eóganacht, on the basis of their prowess in stag-hunting.

Heraldry developed early in the 12th century,

in France, and came to Ireland with the Cambro-Normans (see p. 195). The heavily armored warriors identified themselves in battle by the unique heraldic design on their shields. These designs were hereditary within the male lines of families and were granted and monitored by the king's heralds. The system was not widely adopted by Gaelic families until the 15th century, but when they did so, many of them incorporated ancient animal symbolism, which is why the MacCarthys and O'Sullivans, the principal Eóganacht families, have stags in their arms.

Other families used different symbols that they later incorporated into coats of arms. The oak tree, for example, was especially revered in Connacht, where druids planted them near forts. Oaks appear in the arms of many prominent families there, such as the Flanagans, O'Beirnes and O'Conor Don. The famous Red Hand of Ulster was the *Lamhdearg* (*Labraid*), the

The coats of arms of MacCarthy, O'Connor (of Co. Kerry), O'Sullivan and O'Neill, painted by leading heraldic artist Tom Meek (contact email: tapmeek@bt internet.com) for *Family History Monthly*.

symbol of the sun god Bolg (or Nuadu), and was also equated with the hand of Heremon (see p. 174), which he cut off and threw ashore so that he could claim to be the first Milesian to have touched Ireland. Besides appearing in many Ulster families' arms, it was also used by James I with horrible irony as the badge of the order of baronets he created for the purpose of leading the Plantation of Ulster — the planned process of English colonization of the province of Ulster during the early 17th century.

The Irish Office of Arms was created by Edward VI in 1552, with Bartholomew Butler as the first Ulster King of Arms, as the Chief Herald in Ireland was then known. He and his successors were mainly concerned with ceremonial functions, such as marshaling state processions, but they also controlled the use of heraldry among the king's subjects — a sphere of influence that spread across the whole island in the 17th century.

Visitations and other heraldic records

Irish heraldic record-keeping was very poor until the time of Sir William Betham (see p. 140), to whom modern genealogists owe so much. In the 16th and 17th centuries, however, Heraldic Visitations were made of the parts of Ireland where English families were most plentiful in order to discover who was using coats of arms. If people could prove their right to do so by male lineal descent from someone to whom arms had been granted by the heralds, their pedigrees were recorded. If not, they were forced publicly to "disclaim" the arms or quietly invited to pay for a new grant.

Visitations were discontinued at the end of the 17th century as they entailed expensive and often dangerous traveling. Instead, families wishing to record their right to arms brought their pedigrees to the GO where they are recorded as Registered Pedigrees (GO 156-82, indexed in GO 469). These also include records of noble descent recorded by Wild Geese (see p. 207), who required such evidence for membership of European orders of nobility and

Part of a page of *Some Funeral Entries* (c. 1632–1729, from British Library Add. Ms A820) showing the level of detail you might find on armigers (people entilted to use coats of arms), their families and servants (courtesy of SoG).

Visitation pedigrees

Visitation pedigrees (GO 47-9, indexed in GO 117) may go back a couple of generations or cover many centuries. They usually only give dates or ages for the living generations. They cover:

- Dublin and parts of Co. Louth 1568-70
- Drogheda and Ardee 1570
- Swords 1572
- Cork 1574
- Limerick 1574
- Dublin City 1607
- Dublin County 1610
- Wexford 1610

(592) (Arms.) Sr Basill Brooke of Borigall, Kn^t, Died the 25th of July 1633. He mar^d Ann Dat^r of Thomas Leecester of Toft in Chester by whome He had Henry who mar^d Elizabeth Dat^r of Capt John Winter of Durham in Glocestershire ; Ann mar^d to Richd Crofton of Lisdorn in the County of Roscoñon ; and Elizabeth not mar^d. He was buried in St Warbroughs Church Dublin the 26th of July.

(593) (Arms.) Page 249. The R^t Honble Lady Sarah [Boyle] Baron^{ss} of Geshill Dat^r of the R^t Honble Sr Rich^d [Boyle] Kn^t Earle of Corke, Visc^t Dungarvan Baron of Youghall Lo^d High Treasur^r of Ireland and one of the Lo^d Justices. She first mar^d Sr Thomas Moore, Son & Heir of Sr Garrett Moore, Kn^t, Lo^d Moore, Baron of Mellefont, and Visc^t Moore of Drogheda, by whom She had no issue. After mar^d to the R^t Honble Lo^d Digby Baron of Geashill by whome Shee had Issue Kildare Digby, Lettice and Katherin Digby, She was Interr'd in the Cathedll Church of St Patricks Dublin the 12 of Augt 1633.

Walter the Groom wth a Black Staff
Poore 2 and 2
Henry Cream wth a Black Staff
Sr Will: Fentons Serv^{ts}
Sr Adam Loftus Serv^{ts}
Sr Will: Parsons Serv^{ts}
Visc^t Ranelagh's Serv^{ts}
Earle of Killdare's Serv^{ts}
Lo^d Digby's Serv^{ts}
The Footman & Will. Coniers wth a Black Staff
Mr George Boyle wth ye Pennon
Antony Bragg & Will: Gibon
Pierce Grogan & Rory Donell
Edward Leg & John Leg
Mr Woodward & Mr Bradley
Mr Hammat & Mr Loyd

chivalry. By 1698, the hiatus in records after 1610 had led to many family records being badly out of date. From that year, confirmations of arms (GO 103-11) were issued to people simply if they could prove their family had been using arms for a century or three generations.

Much other genealogically-linked heraldic information appears in the GO's papers. Grants of new armorial bearings are in GO 103-111g). Between 1588 and 1691, the heralds marshaled many funerals of armigers (people entilted to use coats of arms) and created Funeral Entries (GO 64-79, indexed GO 386) recording the deceased's name, spouse, children and arms. Royal Warrants for changes of name (GO 26, 149-154a) date from 1784.

The office of Ulster King of Arms held its authority, despite other political changes, until 1943. Heraldic authority in Northern Ireland was then transferred to Norroy and Ulster King of Arms, stationed at the College of Arms, London. The Irish Free State appointed Edward MacLysaght to the newly created office of Chief Herald of Ireland, and Ulster's old office in Dublin became the Genealogical Office (GO),

which is now part of the NLI.

MacLysaght wrote that,
"we were at first inclined to adopt the British attitude in heraldic matters; but after a few years the peculiar conditions existing in Ireland, politically and historically, induced a modification of outlook..."
Thus, while maintaining the English system of granting new arms to worthy individuals and allowing the use of existing arms to those who could prove their male lineal descent from original grantees, the GO took a new approach to the arms of the Irish *septs*, deciding these were "by custom regarded as appertaining to all members of a sept." They had arisen, in other words, as arms used by a group of people who defined themselves by having the same male-lineal ancestor, as opposed to arms used under the English system, which could only be used by male-lineal descendants of an ancestor *to whom those arms were granted*.

The *septs* concerned are those whose arms are illustrated in part three of MacLysaght's *Irish Families*. The essay on heraldry that accompanies it is fascinating because MacLysaght was in the unique position of defining the rules of modern

Coats of arms of "Hughe O'Neyle" (O'Neill), Earl of Tyrone (d. 1616) and Donell McCarthy Mor, Earl of Clancare (d. c. 1601), from a manuscript in the National Library of Ireland. They show potent Irish symbols. The Red Hand of Ulster (see p. 168-9) was the emblem of the O'Neill's ancient homeland in northern Ireland. The stag was revered in Munster in ancient times, so was used as an emblem by the MacCarthy Kings of Munster (GO Ms. 222, courtesy of the National Library of Ireland).

Irish heraldry. Simply having the same surname as a *sept* is not enough, but if you can prove that your ancestors belonged to one, or can show descent from someone who used the arms historically (and therefore, by inference, by right of blood), regardless of how many generations ago that was, then the arms "may be displayed without any impropriety." If you want to bear them with recognized authority, you can seek a Confirmation of Arms from the Chief Herald.

Many books assign arms to names sloppily. Where an Irish family name has no associated arms, those of an English family who coincidentally bear the same name are cheerfully assigned to it. According to MacLysaght, the heraldic illustrations in various recent editions of O'Hart are particularly flawed in this respect.

The new Genealogy and Heraldry Bill, under discussion in 2007, was created by Michael Merrigan, director of the Genealogical Society of Ireland. It proposes to establish licensed heraldic agents under the authority of the Chief Herald, who will create certificates of arms far more cheaply than under the old system. The aim is to encourage as many people and organizations as possible to enjoy using coats of arms. Emeritus Arms will also be presented to worthy people in lieu of an honours system.

Most printed pedigree material includes notes on the relevant family arms. Arms can also be looked up in B. Burke, *The General Armory of England, Scotland, Ireland and Wales* (1842, repr. 1884 and *Burke's Peerage*, 1961) and P. Kennedy, *Kennedy's Book of Arms* (1816, repr. 1967). To identify a coat of arms, you can use J.W. Papworth and A.W. Morant, *An Alphabetical Dictionary of Arms belonging to Families of Great Britain and Ireland* (1874, repr. as *Papworth's Ordinary of British Armorials*, 1961).

Crowley coat of arms

Arms of the Crowleys (painted by the author).

This *sept* is from Moylurg, Roscommon, and now mainly — but not exclusively — found in Co. Cork. They are blazoned *Argent, a boar passant Azure between three crosses crosslet Gules*, with the crest *A boar's head couped Azure*. These are deliberately based on those of MacDermot, whose earliest coat, granted in 1617, shows a red fess between three blue boars; a later coat, granted in 1765, shows three blue boars' heads between a red chevron charged with three gold crosses crosslet. The Crowleys' arms clearly proclaim their descent from the MacDermots. The origin of the boar is uncertain, but great boars were seen in many cultures, from ancient Greece to Ireland, as worthy opponents of the finest of warriors. The boar had surely been used from ancient times as the emblem of the Crowleys' and MacDermots' ancestors, the Kings of Moylurg, and may have been a local pre-Christian, tribal totem.

further reading
■ A. Fox-Davies, *A Complete Guide to Heraldry* (T. Nelson & Sons, rev. edn. by J.P. Brooke-Little, 1969).
■ S. Hood, *Royal Roots — Republican Inheritance: the Survival of the Office of Arms* (Woodfield Press, 2002).

CHAPTER 21

Milesius was your ancestor

Ultimately, ancient Gaelic pedigrees stretch back to Milesius. He is a mythological ancestor, but it's a myth that belongs to everyone with Gaelic Irish roots. Ultimately, the myth of Milesius underlies several undoubted truths — that the ancient Irish were closely interrelated, and that much of their genetic inheritance came, like Milesius, from the Iberian peninsular.

The *Lebor Gabála*

The bedrock of Irish genealogy is the *Lebor Gabála Érenn* (*The Book of the Conquest of Ireland*). This wonderful book roots the earliest Irish family trees in the history of Ireland's settlement by giants, gods and men. It was compiled by monks, probably in the 11th century, and is preserved in the *Book of Leinster* (c. 1150) and about 136 later versions and copies. It is based on many earlier poems and tales dating back much further: Nennius's *History of the Britons*, compiled in Britain about 830, contains two crude versions of the tale, presumably obtained from monastic colleagues in Ireland. Precisely what was known before then we can only speculate.

In its fullest form the *Lebor Gabála*, as it is usually known, describes seven waves of settlement into "good and lofty Ireland," all rooted in the Bible's account of the world's origins. First, there came Cessair, daughter of Noah's son Bith, with her father and a group of other refugees from the impending Great Flood. When the Flood came, only Cessair's husband Fintán Mac Bóchra survived, submerged in a cave where he became immortal, taking various forms including the Salmon of Wisdom. He witnessed and is the source for all that followed.

Next came the monstrous Formorians, descended from Noah's son Ham. In some versions they were mere pirates, but in others they were giants, "with single noble legs and single full hands." Thirdly came the Partholónians, led by Partholón, a 5 x great-grandson of Noah's son Japhet, "a royal course across an oar-beaten sea: his quartet of heroes, fair and faithful..." subdued the Formorians, but were wiped out by plague and

The Hill of Tara, Co. Meath, seat of the ancient Irish Kings (see p. 174).

are buried at Tallaght near Dublin. Fourthly, the sails of the Nemedians appeared off Ireland's shores. Led by Nemedh, a great-grandson of Partholón's brother Tait, the Nemedians waged successful wars against the Formorians until Nemedh died of plague, whereupon they were destroyed, some say by the Formorians, others by sickness or flood.

The surviving Nemedians fled in three parties, each led by one of Nemedh's grandsons. One, under Briattan Maol, settled in Britain, giving the mainland its first people (it was important to the Irish to claim that the British were an offshoot of the Irish, not the other way around: the myth runs contrary to Britain's own, which claims descent from a group of Trojans under their leader Brutus). A second party, led by Simon Breac, settled in Greece where they were enslaved and bred into a race of stunted, swarthy laborers, split into three peoples, the *Fir Bolg*, *Fir Domnann* and *Fir Gálioin* (fir means "men"), though some of their racial degeneracy — for thus the tale implies — may have come from subsequent interbreeding with the Formorians. Known collectively as the *Fir Bolg*, they escaped from Greece and sailed north to conquer "the tuneful land of Ireland," but were vanquished a mere 37 years later by the Sixth wave, the *Tuatha de Danann*. They lived on, much reduced, and were the acknowledged ancestors of a few historical peoples such as the Gálioin in Leinster.

The *Tuatha de Danann* were descendants of the third group of surviving Nemedians. Led by Nemedh's grandson Beothach, they had settled in Thrace where they became immensely skilled in the sciences and arts. They were described in *Echtrae Laoghaire* (*Laoghaire's Adventure*) in the *Book of Leinster*, in this way:

"*They march among blue lances,*
Those troops of white warriors with knotted hair,
Their strength, great as it is, cannot be less.

They are sons of queens and kings,
On the heads of all a comely
Harvest of hair yellow like gold.
Their bodies are graceful and majestic,
Their eyes have looks of power and blue pupils,
Their teeth shine like glass,
Their lips are red and thin..."

Tall, beautiful and terrible, they "landed with horror, with lofty deed, in their cloud of mighty spectres, upon a mountain of Conmaicne" in Connacht, defeated the Formorians in the two battles at Moytura (*Mag Tuired*) and established their seat at Tara. They ruled Ireland unchallenged for 150 years until the coming of Milesius's sons.

Milesius was the king of Spain. His family was the senior line coming down from Noah's son Japhet via the latter's great-grandson Phoeniusa Farsaidh, whose first name was the eponym for both the Phoenicians of the eastern Mediterranean and also the ancient Irish warriors called the Fenians. Phoeniusa Farsaidh was King of Scythia, a rather nebulous term for western Asia. He was present at the building of the Tower of Babel and his grandson Gaodhal created the Gaelic language. Their descendants roamed about the Mediterranean living in Crete and Libya, spurred on by a druidic prophecy that they would find a promised land. Gaodhal's 15 x great-grandson Brath founded Galicia in Spain, and Brath's son Brigus (Breoghan) built Braganza in Portugal and sent some of his people, the Brigantes, to Britain. He also built the great Tower of Breoghan on the northwest coast of Spain, from which his younger son Ithe saw Ireland. Ithe sailed there and was entertained by the *Tuatha de Danann*, but was later murdered by them. It was this — and the clear knowledge that Ireland was the long-sought promised land of their family's destiny — that caused Ithe's great-nephews, the sons

Braganza in northwest Portugal, founded, according to Irish legend, by Brigus, grandfather of Milesius (drawn by the author).

of Milesius, to set out with their widowed mother Scota and a great invasion fleet.

Milesius, son of Bile, is also called *Míl Espáne*, the Latin for "soldier of Spain" (O'Hart asserted that *mileadh* is the Irish for "brave"), or Galamh. In Scottish history he is called Gaythelos, and in both traditions his wife was Scota, daughter of a Pharaoh. The earliest versions of the *Lebor Gabála* give them two sons, Heber and Heremon (Eber and Eremon), while later ones add others, including Amergin the family druid, and Donn and Ir (most Irish families have stories concerning sets of brothers who left one place and settled in another, and their number is usually variable!). The brothers reached Tara and demanded the kingship but came to a gentlemen's agreement with the *Tuatha de Danann* to return to their ships and sail nine miles out to give their foes a chance to assemble their forces. The Milesians kept their side of the bargain, but the treacherous *Tuatha de Danann* used their magic to raise a terrible storm that scattered the fleet and drowned Ir. Heber landed in the south and Heremon in the north, coming together to fight the *Tuatha de Danann* at the battles of Sliabh Mis and Tailtiu, "vehemently and whole-heartedly... from morning to evening contending, bonehewing and mutilating one another, till the three kings and three queens of Ireland [of the *Tuatha de Danann*] fell there." The *Tuatha de Danann* were driven into the mountains, lakes and *sídhs* (the ancient fairy mounds) where they remain as the Fairies or "Gentry," a potent, magical force that still lurks just behind the physical veil of modern Ireland.

In fact, you may yet encounter one in your family history. Some families, such as the O'Donahues of Kerry and the O'Dalys of Lisadell (of whom John O'Daly wrote the original version of *Robin Adair*), seem to have been plagued by Fairies. The Hackets of Castle Hacket even claimed a Fairy ancestor. A woman who lived near Bantry in the 18th century went one step further — being covered with fish scales, she was said to be descended from the union of a good-looking fisherman who had been seduced by a *murrúghach* (merrow) — a mermaid.

Meanwhile...

"The princes, with many battles,
Took the kingdom of Ireland;
They did it with brightness, merry the sound,
Eber and Eremon."

They divided Ireland between them, Heber taking the south (*Leth Moga*) and Heremon the north (*Leth Cuinn*). In some versions, the latter slew the former, but in all events the two halves of Ireland were established under separate dynasties, each descended from Milesius himself.

Hand-in-hand with the *Lebor Gabála* are the ancient Irish genealogies that trace the ruling families of Ireland back to the Milesians. The earliest of these trace the two main families, the Connachta in the north (and their offshoot, the Uí Néill) and the Eóghanacht in the south, seated at Tara and Cashel respectively, back to Heremon and Heber, the other ruling families being by implication descendants of the earlier *Fir Bolgs* and Formorians. Later versions added ever more extra lines to incorporate some of these into the Milesian scheme, some springing from descendants of Heremon and Heber, others coming down from Ithe, Ir and yet more sons of Milesius.

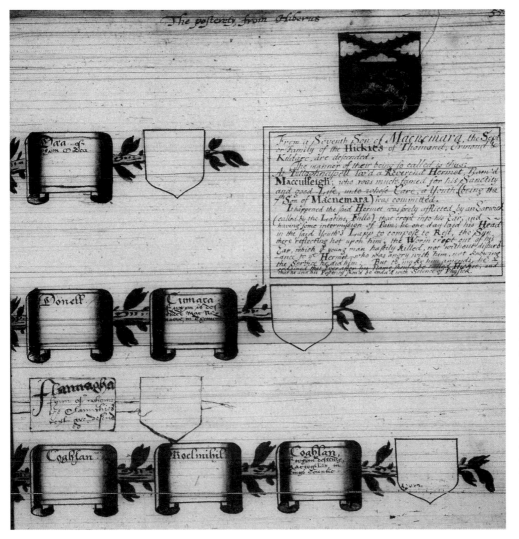

Detail from GO Ms 158 showing the descent of the O'Deas, O'Flanaghans, O'Coghlans and MacNemaras from "Hiberus" (Heber), son of Milesius. It relates the frankly bizarre tale of a son of the MacNemara family who cured his hermit-master by extracting an earwig from his ear and was called Hickie (from the Gaelic *Iceadh* meaning "healer") from that point on. He was the ancestor of the Irish *O'hIcidhe* or Hickey family (courtesy of the National Library of Ireland).

The Milesian pedigree

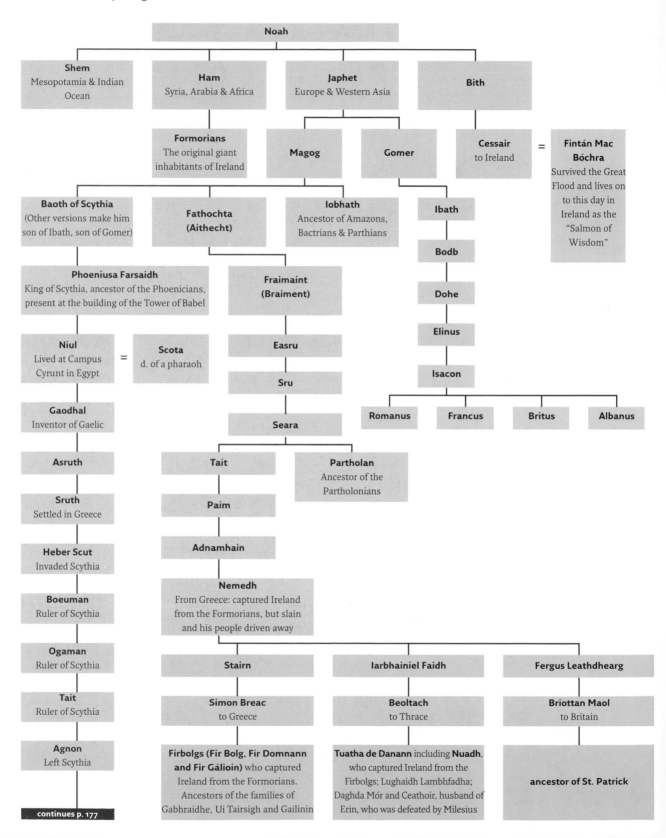

Noah

Shem
Mesopotamia & Indian Ocean

Ham
Syria, Arabia & Africa

Japhet
Europe & Western Asia

Bith

Formorians
The original giant inhabitants of Ireland

Magog

Gomer

Cessair
to Ireland

=

Fintán Mac Bóchra
Survived the Great Flood and lives on to this day in Ireland as the "Salmon of Wisdom"

Baoth of Scythia
(Other versions make him son of Ibath, son of Gomer)

Fathochta (Aithecht)

Iobhath
Ancestor of Amazons, Bactrians & Parthians

Ibath

Phoeniusa Farsaidh
King of Scythia, ancestor of the Phoenicians, present at the building of the Tower of Babel

Fraimaint (Braiment)

Bodb

Niul
Lived at Campus Cyrunt in Egypt

=

Scota
d. of a pharaoh

Easru

Dohe

Gaodhal
Inventor of Gaelic

Sru

Elinus

Asruth

Seara

Isacon

Sruth
Settled in Greece

Tait

Partholan
Ancestor of the Partholonians

Romanus

Francus

Britus

Albanus

Heber Scut
Invaded Scythia

Paim

Boeuman
Ruler of Scythia

Adnamhain

Ogaman
Ruler of Scythia

Nemedh
From Greece: captured Ireland from the Formorians, but slain and his people driven away

Tait
Ruler of Scythia

Stairn

Iarbhainiel Faidh

Fergus Leathdhearg

Agnon
Left Scythia

Simon Breac
to Greece

Beoltach
to Thrace

Briottan Maol
to Britain

continues p. 177

Firbolgs (Fir Bolg, Fir Domnann and Fir Gálioin) who captured Ireland from the Formorians. Ancestors of the families of Gabhraidhe, Ui Tairsigh and Gailinin

Tuatha de Danann including **Nuadh**, who captured Ireland from the Firbolgs; Lughaidh Lambhfadha; Daghda Mór and Ceathoir, husband of Erin, who was defeated by Milesius

ancestor of St. Patrick

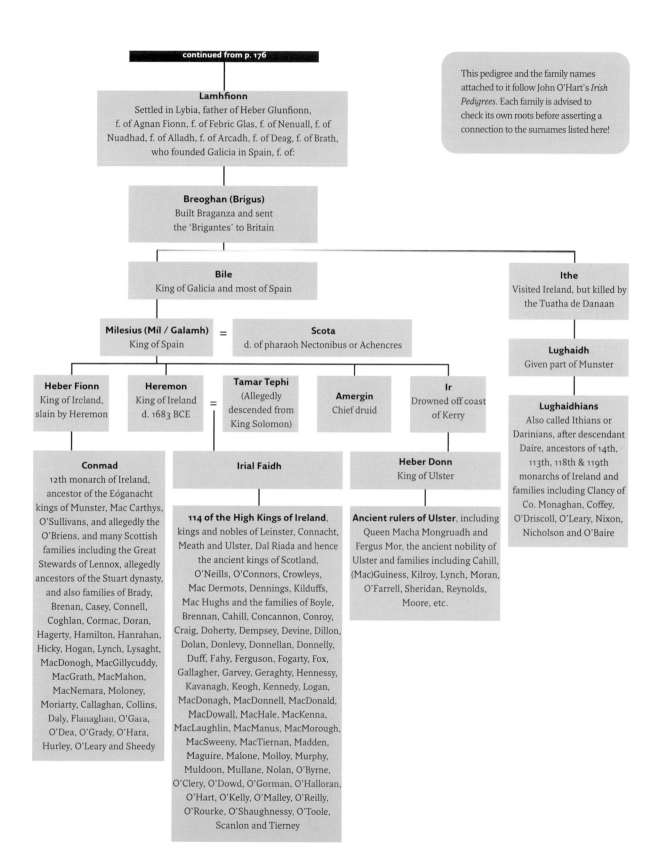

continued from p. 176

Lamhfionn
Settled in Lybia, father of Heber Glunfionn,
f. of Agnan Fionn, f. of Febric Glas, f. of Nenuall, f. of
Nuadhad, f. of Alladh, f. of Arcadh, f. of Deag, f. of Brath,
who founded Galicia in Spain, f. of:

This pedigree and the family names
attached to it follow John O'Hart's *Irish
Pedigrees*. Each family is advised to
check its own roots before asserting a
connection to the surnames listed here!

Breoghan (Brigus)
Built Braganza and sent
the 'Brigantes' to Britain

Bile
King of Galicia and most of Spain

Ithe
Visited Ireland, but killed by
the Tuatha de Danaan

Milesius (Míl / Galamh)
King of Spain
=
Scota
d. of pharaoh Nectonibus or Achencres

Lughaidh
Given part of Munster

Heber Fionn
King of Ireland,
slain by Heremon

Heremon
King of Ireland
d. 1683 BCE
=
Tamar Tephi
(Allegedly
descended from
King Solomon)

Amergin
Chief druid

Ir
Drowned off coast
of Kerry

Lughaidhians
Also called Ithians or
Darinians, after descendant
Daire, ancestors of 14th,
113th, 118th & 119th
monarchs of Ireland and
families including Clancy of
Co. Monaghan, Coffey,
O'Driscoll, O'Leary, Nixon,
Nicholson and O'Baire

Conmad
12th monarch of Ireland,
ancestor of the Eóganacht
kings of Munster, Mac Carthys,
O'Sullivans, and allegedly the
O'Briens, and many Scottish
families including the Great
Stewards of Lennox, allegedly
ancestors of the Stuart dynasty,
and also families of Brady,
Brenan, Casey, Connell,
Coghlan, Cormac, Doran,
Hagerty, Hamilton, Hanrahan,
Hicky, Hogan, Lynch, Lysaght,
MacDonogh, MacGillycuddy,
MacGrath, MacMahon,
MacNemara, Moloney,
Moriarty, Callaghan, Collins,
Daly, Flanaghan, O'Gara,
O'Dea, O'Grady, O'Hara,
Hurley, O'Leary and Sheedy

Irial Faidh

114 of the High Kings of Ireland,
kings and nobles of Leinster, Connacht,
Meath and Ulster, Dal Riada and hence
the ancient kings of Scotland,
O'Neills, O'Connors, Crowleys,
Mac Dermots, Dennings, Kilduffs,
Mac Hughs and the families of Boyle,
Brennan, Cahill, Concannon, Conroy,
Craig, Doherty, Dempsey, Devine, Dillon,
Dolan, Donlevy, Donnellan, Donnelly,
Duff, Fahy, Ferguson, Fogarty, Fox,
Gallagher, Garvey, Geraghty, Hennessy,
Kavanagh, Keogh, Kennedy, Logan,
MacDonagh, MacDonnell, MacDonald,
MacDowall, MacHale, MacKenna,
MacLaughlin, MacManus, MacMorough,
MacSweeny, MacTiernan, Madden,
Maguire, Malone, Molloy, Murphy,
Muldoon, Mullane, Nolan, O'Byrne,
O'Clery, O'Dowd, O'Gorman, O'Halloran,
O'Hart, O'Kelly, O'Malley, O'Reilly,
O'Rourke, O'Shaughnessy, O'Toole,
Scanlon and Tierney

Heber Donn
King of Ulster

Ancient rulers of Ulster, including
Queen Macha Mongruadh and
Fergus Mor, the ancient nobility of
Ulster and families including Cahill,
(Mac)Guiness, Kilroy, Lynch, Moran,
O'Farrell, Sheridan, Reynolds,
Moore, etc.

Is it true?

Until the 17th century, the *Lebor Gabála* and its associated genealogies were accepted unquestioningly. It was a matter of course that all Gaelic families were descended from Milesius: often the English used "Milesian," "Gaelic" and "mere Irish" ("mere" means "only") interchangeably. Mac Firbis had no doubts in 1650, and in 1700 Thady Roddy (*Tadhg Ó Rodaighe*) wrote that "all the families of the Milesian race" could trace back to Adam.

Critical genealogy — questioning sources before accepting pedigrees — began in the 17th century, but was not widespread until the end of the 19th century. Especially in the heady atmosphere of the 19th-century Gaelic Revival, Irish genealogists such as John O'Hart could still take the rather tortuous view that, because the Bible said we all come from the Middle East and the Irish genealogies showed waves of people coming from that region, they must be true.

The latest scholarship suggests not. Francis J. Byrne, one of the foremost modern scholars of the subject, describes the *Lebor Gabála* as, *"a fantastic compound of genuine racial memories, exotic Latin learning and world history derived from Orosius and Isidore of Seville, euhemerised Celtic mythology, dynastic propaganda, folklore, and pure fiction."*

The Bible: that the Milesian pedigree is rooted in the Bible is not surprising. The unquestioned "word of God" was itself a gigantic genealogy, everyone 'begatting' each other since Adam and Eve. When Christian monks and their converted bardic colleagues encountered the ancient Irish traditions, the question was not "are these people descended from Noah?" for of course all humans who survived the Flood were his progeny. Instead, the question was merely "how?" Once a suitable son of Noah was identified, it was simply a question of filling in the generations that *must have* existed in between. Of this scholarly exercise Professor Chadwick wrote "one cannot fail to admire the ingenuity shown in filling up the gap. Eremon, son of Míl, who is represented as leading the Gaedil to Ireland, is placed more than fifty generations before St. Patrick's time, and about thirty generations below Noah." The names used for this filling-up were drawn (rather randomly, I'm afraid) from a mixture of Irish, Biblical and Classical sources.

Milesius: Milesius first appears in written records about 630 CE. The records surrounding him were the work of Christian monks and bards whose aim was to foster a sense of national unity among a patchwork of warring peoples. As the 20th-century scholar Thomas F. O'Rahilly puts it,
"in Ireland at all periods in our history the tendency has been to attach great, and often undue, importance to descent. In the early Christian centuries the ethnic origins of the different sections of the Irish people were vividly remembered, so much so that one of the chief aims of the early Irish historians and genealogists was to efface these distinctions from the popular memory. This they did by inventing for the Irish people generally (apart from the lower classes, who did not count) a common ancestor in the fictitious Mil of Spain."

Milesius's story may have originated with Isidore of Seville, who suggested that "Hibernia" was derived from "Iberia," while Orosius mentions the Spanish tower from which Ithe was supposed to have seen Ireland — innocent details that spawned an epic myth. Fergus Gillespie, Chief Herald of Ireland, has suggested that the myth's potency was aided by the close ties between Irish and Spanish Christianity. At the time, he explains, belief in the divinity of Christ and the existence of the Holy Trinity was under threat from the Aryan "heresy," that saw Christ as simply the highest of created beings. Aryanism had spread all over Europe and Britain, but Spain and Ireland remained resistant and this created a great sense of theological affinity. St. Columbanus wrote of the Irish as *Iberi*, clearly meaning "Iberian" in the sense of "Spanish." As late as the 17th century, the Spanish regarded the Irish as "the Spaniards of the North," one of the reasons why the Wild Geese (see p. 207) were so welcome there: some were the subject of royal decrees declaring them to be Spanish by simple virtue of their Milesian ancestry.

Originally Míl had only two sons, Heber and Heremon. "Eber" means "Irishman" and "Eremon's" root is in *Ériu,* meaning Ireland. O'Rahilly saw them (not implausibly) as parallels of their supposed descendants, Eoghan and Conn respectively.

The races of Ireland: for a long time, historians believed that Ireland was invaded by waves of peoples, especially Celts. Because the *Lebor Gabála* described such waves, it was thought to hold genuine racial memories, albeit in heavily mythologized forms. O'Rahilly

Who was Scota?

Milesius's wife Scota, whose name is Gaelic for "Irishwoman," was slain by the *Tuatha de Danann* at the battle of Slieve Mish and was buried in Glen Scota on the Dingle Peninsula, Co. Kerry, where a burial mound, said to be hers, remains tantalizingly unexcavated. The idea of an Egyptian princess in her chariot, battling the ancient Irish gods, is certainly a stirring one. That she was Egyptian is not surprising when you remember that Milesius's family had spent several hundred years in the eastern Mediterranean, and Egypt was familiar to the monks through the Bible's tales of Moses.

In *Kingdom of the Ark: The Startling Story of How the Ancient British Race is Descended from the Pharaohs* (Simon & Schuster, 2000), Egyptologist Lorraine Evans sought evidence that Scota may have been real. Beads of faïence, a costly glazed pottery, have been found in Bronze Age sites all over the British Isles, including a burial mound at Tara and are virtually identical to those found on the body of Tutankhamen in Egypt. They probably reached Tara having changed hands many times since being in Egypt, but this, and some decidedly eastern-Mediterranean-looking boats of about the right period found at North Ferriby, Yorkshire, offered some tantalizing suggestions that Scota's story might be rooted in fact.

Walter Bower's Scottish version of the story, written about 1435, names Scota's father as Pharaoh Achencres, whom Evans tried to equate with Akhenaten, husband of Nefertiti and father-in-law of Tutankhamen himself. At that point, however, I think Evans's arguments to connect Scota with Akhenaten's daughter Meritaten become far too circumstantial to be even remotely plausible. Ultimately, we must accept that evidence for her existence is seriously lacking. The book is, however, still very much worth a read, and the fact remains that there has been a persistent tradition of Egyptian ancestry behind the Milesian dynasty and all its descendants for a good 1,500 years.

The *Scotichronicon* of about 1435, showing Scota and Gaythelos on their seaborne journey from Egypt to Ireland (picture courtesy of the Master and Fellows of Corpus Christi College, Cambridge).

believed that, while much of the early history was clearly fictitious, "there remains a modest residuum from which important historical deductions can be drawn," and produced a masterful analysis of the *Lebor Gabála* identifying the following "real" invasions:

- **Cruithin** or **Pretain**, the aboriginal inhabitants of Britain, of whom those in northern Scotland were called Picts by the Romans because they painted their bodies. They settled in Ulster, where their descendants included the Dál nAraide and the UíEchach, and in the Midlands as the Loiges (hence Co. Laois), whose descendants include the O'Mores.

A highly imaginative depiction of a male and female Pict, presumably off to war, their otherwise naked bodies covered in paint.

- **Fir Bolg**, also called *Érainn* or *Iverni*. In this theory, the *Fir Bolg* were the Belgae from northern Europe, some of whom also, as

Julius Caesar tells us in his *Gallic Wars*, had settled recently in southern Britain. In Ireland, their descendants included the Dál Riada, Dál Fiatach and Ulaid, the Uí Bairrche in Co. Wexford (hence Barony of Bargy) and many southern peoples, particularly the Corcu Loígde, Corcu Duibne, Ciarraige, Múscraige, Fir Maige, Uí Liatháin and Déisi. As an amusing aside, I should mention the scholar Pokorny who suggested that "Fir Bolg" was from *gae bolgae*, meaning a harpoon, and apparently used this as the basis for arguing that Ireland had once been colonized by Eskimos!

- **Laigin** were the "Iron Age Celts," led to Ireland from Gaul by their own legendary king Labraid Loingsech ("the seafarer"). They include the Osraige (hence Ossory); Uí Drona (hence Barony of Idrone, Co. Carlow); Uí Ceinnselaigh (hence Hy-Kinsella); the Gálioin (hence the Barony of Gallen, Co. Mayo); and Domnainn, the Conmaicne who settled around the upper Shannon, ancestors of the O'Farrell and MacRannall (Reynolds) families and the Uí Maine in eastern Galway and southern Roscommon.

- **Gaeils or Goidels** were descendants of the Helvetic *Quariates*. They were displaced from Narbonne by Roman conquest and reached Ireland about 50 BCE. They called themselves the *Feni*, but the older Irish tribes called them the *Gaodhail* or *Gaeil* from the language they spoke. They were the ancestors of the Éoganacht of Cashel in the south and the Connachta of Tara in the north, two great tribes who had gradually extended their rule over the older peoples, whom they called *aithechthuatha*.

O'Rahilly thought that although the Gaels were the most recent Celtic conquerors of Ireland, the *Lebor Gabála* had created the fiction that they had been there since about 1600 BCE. To make

Dún Ducathair, the Black Fort, on the western coast of Inishmore, dating from the first millennia BCE, but traditionally said to be one of the last refuges of the *Fir Bolg*. As the cliffs are eroded, it is crashing into the sea, stone by stone.

this work, the other invasions had to be pushed back yet further.

The main pedigrees were those of the Gaels (the Eóganacht and Connachta). Many of their subject peoples were made into Gaels by giving them pedigrees going back to younger offshoots of the Milesian stem, many using descents from younger brothers of Heremon and Heber, such as Ir, or even their great uncle, Ithe. They were part of the family, so to speak, but still firmly relegated to junior status.

The fabricators of this history did not try to expunge native traditions; they knew these were far too deeply rooted to be eradicated. Instead, more cleverly, they subverted them, maintaining the essence of the stories but welding them into the great Milesian epic. Recent tales of invasions must have been prevalent among the Laigin (with Labraid Loingsech), Eóganacht (Mug Nuadat) and the Connachta (with Tuathal Teachtmar). In all cases, Milesian pedigrees preserve stories of a great leader invading from abroad, but they have been subverted, for these are "invaders" depicted as Irish princes, wrongfully deprived of their thrones, who led successful return-invasions from overseas.

Similarly, the fabricators could not expunge the ancient gods from folk-memory, so instead they "euhemerised" them — that is, they wrote of them as mortal men, hoping to render their memory impotent. O'Rahilly identified several such gods in the pedigrees. Conn "of the Hundred Battles," ancestor of the Connachta, appears in the pedigree as a grandson of Tuathal Teachtmar. Yet surely, O'Rahilly argued, this Conn was originally a pagan god, the legendary ancestor of all the Connachta including Tuathal Teachtmar himself. The Corcu Loígde of southern Cork claimed descent from Lugaid, son of Dáire, a thunder god similar to the Greek Zeus, but the fabricators made Dáire a human descendant of Milesius's uncle Ithe, with Dáire's father Bolg or Sidebolg, thereby (accidentally) confirming their *Fir Bolg* ancestry. Similarly, the Eóganacht in Munster had as their god Eoghan, from whom descended Mug Nuadat, but later genealogists made Mug Nuadat grandfather of the man Eoghan.

The *Tuatha de Danann*, incidentally, didn't fit into O'Rahilly's system, so instead of equating them to a real race of invaders, he said they had been inserted into the story only to show that the ancient gods of Ireland were mere mortals descended from Noah just like everyone else. A lot of the stories of the *Tuatha de Danann*, however, record what the pagan Irish believed about them — beliefs most of the Christian Irish were clearly loathe to relinquish. And as W.B. Yeats put it, by not being equated with humans very competently, they "preserved a parcel of their ancient dignity, and, becoming the fairies, dwell happily near their deserted altars."

The modern view

O'Rahilly's deconstruction of these stories and pedigrees is an immensely useful work of scholarly archaeology. His view of actual archaeology, though, was rather scathing — *"chafing under the limitations of their science... [archaeologists] often succumb to the temptation to lend a specious semblance of reality to their speculations by linking them arbitrarily with the names of historical peoples."*

In fact, archaeology, linguistics and genetics show that however right O'Rahilly was in many details, his main "invasion" thesis was wrong.

For O'Rahilly, the fact that everyone in Ireland spoke Gaelic, and most thought they had Milesian origins was evidence of the great success of the Gaelic invasion of the Connachta and Eóganacht. The view now is that everyone spoke Gaelic and acknowledged a common origin because Gaelic was the indigenous language of Ireland, and was obviously similar to the languages of the rest of the British Isles. Archaeology shows that Gaelic ogham inscriptions are in fact most frequent in the very areas where O'Rahilly thought the Gaels had *not* settled.

Archaeology has found no mass invasions of the British Isles. Everything points to continuity over thousands of years, and while "Celtic" style metal-work has been found in Ireland, it is not identical to European styles. This suggests that it was copied from European Celtic work by Irish craftsmen not fashioned on Irish soil by Celtic invaders.

Genetic evidence shows that most of the Irish share the same genes, not because of a successful Gaelic invasion, but because the Gaels have been there all along. The other "races" are merely other Irish under different names. Of course, some small groups of warriors may have come from Spain or elsewhere, but most "invasions" were probably internal movements of people.

However, despite being partly made up, the pedigrees probably did, as O'Rahilly thought, contain substantial grains of truth, telling us, for example, that the ancient Connachta claimed descent from an invading ancestor, Tuathal Teachtmar, and ultimately from a god, Conn.

Milesius today

Many serious genealogists, recognizing the mythological aspects of the ancient pedigrees, tend to shun them altogether. It was certainly necessary to make a clean break from the uncritical acceptance of old fables that had dogged genealogy in the past. However, scepticism and outright rejection can go too far — throwing the genealogical baby out with the bath water, so to speak. In many cases, outright rejection of the Milesian pedigrees now is due to

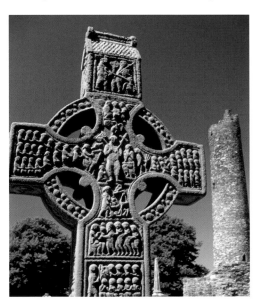

Detail on High Cross, Monasterboice Graveyard, Co. Louth. Such ancient fusions of Christian and pagan Irish art mirror the combination of biblical and barbaric tales prevalent in Dark Age Ireland.

people simply not taking enough time to understand what is, admittedly, a tricky subject. When less serious genealogists find a personal link, they embrace these pedigrees uncritically, insisting that they are 100 percent accurate right back to Noah. The Internet is awash with such pedigrees, some adding dates of birth for each generation and including surprizing new details, such as the British wife of a 1st-century CE Irish king, Feredach Fionn-Feachtnach, who has recently become a daughter of Boadicea, Queen of the Iceni in eastern Britain!

The truth, of course, lies between these extremes. The consensus is that one can often believe the pedigrees as far back as contemporary written records allow, which in Ireland takes us to 431 CE, when Christianity arrived. From that point forwards, besides having different versions of the same pedigree that can be compared critically, there are supporting records such as annals, that give independent evidence of peoples' existence. Some 12,000 people living between the 5th and 12th centuries appear in all, and by-and-large their existence and interrelationships are given accurately. Obviously, one has to take each pedigree on its own merit, and to be especially critical of the point where one family line branches off from an older one — was it really a younger son, or was the line simply grafted on to suit the political expediencies of the time? The most blatant example of grafting occurs with the Dalcasian ancestors of Brian Boru (see p. 192), who ousted the vastly older Eóganacht dynasty from Cashel and promptly claimed descent — and the aura of legitimacy — from a younger branch of the Eóganacht themselves.

Before the 5th century CE, however much as we'd like to, we just can't claim the pedigrees are real. But there are three good reasons for not ignoring them. First, as Byrne says, "*the question of historicity is irrelevant: the texts themselves,* *however legendary their content, stand as documents of the centuries in which they were written.*"

Secondly, there's nothing wrong with studying these legendary pedigrees and being proud of them in their own right. You'd be foolish to say "I am a descendant of Milesius, who was a real man," but by saying "according to the ancient pedigrees, I am descended from Milesius, the legendary ancestor of the Gaels" you are making an accurate statement and also acknowledging the remarkable survival of a genealogical tradition that is among the most ancient in the world.

And thirdly, there's always the chance that the sons of an Iberian lord, who may or may not have been called Míl, really did set off by sea, sometime in our distant past and ran their keel ashore on an Irish beach, destined to become, though they knew it not, the stuff of legend.

further reading

■ D.F. Begley, 'The Peoples of Ireland', *Irish Genealogy, A Record Finder* (Heraldic Artists Ltd, 1981).

■ F.J. Byrne, *Irish Kings and High-Kings* (Four Courts Press, 1973, 2001).

■ H.M. Chadwick, *Early Scotland: The Picts the Scots and the Welsh of Southern Scotland* (C.U.P., 1949).

■ J. Morris, *Arthurian Sources*, vol.. 5, 'Genealogies and Texts' (Phillimore, Chichester, 1995).

■ T.F. O'Rahilly, *Early Irish History and Mythology* (School of Celtic Studies, Dublin Institute for Advanced Studies, 1999).

■ F. Prior, *Britain BCE: Life in Britain and Ireland before the Romans* (Harper Perenial, 2003).

■ Sir A. Wagner, *English Genealogy* (Phillimore, 1983).

■ W.B. Yeats, *Writings on Irish Folklore, Legend and Myth* (Penguin Books, 1993).

■ Many ancient Irish texts such as the *Lebor Gabála* can be found online: **www.isos.dias.ie**, **www.ucc.ie/celt**, **http://members.aol.com/lochlan2/lebor.htm**.

■ Numerous versions of the ancient Milesian lines appear online. Not all are accurate. The following site, however, on the MacLaughlin of Donegal site, seems sound: **www.rootsweb.com/~fianna/history/milesian.html**.

CHAPTER 22

Ancient Irish roots

As you trace your Irish roots, you will find that all Irish family histories were inextricably tied up with the fascinating, often bloody, history of the island itself. And the more you understand Ireland's history, the better a genealogist you will become.

Neolithic roots

Built more than 5,000 years ago (c. 3300–2900 BCE), Newgrange predates the erection of Sarsen stones at Stonehenge by around 1,000 years, and the Great Pyramid of Giza in Egypt by more than 500 years. The stone and turf mound contains a long passage leading to a cross-shaped burial chamber, which has a corbeled roof rising to a height of nearly 20 feet (6 m), still intact today. It is believed that the sun formed an important part of the religious beliefs of the Neolithic people who built it. Every winter solstice, the sun shines directly along the passage into the chamber, entering through a specially-made opening directly above the entrance. The spiral motifs engraved on the entrance stone, "one of the most famous stones in the entire repertory of megalithic art," have similarities to megalithic motifs found all along Europe's western seaboard.

The Irish, like all humanity, evolved as *Homo sapiens* in sub-Saharan Africa about 200,000 years ago but remained a tiny group of hunter-gatherers there until about 70,000 years ago. From that point, we are all descended through our father's direct male line from one male ancestor, dubbed the "genetic Adam," whose DNA clearly gave him the edge over other males alive at the time. Most of "Adam's" descendants remained in Africa but some ventured north, walking to Australia and the Americas, while others remained in Asia. After a long sojourn hunting mammoths on the Russian steppes during the last Ice Age, some descendants of "Adam" followed the migrating herds into Europe. When the ice started to retreat from northern Europe about 10,000 BCE, bands of hunters followed the herds of reindeer and wild horses into Britain.

As the ice caps melted, the sea rose. Ireland was cut off by the rising seas about 8000 BCE, shortly before mainland Britain was itself severed from Continental Europe. Various animals such as otters, snakes and roe deer that lived in Britain never made it to Ireland. Yet a tiny population of humans appeared there about 8000 BCE — whether they were cut off by the rising sea, or they crossed the marshlands between Argyll and Antrim by boat, we don't know. However they got there, this small collection of humans was destined to become the ancestors of the modern Irish. The numbers involved were tiny — even in the early Bronze

Age, Ireland's population may have been no more than 50,000.

At Mount Sandel on the River Bann, Co. Antrim, there is evidence of the earliest Irish making themselves circular, tent-like houses about 8,500 years ago. The first known houses in the British Isles, they comprised hides and brushwood laid across poles. They kept dogs, ate game, fish and berries, hunted with flint-tipped arrows and stone axes, such as those made at Tievebulliagh and Rathin Island, Co. Antrim. In part, they followed herds of animals, but they also explored Ireland using eskers, the gravel ridges deposited by the melting glaciers, that then became Ireland's earliest trackways.

Neolithic roots

Agriculture started in the Middle East about 10,000 years ago and spread very slowly across Europe. This Neolithic "revolution" reached Ireland in about the 4th millennia BCE (about 6,000 years ago); the first sheep, goats, pigs and cattle, their legs firmly tied together, arriving by boat, perhaps from Scotland or maybe, as genetics now suggests, up the Atlantic seaboard from Cornwall via Brittany and ultimately from Spain. Initially, domestic animals would have been herded and hunted very much as if they were wild, but soon stone walls were used to create fields, of which the *Céide* field system, Co. Mayo, is the best known example. In about 3200 BCE we have the earliest evidence, at Ballynagilly, Co. Tyrone, of a stone house, albeit a square one that was probably used more for ritual than domestic duties. Most farms were collections of round communal buildings with steep, thatched roofs, such as those reconstructed at Lough Gur, Co. Limerick.

The period 3000–2000 BCE also saw the building of the great megalithic monuments, used as places for burying and perhaps revering the spirits of the dead — we don't know if there

Just as our forefathers brought farm animals to Ireland by boat some 6,000 years ago, this picture from the 1930s shows a cow being carried in a *currach* to the Great Blasket Island, Co. Kerry. Bulls were not kept on the precipitous island, so cows had to be brought to the mainland each year for insemination. The cow lies on the floor of the *currach*, its legs tied together (courtesy of National Folklore Collection, UCD).

was ever actual ancestor worship — and marking boundaries of ancestral lands. The megaliths included dolmens, with great flat stones raised dramatically above standing ones and passage tombs, especially the awe-inspiring ones at Newgrange, Knowth, Dowth and Loughcrew, Co. Meath, and Carrowkeel and Carrowmore, Co. Sligo, the latter said to be the sepulchre of Queen Maeve, the bewitching heroine of *The Cattle-Raid of Cooley*.

One of the megolithic tombs at Carrowmore, Co. Sligo, showing the dolmen in the centre surrounded by a boulder circle. Knocknarea mountain can be seen in the background, on the summit of which is the great cairn of Miosgan Meadhbha, one of several associated with Queen Maeve.

Newgrange, supposedly the burial place of the High Kings of Tara, was also believed to be the gateway to the infernal realms to which the *Tuatha de Danann* retreated after the arrival of the Milesians in 1699 BCE.

Our Bronze and Iron Age ancestors

The earliest evidence of metalwork comes from Corlea, Co. Longford, where a preserved wooden trackway dating from 2268–2250 BCE seems to have been hewn with metal tools. Irish copper, mined mainly in Cork and Kerry, was mixed with Cornish tin to make bronze. At its height Ireland's "Golden Age" rivaled Homeric Greece in terms of its fantastic bronze and goldwork and its mighty heros and heroic deeds. This is now preserved in legend and connected to everyone with Irish roots by the slender thread of the Milesian pedigrees.

Ironwork first appeared about 500 BCE, ushering in an era of much more intensive farming of both livestock and grain and the building of ring barrows and ditched enclosures, such as those of Emain Macha,

Jagged stone defences at Dún Ducathair, Inishmore. Only the crows inhabit this vastness now, but you get the feeling that the spirits of the dead are never far away.

Ulster. This is the era when scholars from the 18th century onwards believed the Celts had swept in from Europe, displacing Britain and Ireland's ancient inhabitants. In fact, there's very little evidence that a European Celt ever set foot in Ireland: some artifacts similar to the great La Tène style of central European Celtic artwork have been found in Ireland, but these can be easily explained as the result of trade. All evidence from archaeology, genetics and linguistics points to a very limited cultural influence from Celtic Europe. The people and culture of the whole British Isles have roots lying firmly in the original, post-Ice Age settlers.

Genetic evidence

The genetic mapping of Ireland is an infant subject, pioneered by Dr. Dan Bradley, Associate Professor at the Smurfit Institute of Genetics, Trinity College, Dublin, but it has already produced some fascinating results.

Telling people apart by DNA involves looking for mutations on the Y chromosome that men inherit from their fathers, and the mitochondrial DNA (mtDNA) in our X chromosome that we all inherit from our mothers, and then seeking further mutations within those mutations. Dating them is a matter of multiplying the number of mutations by an average time over which mutations are believed to have occurred. This produces results that can be compared for accuracy with other dating techniques, such as carbon dating. Studies of female-line mtDNA in Ireland suggest that most Irish female lines go back to the tiny original population of settlers who arrived in Ireland after the last Ice Age.

There was also a significant presence of the female-line mutations coded as J and T that can be linked to the Atlantic seaboard from the Western Isles right down the West Coast of Spain and Portugal, into the Mediterranean and back to the Middle East. These mutations have already been linked plausibly to the spread of Indo-European languages including Gaelic, and of the Neolithic Revolution — farming — and now indicate that these reached Ireland about 6,000 years ago, mainly via what seems to have been very active maritime travel up and down the Atlantic seaboard.

Male-line Y chromosome DNA has also been studied. Almost all male-line DNA in Europe can be broken down by its unique mutations into eight groups, each descended from a common male-line ancestor, and of these only five are found in any numbers in the British Isles. Of these, Haplogroup R1b, which Professor Sykes has rather confusingly christened "Oisin," accounts for an astonishing 80 percent of Irishmen, indicating that they all have the same male-line ancestor. Initial samples suggest they comprise 73 percent of Leinster's population, 81 percent of Ulster's, 95 percent of Munster's and 98 percent of Connacht's. Leinster's lower percentage is probably due to foreign immigration from the Vikings and Cambro-Normans onwards, especially into Dublin, while far-flung Connacht has seen the fewest immigrants. When Dr. Bradley studied the surnames of those tested he found that membership of the R1b group correlated strongly with having a Gaelic surname.

The R1b mutation is not exclusive to Ireland. It is found all over Europe and beyond, but its highest concentrations, after Ireland, are in Scotland, Cornwall, the Basque region and the rest of Spain. This strongly suggests that it is the DNA of the incoming Neolithic farmers of about 6,000 years ago that largely displaced the men (but not the women) who had been there already. Its great prevalence up the western seaboard of Europe, which has led to its being called the Atlantic Modal Haplotype, may have been reinforced by coastal trade between Ireland and northwest Spain. The areas of highest concentration also equate to the building of dolmens, perhaps indicating that the ideas behind dolmen-building spread within an

Red hair

Red hair, so often linked to Irish blood, actually occurs in less than 10 percent of Irish people, though 75 percent have a genetic propensity to it. According to Dr. Bradley, it is closely linked to freckles, pale skin and lack of ability to tan. The paler the skin, the easier it is to synthesize vitamin D from sunlight, which has always been a rare commodity in rainy Ireland. This bestows a genetic advantage on those with the fairest complexions; red hair was an accidental side effect.

This flame-headed Irish peasant girl, posing for a postcard in the early 20th century, is typically fair-skinned.

The name *Gael*, from *Goídil*, is an Irish version of the name *Gwyddyl*, "savage man" given to the Irish by the Welsh. The name became popular in Ireland when the Viking attacks gave the island its first real sense of national unity. Of course, each *tuath*, or people, generally preferred more local terms for themselves, while some recognized their membership of a wider regional community. *Ulaid* was used for Ulstermen; *Gálioin* and *Laigin* in Leinster; and *Féni* was used by the Midlanders. For the island itself, people tended to use the name *Érainn*, which first appears as a Munster tribal name, *Iverni*, right back in the time of Ptolemy (died c. 168 CE, but whose *Geographia* may have been based on data several hundred years old), hence the Latin *Hibernia*. In the *Lebor Gabála*, Erin was the name of the last queen of the *Tuatha de Danann*, in whose honor the victorious Milesians agreed to name the island.

interrelated population. R1b is lower in the Western Isles of Scotland and England, probably due to influxes of Vikings, Saxons and later immigrants — but interestingly, genetic and archaeological evidence now argues strongly against any substantial influx of Saxons into England either. Despite everything,

the English have their roots in the original inhabitants of the British Isles as well.

These conclusions (of work that is very much in progress) support recent archaeological and linguistic conclusions that the great waves of Celtic immigration from central Europe in the last millennium BCE never happened. Such theories only arose in the last couple of hundred years and were never part of our cultural tradition. What we have always held, in fact, is that our ancestors settled in Britain from northwest Spain. Spanish origins have always been a tradition in Irish families. Many, who have brownish complexions and dark hair, have stories of being descended from shipwrecked sailors from the Spanish Armada of the 16th century. Probably, one or two are, but most families have likely been "Spanish-looking" for substantially longer and before the Armada there were probably earlier tales. In British myth, the leader of the settlement from Spain was Brutus, and Irish attribute this influx to the sons of Milesius. These DNA results certainly don't prove that Brutus or Milesius existed; but they do show that their legends may have contained more truth than has previously been thought.

Gaelic Ireland

Society evolved from small groups of independent farmers into a heavily stratified order, with slaves at the bottom, small farmers in the middle, lords above and regional rulers on top. Druids attended to society's spiritual and moral needs and, we assume, learned and recited the great pedigrees that form the basis of the earliest, legendary ones we have now. The year was punctuated by festivals when extended families came together to feast and arrange marriages: February 1, *Imbole*, was the festival of Brigid, goddess of childbirth; May 1, *Beltain*, celebrated the return of the sun; *Lughnasa* on

This sketch shows a prophet and chief druid (seated), their costume as described in ancient Irish writings: the checked undergarment conforms to the ancient Irish law, which ordained that an *ollamh* (to which class the druids belonged) should have six colors in his garment. The white mantle was common to all druids of the British Isles. The fan-shaped ornament representing the sun and the half-moon, in the chief druid's headdress matches ornaments dug up in bogs and illustrated on sepulchral urns .

August 1 was the great festival of the harvest. The year began on November 1 with *Samhain*, when surplus livestock was slaughtered and offered up for the rebirth of the waning sun. On *Samhain*-eve, the gates of the underworld, hidden below the *sídhs* (the ancient fairy mounds) swung wide, and with a terrible drumming of phantom horses' hoofs the *Tuatha de Danann* thundered forth to haunt the land. The latter was the origin of Halloween; despite centuries of Christianity, the ancient customs have lived on. As Yeats wrote in the 19th century, the Irish remain pervaded with, *"a passion for their lands, and the waters and mountains of their lands remind them of old love tales, old battle tales, and the exultant hidden multitudes. There is no place in Ireland where they will not point to some mountain where Grania slept beside her lover, or where the misshapen Formor were routed, or to some waters where the Sacred Hazel once grew and fattened the Salmon of Wisdom with its crimson nuts; nor is there, I think, a place outside the big towns where they do not believe that the Fairies, the Tribes of the goddess Danu, are stealing their bodies and their souls, or putting unearthly strength into their bodies, and always hearing all they say..."* (W.B. Yeats, 'The Prisoners of the Gods', *The Nineenth Century*, 1898).

The connection between the Irish and their roots was sometimes astonishingly immediate: Yeats once heard a story from an old woman in the Burren concerning an army pensioner called Rippingham, who had the courage to explore an old *sidh* (ancient fairy mound) in Co. Clare. He and his companions went down, and there *"they began to meet people they knew before, that had died out of the village, and they all told them to go back, but still they went on. And then they met the parish priest of Ballyvaughan, Father Ruane, that was dead, and he told them to go back, so they turned and went."*

Halloween divination: Halloween derives from the ancient festival of *Samhain*, the first day of winter. Divination is still popular at Halloween — the girl in this photograph is trying to find out about her future. At this festival, ancient magical powers are believed to be unfettered and accessible to those who dare to invoke them (courtesy of National Folklore Collection, UCD).

Ireland's population was tiny: even by 700 CE there may have been as few as 500,000 people, with numbers increasing and decreasing due to war and famine. Our ancestors lived in farms, fortified against raids with stone walls and earth banks or even on *crannogs* (defended lake islands). Cattle were the most prized livestock as it judged the wealth of kings. This is shown by the extent that Ailill and Maeve, the King and Queen of Connacht, went to steal the Brown Bull of Cooley from Ulster in *The Cattle-Raid of Cooley*. Arable farming focused on oats for porridge and bread, barley for beer and bread, and wheat for high-quality bread. Few vegetables were grown; apples were cultivated but most other fruit grew wild.

Roman Ireland?

The Romans invaded Britain successfully in 43 CE. Written history only hints at a Roman presence in Ireland. Irish legend and historical fact as recorded in Tacitus's *Agricola* combine to suggest that Tuathal Teachtmar (a legendary High King at Tara) may have been the exiled Irish prince who asked the Roman governor in

Britain, Agricola, for military help to regain his throne about 70 CE. In legend, Tuathal Teachtmar reconquered all Ireland with the help, it turns out, of Pictish troops. In reality, in 1996 a massive 40-acre Roman fort was excavated at Drumanagh, Co. Dublin, dating from the 1st and 2nd centuries CE. It would have been used as a beachhead for Roman legions landing in Ireland — perhaps in support of Tuathal himself, and for subsequent trade — but whatever its story, we know that Roman influence in Ireland was negligible. The substantial weakening of Roman rule during the 4th century CE (followed by its collapse in 411 CE) saw extensive Irish raids on the mainland and even the establishment of Irish kingdoms in western Scotland and Wales (see p. 33 — on Aed Brosc and p. 41 on Fergus Mor).

Gaelic families

Once we reach the 4th century CE, we know in detail how Gaelic society worked, though it had probably been this way for several millennia. It certainly remained largely unchanged until the coming of the Normans and survived on until the 17th century.

Saints Patrick and Columba

Roman Britain became largely Christian, and missionaries soon started visiting Ireland. Their success is described brilliantly in Cahill's *How the Irish Saved Civilisation*. Where they could, they eradicated paganism, but they often compromised, and some of the more resistant pagan gods, such as Anu and Brigid, were reincarnated as Christian saints, Ann and Brigid.

Of the missionaries, St. Patrick is the best known. Born the son of a landowner, perhaps of Dumbarton, Scotland (whom legend made a descendant of Briattan Maol, a grandson of Nemedh [see p. 173]), Patrick was captured into slavery in Connacht. He escaped to Britain, but returned in about 435 CE to evangelize, converting the King of Ulster, Eoghan "the Lion," and establishing his bishopric at Armagh, under the protection of the Uí Néill. Other missionaries such as Columba came independently, establishing monasteries. Monasticism was very successful in Ireland: by 600 CE, some 800 monasteries had been founded. Some became rival entities to clans, and church offices became hereditary. Ecclesiastical dynasties were called variously *erenach* or *comharba* ("co-arbs") and sometimes outlasted the monastery or church they were supposed to be safeguarding. For all this, the monasteries proved a durable institution that survived the venality of Gaelic chiefs and the later deprecations of the Vikings, giving Ireland a written culture second to none. We have the monks to thank, too, for recording the ancient legends and genealogies, from which many modern Irish families stem.

Top right: **Croagh Patrick, Co. Mayo, seen from Westport. Every year, a procession bears a statue of St. Patrick to the top of this 2,513-feet-high mountain, to commemorate the 40 days of Lent the saint is believed to have spent here in 441 CE. It was from its summit that he is said to have flung the island's snakes to their doom — and to this day there are no serpents in Ireland.**

Right: **St. Patrick (387–461 CE).**

Under Gaelic Brehon Law, all free men (save outlaws) belonged to families defined by the *fine*, a group of men sharing the same male-line ancestor. The Irish did not choose leaders on the basis of seniority of birth, but rather chose the head of the family, or *ceannfine*, from the best (or strongest!) candidate from the *derbfine*. This was the group of males who were sons, grandsons or great-grandsons of previous chiefs, though precise definitions (whether the relationship had to be within four or five generations, for example) varied. Sometimes, leadership was restricted to a group called the *gelfine*, related through a common grandfather. In royal families, the *derbfine* could also be called the *rígdamnai*, "king-material."

Such "partible leadership" led frequently to internal struggle and murder. The system of *tanistry* was introduced in the 13th century, whereby the head appointed his heir from among the *fine*, thus supposedly ensuring a smooth succession. This did little to decrease the number of violent deaths among eligible candidates and the chosen *tanists*, however. Of the Eóganacht dynasty in Munster between 879 and 1607 CE, 46 percent of all males died violently.

Increasingly during the Middle Ages, the terms *sept*, *sliocht* and *clan(n)* came to be used instead of *fine*. Throughout Ireland's history, of course, new families have branched off old ones. Before surnames arose in the 11th century, families were known variously as *sliocht-*, *sil-*, *clan-* or *cenél-*, followed by an ancestor's name and all denoting common descent from that person.

After surnames arose, they might still adopt such distinctions under the umbrella of a surname: the *Sliocht Ir* and *Clann Mhatha* (hereditary priors of Mohill), for example, were both offshoots of the Mag Raghnaills of Co. Leitrim. There are families in which the use of a particular hereditary surname may, in the 11th

century, have been restricted to the *derbfine* but if that was so in some cases it is not known how widespread the practice was.

Peoples and realms

The next stage up from the *fine* was the *tuath*, "people." This is sometimes translated "clan" or "sept" (but these names were really terms for smaller groups) or even "tribe," which modern scholars don't like, because it suggests distinct customs, language or religion. Like ancient Greece, Ireland was culturally unified; it was only socially that it was fragmented into *tuaths*.

Like the family, *tuaths* were usually defined by a common ancestor and indeed most (if not all) had grown out of what was originally a successful *fine*. Ireland's place names, especially the baronies, contain many echoes of earlier *tuath* names. Because the names of *tuaths* generally arose *before* surnames started, few became surnames. It is often known, however, to which *tuath* a surname belonged. The O'Briens, for example, come from the *Dál gCais* (Dalcassians) of Thomond and the O'Connors, MacDermots and O' Crowleys spring from the *Siol Muireadhaigh* (Silmurray) of northern Connacht. Because of the way new families and *tuaths* grew out of older ones, you may encounter several layers of belonging — the Silmurray, for example, sprung in turn from the *Uí Briuin Ai* (the senior descendants of Brian Orbden, King of Connacht [336–88 CE], not to be confused with the much later, unrelated O'Briens) who were ultimately part of the Connachta. Confusing, certainly, but remember that most countries have completely lost the rich traditions that can so baffle us when we try to disentangle the subtleties of our earlier Irish roots!

These *tuaths* formed the ever-changing patchwork of petty kingdoms of Gaelic Ireland. There were usually about 100–150 *tuaths*, each engaged in complex interrelationships with each

Regional power

Real power in Gaelic society lay not with the High Kings of Ireland, but was regional and lay with the *Rí ruirechs* of the provinces (or fifths) — from whose number the High Kings were theoretically chosen. Ireland's ancient *Cúig Cúigí* ("five fifths"), allegedly dating from the time of the *Fir Bolg* (see p. 173), are what we now call Connacht, Leinster, Munster and Ulster. The fifth province may never actually have existed, but is said variously to have been Meath (with Tara as its capital), or one of two divisions of Ulster or Munster.

Munster, the "kingdom of music and the arts, of harpers... and of skilled horsemen"(according to the poem *Ard Ruide)*, lay in the south and southwest. It derived its name from Mug Nuadat (a supposed descendant of Heber), legendary grandfather of Eoghan, ancestor of the Eóganacht dynasty who ruled from Cashel, Co. Tipperary, from at least the 5th century CE. The dynasty's strongest branches were the O'Sullivans, the MacCarthys and the O'Connells. Within northern Munster was the kingdom of Thomond, ruled by the Dalcassians. At the end of the 10th century, Thomond's king, Brian Boru, ousted the Eóganacht, becoming king of Munster and effective High King of Ireland.

Leinster was "the seat of prosperity, hospitality, the importing of rich foreign wares like silk or wine...the men of Leinster are noble in speech and their women are exceptionally beautiful." Situated in the southeast, it was dominated by Laigin people, thought to have been of *Fir Bolg* ancestry. The kingship at Ailinne, near Kilcullen, Co. Kildare, was filled by the Uí Dúnlainge and Uí Cheinnselaig,

Emain Macha (Navan Fort), Co. Armagh, the capital of the Ulaid of Ulster (see page opposite).

other, all codified neatly in Brehon Law and simultaneously raiding and fighting each other with gusto. Their heads (chosen of course from the *tuath's derbfine*) were called *Rís*, usually translated as "kings," though smaller ones also tend to be translated as "chief," "prince" and so on. The *Rí túaithe* ruled one *tuath*; he was the most local, "petty" king. Greater power was held by the *Ruiri*, who ruled several *tuaths* (the group being called the *morthaithe*). Above these were the *Rí ruirech*, who ruled a province or "fifth," while above all was the *Ard-ri* or *tríath*. Within these strata smaller kings might hold specific roles within the court of the regional king: at the court of the *Rí ruirech* in Connacht, for example, the *Rí túaithes* of the O'Malleys and O'Mulconrys were responsible for warships and poetry respectively.

The *Ard-ri* or High King was enthroned at the *Ràth na Ríogh*, the sacred hill of Tara, and was the overlord of all Ireland. According to the *Lebor Gabála* and the ancient genealogies, there had been a High King since the joint reigns of Milesius's sons Heremon and Heber, the office then being held by various descendants of Heremon, Heber, Ir and Lughaidh (son of Milesius's brother Ithe). The reality is very different: most kingdoms in the but they were dominated initially by Munster and increasingly from the 9th century by Ulster.

Connacht in the west was "the kingdom of learning, the seat of the greatest and wisest druids and magicians," where the men were "famed for their eloquence, their handsomeness and their ability to pronounce true judgement." Connacht was ruled from Cruachan, near Tulsk, Co. Roscommon. Its name comes from Conn of the Hundred Battles, legendary grandson of Tuathal Teachtmar (supposed to have been descended from Heremon) but probably originally an ancient god. From the 5th century, their kings, the Uí Fiachrach and Uí Bruin (the latter the ancestors of the O'Connors) claimed descent from Niall of the Nine Hostages.

Niall of the Nine Hostages ruled at Tara, Co. Meath, "kingdom of Kingship, of stewardship, of bounty in government" near the east coast, in the 5th century CE. His power spread into the north, defeating the Ulaid and the other ancient tribes of **Ulster**, whose ancient capitals were at Aileach (near Burt, Co. Donegal) and Emain Macha (Navan Fort, Co. Armagh). Henceforth, Ulster, "the seat of battle valour, of haughtiness, strife [and] boasting" was ruled by the Uí Néill of the North, and Mide (Meath, perhaps the elusive fifth province of Ireland) by the Uí Néill of the South. The nominal High Kingship at Tara then fluctuated between the northern and southern Uí Néill until Brian Boru's time.

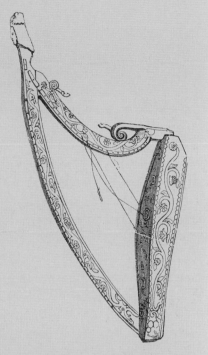

An Irish harp, a symbol of Ireland, especially Munster, the "kingdom of music and the arts." The Irish appear to have had two kinds of harps; a smaller harp strung with single chords used chiefly for religious purposes and probably employed by the druids in their rites; the second, a larger harp, used in public assemblies and perhaps in battle, strung with double chords.

north (*Leath Cuinn*) acknowledged the nominal overlordship of the king at Tara, while those to the south paid lip-service to the king at Cashel (*Leith Mogha*) but even Niall of the Nine Hostages in the 5th century, often referred to as High King, held no greater sway over the whole island than his mighty sword allowed him. Brian Boru (d. 1014 — see p. 194) was the nominal ruler of Ireland and the closest to a true High King, but even he was the mere head of an *ce hoc* confederation of kings (and some Vikings), with authority stopping far short of equivalent monarchs in England or France.

further reading

■ D. Bradley, 'Meet the Family,' *Irish Times*, 2006, www.ireland.com/timeseye/whoweare/p2bottom.htm.

■ T. Cahill, *How the Irish Saved Civilisation* (Sceptre, 1995).

■ B. Sykes, *Blood of the Isles: Exploring the Genetic Roots of our Tribal History* (Bantam Press, 2006).

■ http://freepages.genealogy.rootsweb.com/~gallgaedhil/haplo_r1b_amh_13_29.htm. A very clear, jargon-free explanation of the Atlantic Modal Haplotype, with diagrams.

The invasions of Ireland

Overlaying Ireland's indigenous population are waves of invaders, who have all added their genes to the rich tapestry of Irish roots.

Vikings

Viking longships first appeared off Ireland's shores in 795 CE, as part of the general expansions of the Scandinavians, spurred, it is thought, by food shortages at home. The Irish called their first Viking attackers, who were from Norway, *Lochlainn*, or *Fionn-Gaill*, "fair-haired foreigners." Vikings returned each year, usually attacking monasteries where they could capture treasure and slaves. From the 830s, greater numbers came to the Liffey, Boyne, Shannon and Erne, and in 841 they built

The mighty High King of Ireland, Brian Boru (926–1014), was kneeling in prayer in his tent while the battle of Clontarf raged outside when in burst the Danish leader, Brodir, and cut him down.

permanent bases at Dublin and Annagassan, Co. Louth, followed by ones at Cork, Limerick, Wexford and Waterford. Called *longphuirts*, these bases were used for overwintering, gathering tributes and trade. The Viking king *Turgéis* (Thorgils) established himself at Armagh, stationing longship fleets in Lough Neagh and Lough Ree. He was poised to take over the region, but was defeated and drowned in Lough Owel by Mealseachlainn, King of Meath, in 845.

In 852 came the Danes, called *Danair*, or *Dubh-Gaill*, "dark-haired foreigners." Their king *Amhlaoimh* (Olaf) captured Dublin from the Norwegians in 853. The Irish kings scored occasional victories against them: in 866, for example, Finnliath, king of the northern Uí Néill, destroyed many Viking bases in Ulster. In 902, Dublin fell to the Irish, but in 914 a new fleet that had been menacing northern France appeared at Waterford, capturing Dublin in 917 and defeating the High King, Niall Glúndub, in 919. The tide turned again, however, and on April 23, 1014 the Vikings were defeated at Clontarf and driven into the sea by a confederacy of Gaelic kings led by Brian Boru. Brian was slain, but the great victory was celebrated in *Cogadh Gaedhil re Gallaibh*, "the war of the Gael with the Foreigners," by Brian Boru's bard Mac Laig.

Outside their *longphuirts*, the Vikings had little impact on Irish social life, and Vikings often became Hibernicised. Their legacies were an embryonic sense of Irish unity forged in the face of a common foe, along with ports that remain important to this day. After 1014, Vikings remained under the High King's overlordship in Dublin and Waterford; the latter, ironically, were the first people in Ireland to oppose the coming of the Normans.

Dublin, Waterford, Wexford, Wicklow, Howth and Carlingford are all Norse names. You may have a dose of Viking DNA, especially if your roots are in Leinster, but only a few families can prove Viking genealogical origins. The Arthurs of Limerick, Coppingers of Cork, Esmondes of Wexford, Skiddys of Cork, Sweetmans of Kilkenny and some Woulfes certainly have Viking roots. Some Scottish families with branches settled in Ireland, such as the MacLeods, are also of Viking descent. The majority of proven "Viking" families in Ireland, however, came later as Normans.

The Cambro-Normans

Rolf the Ganger (d. c. 932) was the son of the Jarl of Möre in Norway, of the same Norwegian Yngling dynasty that gave kings to Dublin. He settled in northern France, where Normandy means "land of the north-men." Rolf's 3 x great-grandson, William the Conqueror, Duke of Normandy, invaded England in 1066. In 1169, William's great-grandson Henry II gained control of Ireland.

Back in 1166, Diarmait Mac Murchada (Mac Murrough) (d. 1171), King of Leinster, had failed in his bid to become High King. His rival, Ruaidrí Ua Conchobair (Rory O'Connor) of Connacht, drove him into exile in Wales. Henry II allowed Diarmait to recruit an army here, which he did with the help of Maurice FitzGerald and Robert FitzStephen (both sons of the Welsh princess Nest), and Richard (FitzGilbert) de Clare, Earl of Pembroke (d. 1176), known as "Strongbow," who later married Diarmait's daughter Eva (Aoife). Robert FitzStephen landed at Baginbun, Co.

Wexford, in May 1169, followed by Diarmait and Strongbow in Waterford. The Normans quickly gained control of much of eastern Ireland and, when Diarmait died in 1171, Strongbow declared himself Lord of Leinster. Henry II landed at Waterford that October mainly to ensure that he, and not his vassal Strongbow, became overlord of Ireland. The Normans and many Irish kings submitted to him — as a powerful unifying force, he was not entirely unwelcome — and later the Pope, who happened to be English, gave holy sanction to Henry's

The 8th-century Ardagh Challice was found in 1868 at Ardagh, Co. Limerick, by Jimmy Quin and Paddy Flanaghan, who were out digging potatoes. It was probably hidden there by a Limerick Viking in the 12th century.

The marriage of Eva of Leinster and Richard "Strongbow" de Clare, the 2nd Earl of Pembroke and conqueror of Ireland.

overlordship of Ireland. Together with Hugh de Lacy, constable of Dublin, Strongbow crushed those Irish kings who resisted him and Ireland was subdued. In 1175, by the Treaty of Windsor, the High King, Ruaidrí Ua Conchobair, acknowledged Henry II's overlordship of Ireland. When Ruaidri died in 1189, the High Kingship ended — though his heirs argued otherwise — and the English monarchs succeeded as Lords of Ireland.

The "Normans" were mainly drawn from the *Advenae*, the Normans who had only just invaded and settled in Wales. The thrust into Ireland was a natural westward progression — you can see the Wicklow mountains from Pembroke. They included the Prendergasts, so-named after their lordship of Prendergast near Haverfordwest; De Lacys, De Courcys, De Nugents and Nangles (Neagles). Many *Advenae* lords had intermarried with Welsh women, making their sons part Welsh, and therefore much better suited than pure-bred Normans to assimilate into Gaelic life. Thus, while they are conventionally called Anglo-Normans (Normans from England), the more fitting term is Cambro-Normans (Normans from Wales).

The troops the Anglo-Normans brought included many pure-blooded Welshmen. Gerald of Wales, the great chronicler of the invasion, writes, for example, that Robert FitzStephen's 300 archers were the "flower of the south of Wales." Of course, some Welshmen were already in Ireland. Geoffrey Keating, writing in the 17th century in *Forus Feasa ar Éirinn*, claims that "*Ireland was a place of refuge for the Welsh whenever they suffered persecution from the Romans or Saxons... large numbers of them with their families, followers and cattle used to repair for refuge to Ireland where the Irish nobles would give them land.*" However, the influx that came with the Normans was the first for which we know any names. Walsh, "Welshman," is Ireland's fourth most popular surname. Brannagh is an Anglicization of *Breathnach*, the Irish for "Welshman": hence, the first known Walsh was called "Haylen Brenach, alias Walsh" — son of "Philip the Welshman." He was the ancestor of many of the Walshes of southeast Ireland, but there were certainly others: the Waleses of Tirawley, Co. Mayo, claim descent from Walynus, a Welshman who came to Ireland with Maurice FitzGerald in 1169, while the Barratts of Tirawley descend from Walynus's brother, Barratt. The 17th-century genealogist MacFirbis knew that these Walshes and Barretts, along with the Joyces, MacHales, Wallaces, Tomlins, Hostys, Lawlesses and Cusacks, were descended from Welsh settlers.

The Normans also brought in people from Flanders. Henry I had established a colony of Flemings at Ros near Haverfordwest, Pembrokeshire, which contributed to the retinue that Maurice de Prendergast brought to Ireland. Maurice's neighbor, Richard Fitzgodebert, was a Fleming who went to Leinster with Dermot MacMurrough in 1167; his descendants took their surname, de la Roche (hence Roach), from Richard's rock-castle in Haverfordwest. Many Flemings settled in the Wexford baronies of Forth and Bargy, where names like Codd, Rossiter, Sinnott and Whitty are still common.

Trim Castle, Co. Meath, the largest Norman castle in Europe, was built by the de Lacy family, a Norman noble family that took a major role in the Norman invasion of Ireland.

The Fitzgerald-Barry pedigree

The pedigree on the next two pages shows part of the complex web of families centered around the Cambro-Norman invasion of Ireland in the 12th century. "Fitzgerald" meant "son of Gerald" in Norman-French and was used by the sons of Gerald of Windsor. The earlier ancestry of the Fitzgeralds is almost certainly fanciful and heavily influenced by the Milesian genealogies: having seen how those all ultimately went back to the Mediterranean, the Fitzgeralds obviously wanted something similar, hence the line back to the lords of Biscay; other versions deduce them from Trojans. The surname Fitzgerald is now found all over Ireland but mainly in Kerry, Cork and Limerick. President John Fitzgerald Kennedy, assassinated in 1963, was the son of Joseph Patrick Kennedy and Rose Elizabeth Fitzgerald, daughter of John Francis Fitzgerald (d. 1950), whose own father Thomas Fitzgerald was born in Bruff, Co. Limerick, in 1835.

The Barrys come from Odo de Barri, whose son William married Angharat, daughter of Gerald of Windsor. Their son Gerald de Barri, called *Giraldus Cambrensis* or "Gerald of Wales," wrote *The Conquest of Ireland*, based on his family's involvement with those events and a topography of Ireland, based on his travels there with Prince John in 1185. In another work, *The Journey through Wales*, Gerald explained his own surname:

"Not far from Cardiff there is a small island just off the shore of the Severn Sea which the local inhabitants call Barry. It takes its name from St. Baroc, who used to live there… a noble family resident on the coast of South Wales has taken its name from the island, because it owns it and neighboring estates… It is an odd thing that in a rock by the sea where one first lands on the island there is a small crack. If you press your ear to it, you can hear a noise like that of blacksmiths at work… one could well imagine that a sound of this sort would come from the sea-waters rushing into hidden orifices beneath the island…"

Through his nephew Robert de Barry, the surname gave rise to several lines of Irish aristocrats, Barry Mor (hence Barrymore), Barry Og and Barry Roe, and one line from Adam Barry that became MacAdam. There were so many cadet branches that it is now a very popular Irish surname: almost half of all Irish Barrys live in Cork where the family first received lands. It is also numerous in neighboring Limerick and Waterford, where my own great-grandmother Mary Barry was born in 1870 at Ballyin near Lismore.

Despite being a priest, Gerald's uncle David Fitzgerald, Bishop of St. David's, had a daughter who married Walter, son of Wyzo, a Flemish knight who was part of the earlier Norman conquest of Wales. Walter's granddaughter

Gwenllian married Gwgan ap Bleddyn, whose descendants used his name, Gwgan, as a patronymic surname, Anglicized to Wogan. Their descendant Sir John Wogan came to Ireland as a judge in 1295, and from him descend the Irish Wogans, of whom the most famous is Terry Wogan, disc jockey and chat show host in Britain.

The pedigree shows the diversity of blood that poured into Ireland due to the conquest, and also how Irish royal blood entered England through the marriage of the main conqueror, Strongbow, to Aoife, daughter of Dermot Mac Murrough, King of Leinster. Aoife and Strongbow's daughter Isabel married back into the Norman aristocracy and thereby Irish blue blood has infused the veins of a vast swathe of the British population, including anyone who can prove descent from the de Bohuns, Marshalls and indeed the Plantagenet kings themselves.

My great-grandparents William Denning and Mary Barry, pictured at Battle, Sussex. Mary's surname suggests that she was among the descendants of the Cambro-Norman invaders of Ireland in the 12th century.

The Fitzgerald-Barry pedigree

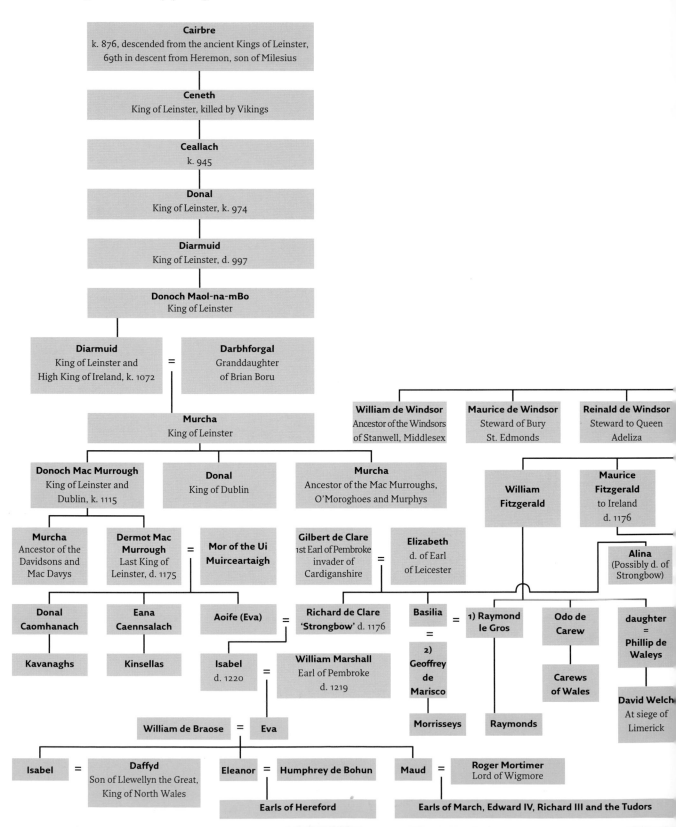

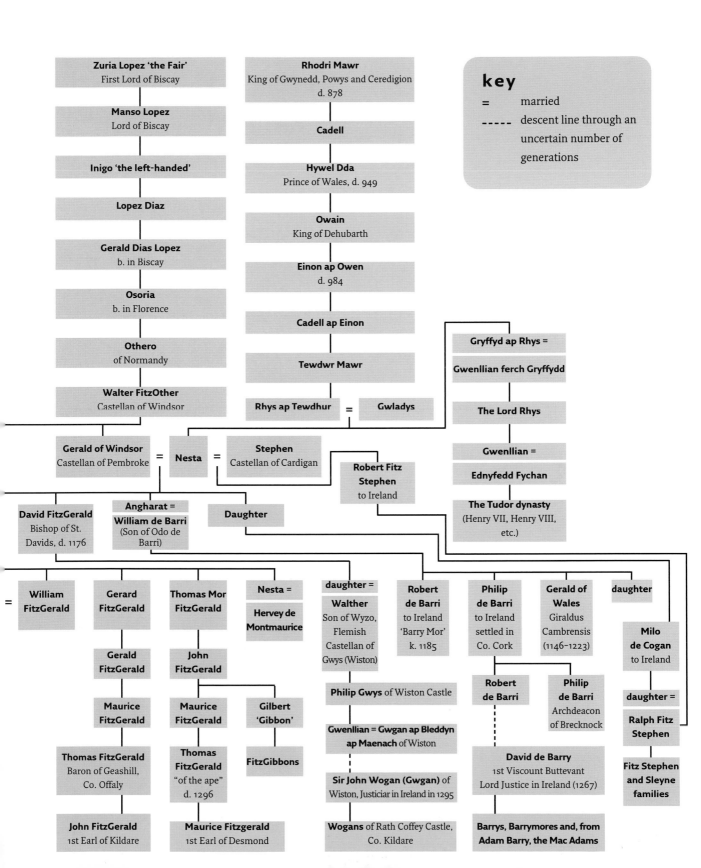

key

= married

----- descent line through an uncertain number of generations

Zuria Lopez 'the Fair'
First Lord of Biscay

Manso Lopez
Lord of Biscay

Inigo 'the left-handed'

Lopez Diaz

Gerald Dias Lopez
b. in Biscay

Osoria
b. in Florence

Othero
of Normandy

Walter FitzOther
Castellan of Windsor

Rhodri Mawr
King of Gwynedd, Powys and Ceredigion
d. 878

Cadell

Hywel Dda
Prince of Wales, d. 949

Owain
King of Dehubarth

Einon ap Owen
d. 984

Cadell ap Einon

Tewdwr Mawr

Rhys ap Tewdhur = Gwladys

Gryffyd ap Rhys =

Gwenllian ferch Gryffydd

The Lord Rhys

Gwenllian =

Ednyfedd Fychan

The Tudor dynasty
(Henry VII, Henry VIII, etc.)

Gerald of Windsor
Castellan of Pembroke = Nesta = Stephen
Castellan of Cardigan

Robert Fitz Stephen
to Ireland

David FitzGerald
Bishop of St. Davids, d. 1176

Angharat =
William de Barri
(Son of Odo de Barri)

Daughter

= William FitzGerald

Gerard FitzGerald

Thomas Mor FitzGerald

Nesta =

Hervey de Montmaurice

daughter =

Walther
Son of Wyzo, Flemish Castellan of Gwys (Wiston)

Robert de Barri
to Ireland 'Barry Mor' k. 1185

Philip de Barri
to Ireland settled in Co. Cork

Gerald of Wales
Giraldus Cambrensis
(1146–1223)

daughter

Milo de Cogan
to Ireland

Gerald FitzGerald

John FitzGerald

Philip Gwys of Wiston Castle

Robert de Barri

Philip de Barri
Archdeacon of Brecknock

daughter =

Ralph Fitz Stephen

Maurice FitzGerald

Maurice FitzGerald

Gilbert 'Gibbon'

Gwenllian = Gwgan ap Bleddyn ap Maenach of Wiston

Fitz Stephen and Sleyne families

Thomas FitzGerald
Baron of Geashill, Co. Offaly

Thomas FitzGerald
"of the ape"
d. 1296

FitzGibbons

Sir John Wogan (Gwgan) of Wiston, Justiciar in Ireland in 1295

David de Barry
1st Viscount Buttevant
Lord Justice in Ireland (1267)

John FitzGerald
1st Earl of Kildare

Maurice Fitzgerald
1st Earl of Desmond

Wogans of Rath Coffey Castle, Co. Kildare

Barrys, Barrymores and, from Adam Barry, the Mac Adams

Norman dynasties

By 1250, the Normans had spread all over Ireland, seizing the fertile plains and building motte and bailey castles to strengthen their grip: the greatest is Hugh de Lacy's at Trim, Co. Meath, built about 1200 (see p. 196). Ancient dynasties were rapidly displaced — the Eóganacht families of McCarthy and O'Sullivan were driven from Cashel and into the southwest, and the Kavanaghs, O'Tooles and O'Byrnes were hounded from Leinster into the Wicklow Mountains. The Normans established great dynasties, such as the Butlers of Ormonde; de Burghs (Burkes) in Connacht; Fitzgeralds in Desmond; de Lacys in Meath; and de Courcys in Ulster.

Some remained apart from the Gaels. The Butlers of Ormonde, for example, despite speaking fluent Gaelic, never lost their sense of "Englishness," but they were unusual. Mostly, "English" influence soon waned in the face of constant feuds between barons and Gaelic lords, who formed all sorts of alliances between and against each other, and of course most "Normans" were part-Welsh anyway. Some married into Gaelic families, adopted Brehon Law and quickly became Gaelicized — *Hiberniores Hibernicis ipsis* (or *Hiberniores ipsis Hibernicis*), "more Irish than the Irish." They assumed the roles of the Gaelic lords they had displaced and some took Gaelic titles, such as *An Fáltach*, the head of the Wall family of Limerick and *An Condúnach*, head of the Condons in Co. Cork.

Several Norman families actually became clans and *septs*. The McQuillins of the Route

Galloglasses

Called in Gaelic *gallóglach* — "foreign warrior" — the Galloglasses were mercenaries from the Hebrides and other parts of western Scotland, with a mixture of Pict, Irish and Viking blood. They came to Ireland, especially in the 11th and 12th centuries, initially to fight for the native chiefs of north Connacht and Ulster, especially the O'Neills, O'Donnells and Maguires, against the Cambro-Normans. Fighting on foot, these stocky men formed an impenetrable barrier bristling with two-handed swords, spears, halberds, battle axes and *skeans* (daggers) that could stop an otherwise devastating Norman cavalry in full charge. Later, Galloglasses were also employed by Normans, such as the Fitzgeralds in Munster and the De Burghs in Connacht. Some were granted lands by their employers and settled in Ireland, the most prominent being the Irish MacDonalds, MacSweenys, MacSheehys, MacLeods and MacCabes. The latter were Mac Cába, Cába being a personal name meaning "caped one" and came to Bréifne, the ancient land covering modern Cavan and west Leitrim in about 1350 in the pay of the O'Reillys and O'Rourkes. The chief of the MacCabes became Constable of the two Bréifnes and survived even Cromwell's incursions, but they lost everything after fighting on James II's losing side in the Battle of Aughrim in 1691 (see p. 205).

The Gaels had mercenary bands too, much more lightly armed and deliberately barefooted, called *ceithearnachs* (kerns). Uniquely, however, one Gaelic *sept*, the O'Crowleys, became Galloglasses, leaving their native Roscommon to serve as mercenaries for the O'Sullivans in Co. Cork.

Some wonderful little Galloglasses (ABOVE) are shown on John Goghe's map *Hibernia*, 1567 (LEFT).

(*Mac Uighilin*) were the Hibernicised Mandevilles. The transformation of the de Nangles to Costellos (see p. 148–54) is another good example. Similarly, the MacRudderys were originally FitzSimons and the MacCorishes were de Birminghams. The descendants of William de Burgh, whose senior line consisted of Earls of Ulster and later Earls of Clanrickarde and Viscounts Mayo, became a clan with offshoot *septs*, the *MacSeoinin* (Jennings) and *MacGiobúin*, the former, for example, founded by "Little John" (*Seoinín*) Burke. Only one prominent Gaelic family, the MacDermots of Rathdown, made the reverse journey to become Normanised: having supported Strongbow (Richard FitzGilbert de Clare), they became the *Fitz*Dermots.

The English influx

Besides constant feuds between the nobles, Normans and Gaels alike, Medieval Ireland saw occasional large-scale rebellions and invasions, such as that of Robert the Bruce's brother Edward, who led a Scots army into Ulster in 1315 where it was defeated by John de Bermingham at the Battle of Faughart, Co. Louth, in 1318. Edward III and Richard II sent armies to try to quell Irish rebellions but despite this the Irish kings began to recover their ancient authority. When Niall Mór O'Neill became king in Ulster in 1364, the bards sang that "Ireland is a woman risen again/from the horrors of reproach/she was owned for a while by foreigners/she belongs to Irishmen after that."

After the main Cambro-Norman influx, relatively few English families voluntarily settled in Medieval Ireland. Notable exceptions were the "Tribes of Galway," the merchant families such as the Frenches (p. 142) who settled in Galway. The 16th century saw a handful, like the Fleetwoods, Goldsmiths and Springs, not to mention Walter Cowley, who arrived in 1537 to become Solicitor General, the ancestor of the Irish-born Duke of Wellington.

Most post-Norman families, like Cowley's, came either as merchants or administrators, but if their aim was to farm they stuck to the area around Dublin, hoping to be safe from the barbarous Gaels. To protect them the administration in Dublin created the Pale. We hear of this first in 1495 when instructions were issued for "ditches to be made aboute the Inglishe pale." It covered the four fairly Anglicized counties of Kildare, Dublin, Louth and Meath, and was generally called the *marghery* or "land of peace," as opposed to the rest, "the land of war."

Rebellion and Plantation

In the 16th century, the Tudors were keen to promote and strengthen their power throughout their realms. In Ireland, Henry VIII crushed a small rebellion by Thomas FitzGerald, Lord Offaly, the son of the powerful Earl of Kildare, and strengthened the garrison at Dublin Castle. Elizabeth I appointed first Lord Sussex and then Sir Henry Sidney as Lords Lieutenant in Ireland, first to appease the Gaelic lords and, when that failed to work, to dispossess them of their land and create plantations of English settlers. Two rebellions ensued, each so brutally crushed as to fuel ever-greater loathing of the English.

Ireland's next population influx was due to the settlement or "planting" of English settlers in Ireland. Philip and Mary's mid-16th century "transplantation" was aimed at forcing the chiefs of the O'Mores, O'Conors and O'Dempseys off their land in central Ireland. They created two new counties, King's and Queen's (Offaly and Leix [Laois]), centred around Phillipstown and Maryport. The plan failed: few English wanted to venture so far inland, and the chiefs put up a stubborn resistance, though eventually O'Conor died and O'More gave up and accepted alternative lands in Co. Kerry.

These depictions from the margin of Spede's map of Ireland, 1609, show something of the attitudes of the time towards the "wild" Irish peasantry.

The Gentleman of Ireland
The Gentlewoman of Ireland
The Wilde Irish man
The Wilde Irish Woman

Of all Ireland in the late Tudor period, Ulster remained the most Irish. Despite having surrendered their ancient rights to Henry VIII in favour of English titles, Hugh O'Neill, Earl of Tyrone, Hugh Rory O'Donnell, Earl of Tyrconnell, and Cúchonacht Maguire, Lord of Fermanagh, remained to all practical purposes kings of their ancient lands. In 1594 a further wave of resistance erupted when Hugh O'Neill, Earl of Tyrone, expelled English officials from Ulster and asked the King of Spain to help him expell the English forever. Initially, the Gaels were successful, defeating the Anglo-Irish forces at Benurb and Yellow Ford in 1596. In 1600, O'Neill, now proclaimed "Prince of Ireland," marched south and the next year 4,000 Spanish soldiers landed at Kinsale, Co. Cork. O'Neill marched his brave but disorganized army south to meet them, but the combined force was crushed by Lord Mountjoy's army on Christmas Day.

The chief rebels were shown exceptional leniency, but in 1607, fearful of belated reprisals, O'Neill, O'Donnell and Maguire fled abroad, taking 99 of their most prominent nobles with them. The "Flight of the Earls" marked the start of collapse of the Gaelic order that had so successfully survived the Cambro-Norman invasion.

James I, like his predecessors, saw the Plantations as a means of enhancing royal power in Ireland, while Lord Lieutenant Wentworth and Cromwell used the system for raising money and rewarding loyal troops. The land used was either already in Crown hands or it was confiscated from Gaelic lords for supposed misdemeanors or bought from bankrupt lords, such as the O'Neills of Clandeboye in Ulster. Some Irish lords, such as Clanricard, Thomond and Antrim, actually encouraged Protestant settlement on their land. While methods varied, the usual one was to grant land to "undertakers," Protestant landlords who undertook to settle

Elizabeth I's plantations aimed at creating Protestant settlements in Ireland that would spread Protestant "civilization" by example to the "wild" Gaels. The plan was encouraged enthusiastically by Sir Walter Raleigh, who brought many settlers from his native West Country. Settlement focused on Munster, especially on the confiscated lands of the Fitzgerald Earls of Desmond, and other rebels in Cork, Limerick, Tipperary, Waterford and Kerry. Prominent Tudor planter families included the Spensers, Raleighs, Coutenays, Cliftons, Hattons, Hydes, St. Legers, Carews, Dennys, Brownes and the Boyles of Faversham, Kent, who became Earls of Cork, from whom came Robert Boyle (1627–91), the pioneering physicist.

the land with an agreed number of Protestant settlers. The Scottish and English undertakers in Cavan, Donegal and Fermanagh (1612–13) are listed in *Historical Manuscripts Commission Report 4* (Hastings MSS).

The Plantation of Ulster was greatly aided by the Flight of the Earls in 1607. It enabled the Crown to confiscate vast tracts of land in Armagh, Cavan, Coleraine (now called Derry), Fermanagh and Tyrone, forcing remaining Gaelic proprietors into marginal land, such as the bogs. Londoners were brought in — hence Derry becoming Londonderry. So too were troublesome elements of Anglo-Scottish Border families, such as the Grahams, Armstrongs, Hetheringtons and Elliots, in the hope that a change of scenery would temper their internal feuds. Lowland Scots were favored because James I was king of both England and Scotland, and also because he feared an alliance between the Ulstermen and their cousins in the southwestern Highlands. Land went to undertakers such as Hugh Montgomery and James Hamilton at sixpence an acre, and they brought in planters, with surnames including Gordon, Sincair, Stewart, Ross, Patterson, Frazer, Morrison and Kerr.

By 1641, some 22,000 English planters were taking root in Munster, and a further 15,000 English and Scots in Ulster. The Irish, for the most part, loathed the system and while some early planters became Hibernicised, most remained isolated. They were attacked periodically, in Munster in 1598 and Ulster in 1615. In 1641, fuelled by Lord Lieutenant Wentworth's publicly declared intention to confiscate further Catholic-held land and emboldened by impending civil war in England, Ireland again erupted in violence. Hugh O'Neill's nephew Owen Roe O'Neill raised the Gaels of Ulster, and great numbers of Protestant planters were massacred. The

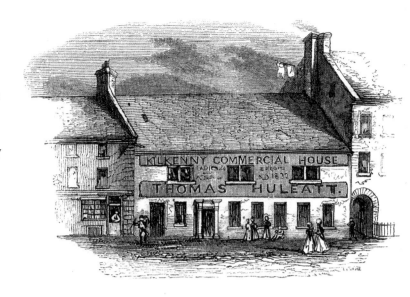

Catholic lords formed a confederacy at Kilkenny, which Charles I's queen Henrietta Maria and her political advisor, Henry Jermyn, Earl of St. Albans, tried desperately to recruit to the Royalist cause. The Protestants were largely sympathetic to Parliament, but were led by the new Royalist Lord Lieutenant, Lord Ormonde. A Scots Protestant army entered Ulster to help the beleaguered Scots planters and a papal envoy, Rinuccini, came from Rome to stir up the Catholics against the English. Huge numbers on all sides died for no real purpose.

The period is chronicled in M. Hickson (ed.), *Ireland in the Seventeenth Century or The Irish Massacres of 1641–2* (Longmans, Green & Co., 1884), with a manuscript index (by P. Manning) at the SoG. The depositions make harrowing reading. Twenty-five-year-old Edith Gardiner of Portumna, Co. Galway, related that her husband agreed to surrender the church steeple of Roskerke Abbey, in which he was being besieged, to the Burkes of Rappagh, in return for safe passage for herself and her mother into Co. Roscommon. Despite being escorted by one of the Burkes who was a friar, Edith and her mother were attacked and "stript...to the skin" by their own guards. They made it to the English garrison at Abbey Boyle, Co. Roscommon: Edith

A 19th-century sketch of the small house in Kilkenny at which the Catholic confederates assembled in 1642, after "the grand rebellion" of 1641.

The government made "Books of Survey and Distribution" in about 1641 and 1666-8 to record who owned what, mainly as a basis for redistribution of land. Those for Clare, Galway, Mayo and Roscommon are published, and others are in manuscript form at the NLI, as listed by Grenham.

Between 1655 and 1667, Sir William Petty made his detailed "Civil Survey" which included descriptions and proofs of landholding, such as deeds and wills. This survives for Cork, Derry, Donegal, Dublin, Kildare, Kilkenny, Limerick, Meath, Tipperary, Tyrone, Waterford and Wexford, and is published by the Irish Manuscripts Commission.

In 1659, Petty also made a list of everyone — called "tituladoes" — with title to land, recording numbers of Irish and English people in each townland and the main Gaelic names for each barony. Records survive for all counties (*except* Cavan, Galway, Mayo, Tyrone and Wicklow) and were published as *Pender's Census*, so-called after its 1939 editor, Seamus Pender (repr. GPC, 1997).

Certificates of Transplantation created under Cromwell were destroyed in 1922, but many details survive in older genealogical research papers and family histories. Transplantation was often between specified areas as detailed in local histories. Limerick landlords, for example, were sent to Galway, though in fact about 20 families disobeyed and went to Co. Clare: among these were the ancestors of the great Irish genealogist and surname expert, Dr. Edward MacLysaght.

Many of the families who acquired land appear in printed and manuscript sources (see p. 157-9). O'Hart, though much criticized on other fronts, provides a vast list of pedigrees and transcripts of original sources in volume 2 of his *Irish Pedigrees*.

later rejoined her husband, but her mother, traveling on to "the Boyle," was murdered. Edith's party of feckless escorts had included "one Gilduffe," perhaps an ancestor of the Revd. Patrick Kilduff (see p. 111).

In 1649, Charles I was executed in London and Cromwell came to power. A brilliant and brutal general, Cromwell invaded Ireland that year and quickly established control. He left in 1650, but campaigns by his generals against far-flung rebels lasted until 1652.

In 1641, the English Parliament had passed the *Adventurer's Act*, a money-raising venture that allowed land to be confiscated from disloyal Irish landlords and sold to investors called "Adventurers." Cromwell's campaign had cost £3.5 million. To make this back, he had similar legislation passed in 1652. The leading 105 Irish lords who had opposed him were either executed, banished or transported to the Americas, and their land was seized. Many more, who had simply not shown "constant good affection" to Parliament, were fined and transplanted — deprived of their land in return for worse plots (the size, relative to their original ones, being calculated by their degree of "guilt") in the extremities of Clare and Connacht — "to Hell or to Connacht," as people said at the time.

Sir William Petty organized a government survey to establish the land available and decide who should receive it. In all, Petty estimated, 11 million out of Ireland's total of 20 million

The Siege of Derry, 1688–9. By November 1688, the walled city of Derry (Londonderry) was the only one in Ireland whose garrison was not loyal to Catholic King James II. The Earl of Antrim was ordered to replace it with a more reliable force. Tradition has it that 13 apprentice boys seized the city keys and locked the gates ahead of the approaching Catholic army which then besieged the city for 105 days during which some 4,000 people died (about half the population). The siege is commemorated annually by a parade of the Apprentice Boys of Derry.

acres was confiscated and reassigned, mainly in Dublin, Kildare, Carlow, Cork, Armagh, Down, Antrim, Laois, Offaly, Meath, Westmeath, Limerick, Tipperary and Waterford. It was a massive shift in landownership.

The benefiting Adventurers were mainly London merchants or soldiers in Cromwell's army, but for the most part soldiers' shares were bought up by larger landholders, including many of the longer-standing Protestant-landowning families, who used the 1650s to build up their estates. One of the worst effects of the system was to create many absentee landlords living on the mainland for whom the newly acquired estates were mere sources of profit.

The Jacobites

The Catholic James II succeeded his Protestant brother Charles II in 1685. He appointed the Catholic Duke of Tyrconnell as Lord Lieutenant in Ireland with the intention of reversing the Protestant plantations and restoring the Catholic lords. In 1688, James's Protestant nobles overthrew him in favour of his Protestant daughter Mary and her husband William III of Orange. James fled to France and then to Ireland, landing at Kinsale in March 1689. He ruled briefly, with a government of Catholic favorites, including Harry Jermyn, Earl of Dover, and an army of around 6,000 led by a mixture of French officers and Irish Catholic lords. More on this army is given in O'Hart and J. D'Alton, *Illustrations, Historical and Genealogical of King James's Irish Army List 1689* (2. vols., Dublin, n.d.).

The Protestants of Derry were besieged and while the brave citizens held out, William sent a force under General Schomberg to Ireland. The two sides met at the Battle of the Boyne on July 1, 1690, and James's forces were defeated. James fled back to France, but his followers, the "Jacobites," fought on. They were crushed at the Battle of Aughrim on July 12, 1691, and the

remnants retreated to Limerick. When the city surrendered to William's forces on October 3, 1691, the Jacobite cause — and that, incidentally, of Gaelic Ireland — was over.

The round of confiscations in the aftermath of the Jacobite war marked the last of the wholesale transfer of Irish landownership from native Gaels to Protestants from England, Scotland and even abroad, for Schomberg, a German, became Duke of Leinster.

The Anglo-Irish

Those outsiders who actually settled on the estates they had acquired through the whole process of land transfer were termed "Anglo-Irish," but tended to call themselves the "Protestants of Ireland" (1690) and "The English of this kingdom." By the 1720s "Irish gentlemen" was the more normal term, the ancient Gaelic gentry having been so effectively decimated.

Gaelic survival

The Gaelic landlords who survived were few and far between. In 1600 about 90 percent of Ireland was in Irish hands: by 1700, only 14 percent remained. Many survivors were those who had already converted to Protestantism; others did so during these troubled times, and survived.

Protestant King William III (William of Orange) advancing at the Battle of the Boyne, on 1 July 1690, where his troops defeated the supporters of the exiled Roman Catholic King James II, who was trying to regain his throne. Protestant celebrations commemorating the battle are held in the north every year on 12th of July and include the parade of the Orange Order, which pays tribute to William of Orange's victory.

Amazingly, some Catholic Gaelic lords remained in isolated areas, avoiding confiscation simply by not leaving when they were told to or returning when they found that nobody had occupied their land. They were then subject, however, to the deprecations of the Penal Laws (see p. 80), which further weakened these last survivors of the old order.

Most Protestants who survived the violence of the 1640s and the ensuing famine understandably developed a siege mentality that led them to give unqualified support for Cromwell and William of Orange. As we know, this polarization survived unadulterated down the centuries. Among the Northern Irish

Protestants are many who still remain highly resistant to severing links with the mainland. However, the overall effect of the Plantations should not be over-emphasized. MacLysaght noted that, contrary to expectation, non-Irish surnames are only in the majority in two counties, Antrim and Down, and this is mainly because of economic migration to the cities of Belfast and Derry in the last two centuries. Most planters in the countryside at the lower economic level, it seems, became broadly integrated with the native population.

Great though the disruption was, the effect on tenants was fairly minimal. The men in charge might have changed, but the peasants remained,

Wild Geese sources

The rather romantic subject of Wild Geese is well documented. The NLI has the early 18th-century papers of James Terry (NLI Ir.9292 T.7) concerning Wild Geese families. The GO's Registered Pedigrees (GO 156-82, indexed in GO 469) include many Wild Geese, for they often required proof of their noble ancestry to join foreign chivalric and noble orders. Foreign archives contain much that is of use: Dr. R.J. Hayes, when director of the NLI, had large parts of this microfilmed, making it available in the NLI. The microfilms include the Archives de la Brigade Irlandaise (from the French Army Archives at the Chateau de Vincennes), whose detailed records include precise places of origin. Descendants of these exiles often have much fuller, unbroken pedigrees than families who remained in Ireland or left much later.

O'Hart (vol.. 2) prints many useful lists of Irishmen serving in foreign regiments. Much has been published on this subject in its own right, including:

- G.T. Griffin, *The Wild Geese: Pen Portraits of Famous Irish Exiles* (Jarrolds Ltd, 1938).
- R. Hayes, *Biographical Dictionary of Irishmen in France* (M.H. Gill & Sons, 1949).
- C.E. Lart (ed.), *Saint-Germain-en-Laye, The Parochial Registers; Jacobite Extracts 1689-1720* (St. Catherine's, 2 vols., 1910).
- Marquis de Ruvigny, *The Jacobite Peerage* (1904, repr. Charles Skilton, London, 1974).
- M.G. McLaughlin, *History of the Irish Brigades* (P. O'Shea, 1874).
- T. O'Connor, *The Irish in Europe, 1580-1815* (Four Courts Press, 2001).
- M. Walsh, *Spanish Knights of Irish Origin; Documents from Continental Archives* (Irish Manuscripts Commission, 1960).

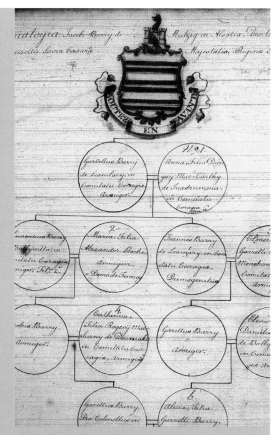

A genealogical table of "Jacobi Barry" (James Barry), one of the Wild Geese, from Co. Cork, who appears to have become a Colonel in the army of the Queen of Hungary (courtesy of the National Library of Ireland).

heads to the soil, unmoved. Where the Potato Famine did not decimate them or cause them to migrate, Irish families are, for the most part, still living exactly where they have always been.

The Wild Geese

Under the Treaty of Limerick, many Jacobite officers were permitted to leave Ireland. Some 11,000 exiles, mainly from Gaelic or Cambro-Norman families, went abroad to seek employment in the armies of the Catholic countries, especially France, Portugal and Spain. But they were only the latest wave of "Wild Geese" to fly from Ireland. The phenomena had started in 1607 with the Flight of the Earls, who ended up in Rome, and continued throughout the century, especially due to the campaigns and confiscations of Cromwell. Thus, Irish Brigades or Regiments had become commonplace in the armies of the Catholic powers. Their members proved loyal supporters of Charles II while he was in exile in France in the 1640s and early 1650s, and many of their members later joined James II in Paris and followed him to Ireland in 1689. While figures varied daily, roughly 34,000 Irishmen served in foreign armies by the end of the 17th century — the start, in effect, of the Irish Diaspora. And, thanks to the continued persecution of the Irish Catholic in the 18th and 19th centuries, the tradition continued.

In France, the Irish Brigade developed out of the Brigade formed by Col. Arthur Dillon and other exiles from the Cromwellian war. One of its number, Patrick Sarsfield, later led 12,000 veterans in James II's army. As the Irish Brigade, it won glory under its leader Major Dan Mahoney for its role in defeating the Austrians at the Battle of Cremona in 1702. In 1744, they had the pleasure of beating the British at the Battle of Fontenoy, advancing under the battle cry "Remember Limerick and the treachery of the English!" In all, about 100,000 Irishmen served in its ranks throughout the 18th century: most married French girls, but their families never forgot their Irish roots.

Famous Wild Geese include Richard Hennessy from Ballymacoy near Mallow, Co. Cork, who joined the Irish Brigade in France in 1740, aged 26. Having been asked to send a couple of barrels of brandy home to friends, he founded a trading firm in the town of Cognac. Perhaps the most prominent of the Wild Geese, however, was Marshal (Marie-Edme-) Patrice de MacMahon (died 1893), a descendant of Mahon, brother of Brian Boru. A third-generation Wild Goose, Patrice's grandfather had gone to Paris to study medicine at the Irish College. Patrice became a Marshall of France, served with great credit in the Franco-Prussian War and became President of the Third Republic in 1875.

The struggle for freedom

The campaigns of Hugh O'Neill in the 1640s and James II in the later 17th century both fuelled the concept of Ireland as a proud yet suppressed nation. It was not until the late 18th century, however, when revolution had rocked America and France, that Irishmen began to take organized steps to regain their freedom.

The Kavanaghs

MacLysaght writes of the Kavanaghs (the ancient dynasty driven from their lands by the Normans) that,

"several Kavanaghs were officers in the Irish Brigade in the army of France and a branch of the family settled in that country, but it was in Austria they chiefly distinguished themselves... Brian Kavanagh, one of the many Kavanaghs who fought for the Stuart cause, [was] described as the tallest man in King James's army; while among the Wild Geese... Morgan Kavanagh, who rose to be Governor of Prague in 1766, was said to be the biggest man in Europe."

Convicts

For many Irish people convicted of crime, the choice was often death or transportation. For this reason, criminal records are often synonymous with those of migration. The NAI has an index to prisoners' petitions and cases 1788-1836; state prisoners' petitions 1798-99 and papers relating to free settlers (mainly the wives and families of convicts who volunteered to go abroad with them); transportation registers 1836-57; and Convict Reference Files 1836-56 and 1865-8.

Unindexed material, which can be extremely time-consuming to research, is covered in R. Lohan, 'Sources in the National Archives for research into the transportation of Irish convicts to Australia (1791-1853)', *Journal of the Irish Society for Archives* (Spring 1996).

For prisoners in Ireland, there are lists of people awaiting trial in Irish gaols, those admitted to bail, convictions in courts and petitions for leniency. Most are at the NAI, the earliest dating from 1796 (insolvent prisoners discharged out of the Four Courts Marshalsea between 1796 and 1798). Kilmainham Gaol registers date from 1798. Also notable for the period up to 1840 are gaol registers for Cork City, Cork County, Galway, Grangegorman Female Prison (now Port Laoise), Sligo and Trim. Many more gaols were built after 1840.

In contrast to attitudes of the past, having a "black sheep" in the family is considered rather fascinating. As Dublin-born playwright George Bernard Shaw (1856-1950) said, "If you cannot get rid of the family skeleton, you might as well make it dance!"

This certificate of freedom (commonly referred to as a ticket-of-leave), dated June 5, 1838, demonstrates that an Irish convict, Francis Neill, has completed his seven years of obligatory labor in the penal colony of New South Wales, Australia, and is now restored to conditional freedom. He was now free to live, work and raise a family there should he so wish.

Two secret societies, the Defenders and United Irishmen emerged, both of whom participated in the Insurrection of May–August 1798. Risings took place all over Ireland and there were atrocities on both sides — the government massacred 350 rebels at Tara, for example, and the rebels killed 200 Protestant prisoners in a barn at Scullabogue, Co. Wexford. In August, 1,019 French soldiers under General Humbert landed at Killala Bay, Co. Mayo and defeated government forces before being routed at Castlebar and surrendering at Ballinamuch, Co. Longford. The insurrection was finally quelled, at the cost of some 30,000 lives.

Sir R. Musgrave, in *Memoirs of the Different Rebellions in Ireland... with a particular detail of that which broke out the 23rd of May 1798...* (4th edn.,

Round Tower Books, 1995) chronicles these events and includes many names. In a list of Protestants massacred in Ferns, for example, is Thomas Crowly, shoemaker, killed at Enniscorthy on May 28, leaving a widow and five children in Ferns.

The result was the Act of Union of 1800, creating the United Kingdom of Great Britain and Ireland, moving Ireland's government to Westminster, the exchequer following in 1817. The move had a devastating effect on Ireland's economy and morale. Dublin, which had been the second city of the Empire, became a mere provincial capital and the great building works that had adorned it in the 18th century ceased.

The rebellion generated a series of claims made for financial losses it had caused, particularly by landowners in Carlow, Dublin,

Kildare, Wexford and Wicklow. The records are in the NLI (and on Eneclann CD). In Co. Leitrim, for example, William Hamilton of Blackrock made a claim "on behalf of the children of Edw. Hamilton of Drumkerin, deceased," presumably a close relative of theirs, for the loss, at Drumkerin, of "horses, spirits, oats, hay, and potatoes," valued at £71-10-3$^1/_2$. Ann Nevill of Carrick-on-Shannon, meanwhile, had lost millinery worth £46-14-11$^1/_2$ on the "Great road, leading from Dublin to Carrick-on-Shannon."

The Battle of Widow McCormack's Cabbage Patch

The struggle for freedom continued throughout the 19th century. Daniel O'Connell (1775–1847) led an unsuccessful campaign for the repeal of the Act of Union within Parliament, while the secret lodges of the Ribbonmen (mainly Catholic farmers, tradesmen, laborers and publicans) and the Young Ireland movement spread the aspiration of freedom through revolution.

In 1848, the Young Ireland movement staged a rebellion in Counties Dublin, Kilkenny and Tipperary against British rule. Poorly organized and easily infiltrated by British spies, the rebels raised only a motley army of badly-armed peasants, led somewhat reluctantly by a nationalist politician, William Smith O'Brien (1803–64). He made his last stand at Ballingarry, Co. Tipperary, forcing a party of police to take refuge in Widow McCormacks' farmhouse where two of the rebels were killed before being dispersed by soldiers. O'Brien was convicted of High Treason but a petition was raised and sent to the Chief Secretary's Office, Dublin. It comprises some 80,000 names of Irish people in Ireland and mainland Britain. It saved his life — he was transported to Tasmania instead (and was later pardoned and allowed to return home). The petition, transcribed by Ruth Lawler, is at **www.originsnetwork.com**.

Evacuation lists

In 1803, the government feared another French invasion and drew up plans to evacuate the eastern parts of Counties Antrim and Down and an "agricultural census" of crops, animals and transport listed under their owners. Those for Antrim are in the NLI Official Papers and the PRONI, and those created for Down are in the 1st Marquis of Londonderry's papers at the PRONI.

Many Irish names in other petitions at the Chief Secretaries' Official Papers at the NLI are calendared 1790–1831 and card-indexed 1832–80. Topics include other pleas for mercy and such matters as applications from towns wanting to host the Quarter Sessions. Obviously, searching here is a lucky-dip, but potentially worth the effort if you find your family. The struggle for freedom continued into the 20th century, as related on p. 81–3.

William Smith O'Brien, the Irish nationalist and rebel, at Kilmainham Gaol in Dublin. He joined Daniel O'Connell's Repeal Association, and later the Young Ireland party.

CHAPTER 24

Modern chieftains

The Old Gaelic order may have been crippled, but it never died. Since Independence, Ireland's old clans have been reforming, and the chieftains have re-emerged. Your family may already have one, or the search for the heir could still be on: it could be you!

By the Tudor period, much of Ireland beyond the Pale was still ruled by local chieftains. Many were of ancient Gaelic descent, but some had been displaced by Cambro-Norman lords who had long since adopted Gaelic ways. In the ensuing century, however, the Gaelic order was destroyed. Some chieftains submitted to the English and received titles from the

A highly romanticized imagining of an ancient warlord or chieftain.

Crown. Others fled abroad as Wild Geese. Many were simply impoverished and fell into obscurity. The descendants of chieftains, however, were often remembered and recognized by descendants of their clans and *septs* but on an entirely unofficial basis, for their role had no legal function. The sole exception was O'Conor Don, senior lineal descendant of the O'Connor Kings of Connacht and thus of Roderick O'Connor (d. 1198), the last High King of Ireland. In 1900, he was recognized as head of his clan for the rather patronizing purpose of carrying the Irish standard at Edward VII's coronation.

In 1956 under Dr. MacLysaght, the GO started tracing the senior male-lineal descendants of the last officially inaugurated 16th- or 17th-century Gaelic chieftains. This was done partly to right the old wrong done to Gaelic Ireland by the English, but also to stop bogus chieftains making false claims to dormant positions. Tracing the true chieftains was often no easy task, but eventually the following were found and recognized officially as Chiefs of the Name:

- *O'Brien of Thomond*
- *O'Callaghan*
- *O'Conor Don*
- *MacDermot, Prince of Coolavin*
- *MacDermot Roe*
- *O'Donnell of Tirconell*
- *O'Donoghue of the Glens*
- *O'Donovan*
- *Fox (An Sionnach)*
- *MacGillycuddy of the Reeks*
- *O'Grady of Kilballyowen*

- *O'Kelly of Gallagh and Tycooly*
- *O'Morchoe*
- *MacMorrough Kavanagh*
- *O'Neill of Clannaboy*
- *O'Toole of Fer Tire*

A further seventy 16th-century chieftains were identified (see MacLysaght's *More Irish Families*, p. 20) using State Papers, fiants and so on. In a handful of cases likely claimants are still seeking proof (see **http://homepage.eircom.net/ ~seanjmurphy/dir/chiefs.htm**), but in most cases senior descendants could not be traced. All the records of the project are in GO 610-27.

Unfortunately, in 1992, a claimant to the title MacCarthy Mor was recognized, who then made in the region of $1 million selling titles without actually having any right to do so. When it emerged that his initial claim to the chieftainship had been false anyway, recognition of him was withdrawn. Since 2001, the GO has been forced, due to this scandal, to suspend its recognition of any Irish chieftains.

One genuine chieftain who was recognized up to 2001 was The MacDermot, Prince of Coolavin. He tells me that his title derives from,
"the last King of Moylurg, Turlough MacDermot who died in 1576. From that time the head of the family was referred to simply as chief (the Irish for which is taoiseach*). The name The MacDermot along with all the other Irish 'The's comes directly from the translation into English. The chief of an Irish clan, in Irish, was always referred to only by his patronymic, e.g. Mac Diarmada, O Conchobair (O Conor), etc. All other MacDermots would have their given names preceding the surname, which itself would be preceded by a brief genealogical description, e.g. Francis mc Rory mc Niall MacDermot (my son).*

The term Prince of Coolavin was adopted later, the first being Hugh, who died in 1707. The title itself was not granted from above (the British crown and parliament would certainly not have granted titles to Gaelic Irish chieftains); rather it arose by popular usage. *Irish chieftains had renounced all titles to the Crown in the 1585 Composition of Connacht. When MacDermot was finally compelled to leave Moylurg and find a new home in the barony of Coolavin his family could not be divested of royal antecedent and continued to regard themselves as princes and, more importantly, were so considered by the people among whom they lived. To this day this local custom survives."*

I also asked him what being The MacDermot in 2006 actually entailed. He replied, *"being The MacDermot in the modern world is something of a curiosity. Certainly it brings no privileges with it and the old Gaelic titles are [no longer] recognized by our republic [Éire]... I keep our clan together by operating the website [*www.macdermot.com*], organising gatherings, maintaining and developing family archives, providing whatever genealogical assistance I can and generally being there for those who feel the need to communicate with us. I provide a focal point. The maintenance of Coolavin, our family home, not just for the direct family but also for all MacDermots, is of course an important element of what we do."*

A 21st-century prince: Rory MacDermot, The MacDermot, Prince of Coolavin.

further reading
■ E. MacLysaght, *More Irish Families* (Irish Academic Press, 1982).

CHAPTER 25

Genetics

The new science of genetics is revolutionizing genealogy. It is confirming some ancient pedigrees that were once held in grave doubt, and making us rethink others we once assumed were almost certainly true. DNA testing is available to us all, and especially in a country where recent records are relatively poor, the results now often provide the keys needed to reconnect families separated by the diaspora.

Most of these Limerick children will have had very similar DNA, suggesting where their common ancestors may have come from thousands of years ago. The subtle differences between their individual genetic signatures, as passed down to their descendants, helps us now to tell different families apart.

Surnames are usually inherited down male lines from a common male ancestor, and so too are Y chromosomes. DNA testing turns out to be a great way of seeking new proof for ancient pedigrees that claim male-lineal connections between people of the same or different surnames. A lot of ancient pedigrees have recently been dusted off and studied in genetics labs — with some extraordinary results.

Common genetic ancestors

All men inherit their Y chromosome from their fathers. Men of a certain lineage, usually therefore of the same surname, should consequently have inherited the same Y chromosome. DNA tests work by breaking down strands of DNA, such as the Y chromosome, and giving them numerical "signatures." It's therefore quite easy for non-geneticists to compare these numbers: if two men's Y-chromosome signatures match, they're of the same male lineage and if they don't, they're probably not.

Many Irish Gaelic and Cambro-Norman families often comprise many living people with the same surname and an ancestor who was invariably a warrior, often himself a member of an earlier dynasty. This is hardly surprising. Membership of the dominant male group, be it (for example) the Uí Néill in the 5th and ensuing centuries (see p. 165) or the Barry-Fitzgerald dynasties in the 12th and later centuries (see p. 197), conferred considerable advantages on its members: control of land and wealth and therefore better diet and training in arms, resulting in these males having access to the most desirable women and being able to rear more children, who

could themselves spread their genes further. The very structure of the *fine* and the clan system was therefore conducive to creating and promoting certain male lineages over others. These circumstances make Ireland a rich hunting ground for geneticists, and this is all entirely to the advantage of people seeking Irish roots.

Recently, a series of genetic studies have been undertaken to see if historical characters who are supposed to have become ancestors to a vast number of modern descendants can be identified by distinctive DNA signatures within their supposed progeny. The MacDonalds, McDougalls and MacAllistairs claim descent from Somerled, Lord of the Western Isles of Scotland, a descendant of Colla Uais (supposedly a cousin of Niall of the Nine Hostages). Tests, mainly focused in Scotland, have revealed that 25 percent of MacDonalds, 33 percent of McDougalls and 40 percent of MacAllistairs — an estimated 200,000 men in all — had a common Y chromosome. It cannot be proven that this was inherited from Somerled, but it is the most plausible explanation (similar tests revealed what is likely to be the genetic signature of Leod, Viking ancestor of the MacLeods, and one, found in an estimated 16 million men right across Asia, centered on Mongolia, that seems likely to be that of Genghis Khan himself).

In Ireland, the Trinity College team have found that about 12 percent of all Irishmen and about 20 percent of men in northwest Ireland and the area of Meath, Westmeath and Longford have a fairly recent common genetic ancestor. Besides being located in the heartlands of the Uí Néill — the dynasty of Niall of the Nine Hostages — the Dublin team found that it was particularly prevalent among surnames such as O'Doherty and McLoughlin that claimed Uí Néill origins. Significant matches were also found in Connachta families,

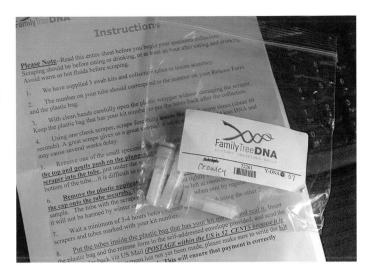

A DNA sample ready to be posted to the lab.

such as O'Flannagan and McGovern, who claimed descent from Niall's half-brothers, indicating that they were indeed related, as their genealogies had asserted all along — though not necessarily, of course, in exactly the way the pedigrees suggested. Genetically, the common ancestor *could* have lived as long ago as 2,500 years earlier than Niall's day! However, the families claiming descent from the Three Collas (such as the MacDonalds and the Maguires of Fermanagh) had clear differences to the Uí Néill signature, indicating that recent scholars had been right in doubting their true genealogical connection to Niall.

The experiment produced further surprises. Besides many families in northern Ireland, Niall's DNA signature appears in Scotland and even in English families with surnames such as Blanchard, Knowles and Drake. One explanation could be that long before they acquired their surnames, these families resulted from Uí Néill raids on the mainland. Most surprising, though, was that most O'Neills tested did not match the Uí Néill signature! The main line, it seems, descended from an undisclosed illegitimacy or adoption: the genealogy is right, but at some point a baby claimed by its mother to be the son of an O'Neill was nothing of the sort.

Starting a DNA project

Through the DNA firms, you can have your Y chromosome and mtDNA tested and assigned numerical sequences. Firms offer tests on 12, 25, 37 (or sometimes more) markers. It is generally agreed now that 12 markers is too few — if you can afford it, go for 25 or more (currently in the region of £100 [$200 US] plus). You can then compare your numerical sequence with others who have already been tested. Exact matches with someone else at 37 markers indicates that you are related within a couple of generations. A match that includes a number out by one indicates a link somewhat further back, and so on — the fewer similarities, the less your chances of being related.

Surnames are generally inherited down male lines. In Ireland, having a Gaelic "Mac" or "O" surname carries a strong implication of being descended from the person commemorated in the surname. By comparing Y-chromosome signatures of people with a common surname, you can see if they all match up. If they do not, you may find a core group who do, and may therefore have the DNA of the founder, while others with the same surname may not share this group's DNA. This may be because the surname actually had two or more origins, there

Crowley DNA

Tom Crowley, former *Taoiseach* of the Crowley Clan, was instrumental in setting up a major Crowley DNA project with FamilyTreeDNA. The project has so far tested 45 Crowleys. According to him, roughly three-quarters of these have DNA similar to within three or four markers of each other. This means that they are related, though further back, and the results tie in very well with the idea that they all descend from a small group of related Crowleys who came to Co. Cork in the 13th century.

Some, who thought they had Irish Crowley ancestry, have found their DNA does not match this "norm" at all. These people may be from English Crawley/Crowley families who settled in Ireland. Some Crowleys living abroad who hoped they were Irish on the basis of their surname are finding that they may actually be of English origin. A group in South Carolina have found that while the original Crowley there probably did come from Ireland, their male-line DNA actually belongs to a non-Irish family that had been living in the locality for several hundred years and whose DNA had entered the Crowley family, presumably by adoption or an act of infidelity by a Crowley wife. They have my sympathies, as do the Crowleys of Co. Clare. Their story was that their ancestors came there in 1603, when O'Sullivan Bear marched north from Co. Cork to join the Great Rebellion against the English. Crowleys are known to have marched with him, but one, having slaughtered his horse to make a *currach* to cross the Shannon, is said to have decided to go no further. That may be true, but their DNA doesn't match those of the Cork Crowleys at all.

So what of the Crowleys of Annaduff, Co. Leitrim? A descendant of theirs, Scott Crowley, sent a DNA sample off to FamilyTreeDNA. Six weeks later, 37 markers had been tested, producing a string of 37 numbers that could be compared to the rest. The firm's website offers several ways of doing this and also of uploading the results to a wider database, **www.ysearch.org**, which is open to all. You can seek exact matches or decide how wide a range of "genetic difference" (mismatches in your 37 numbers) you want to set, and contact anyone who has resultant matches with you. DNA tests have revealed many surprises, and Scott's was no exception, for he did not match any of the Crowleys. His closest match in the entire database was to a Thomas Walsh of Co. Waterford. However, it is early days: his DNA signature will remain in the databases forever, and as increasing numbers of people are tested, more matches will appear, and a clearer picture will emerge. In Scott's case, his DNA test is an investment that will doubtless yield future discoveries.

Of the group's members, four had identical matches across 37 markers and were probably therefore very close relatives. Three of these are from Crowleys from the Beara Peninsular, Co. Cork — Tom Crowley himself, a descendant of a family who lived near Tom's recent ancestors, and another from "over the mountain," about five miles away. A fourth was from Bantry, about 40 miles away. Interestingly, Lord Bantry's family owned both areas, potentially explaining movement from one place to another. All four families can be traced back to about 1800, but none quite far enough (due to lack of records) to prove a genealogical link: DNA confirms, however, that a connection existed, probably not much further back than this.

O'Gara DNA

It was hoped that genetics would solve the O'Gara's long-running family mystery. The main O'Gara line was in Co. Sligo, sprung from a line of warriors coming down to Fergal O'Gara, the 17th-century Lord of Moygara and Coolavin, a patron of the Four Masters (see p. 157). Fergal's family was dispossessed of its lands by Cromwell in 1648, and his grandson Oliver was one of the Wild Geese, a distinguished soldier who became a Count of the Holy Roman Empire.

The O'Garas of the Glencolumbkille/Kilcar area of Co. Donegal knew they were descended from four brothers, who arrived in the area at some indefinable point in the past, one of whom subsequently returned "home." Persistent tradition linked these brothers to Fergal's family, yet no amount of original records or oral history, both of which a descendant, Joseph O'Gara, has collected assiduously, would provide an answer. Who were the brothers? How many were there? Where did they originate?

When family DNA testing was new, I suggested setting up a project with FamilyTreeDNA. All the Donegal O'Garas who have been tested have matching DNA. O'Garas in Sligo, Mayo and Roscommon have been tested as well — their DNA all matches up with each other — but not with the Donegal O'Garas. DNA has *not* cosily confirmed that the Donegal O'Garas came from Fergal's family; they are still waiting for new matches to emerge to suggest who their true kin may really be. However, the brothers may yet have been of the Sligo O'Garas — but at some point an undisclosed adoption or illegitimacy may have disrupted the genetic line.

may have been undisclosed adoption or illegitimacy in the family, or peasants may have adopted the surname of their lords — but the latter, though much discussed, is thought to have been a rare occurrence.

DNA-testing firms are encouraging everyone to set up surname projects, whereby people of a surname have tests and see how they match up. Firms' websites include instructions on how to find out if a project exists, or how to set one up if it does not. The advantage of such projects for descendants of the Irish Diaspora who do not know their place of origin in Ireland can be huge. If just one person who does know their place of origin joins a surname project, then anyone with an exact or almost-exact match to them will have a very reasonable chance of finding their genealogical roots in the same area. Though this method takes no account of random migrations of individuals within Ireland, it will invariably prove a useful guide.

It is fitting to be able to end this book not by bemoaning the loss of records in 1922, but looking forward to the wealth of new information geneticists will yet be able to unlock from all those who share that most wonderful of ancestral privileges — Irish roots.

Learn more about genetics

■ C. Pomery, *DNA and Family History: How Genetic Testing Can Advance your Genealogical Research* (TNA, 2004) and associated website www.dnaandfamilyhistory.com.

■ Details of the 'Uí Néill' signature are at www.ysearch.org/research_comparative.asp?uid=G4EF6&vallist=M5UKQ and www.familytreedna.com/matchnialltest.html with a clear analysis at http://members.aol.com/lochlan/dna.htm.

Testing firms

■ www.familygenetics.co.uk/

■ www.dnaheritage.com/

■ www.oxfordancestors.co.uk/

■ www.familytreedna.com

Project co-ordination

■ www.theclansofireland.ie/dna.html aims to become an umbrella for family DNA-testing projects.

Sites for comparing your results with others

■ www.ybase.org

■ www.ysearch.org

■ http://smgf.org:8081/pubgen/site34.jsp

■ www.ystr.charite.de

Useful addresses

England and Wales

Ancestors Magazine
The National Archives
Kew
Surrey TW9 4DU
0208 3925370
www.ancestorsmagazine.co.uk/

Army Medals Office
Government Office Buildings
Worcester Road
Droitwich
Worcestershire WR9 8AU
01905 772323
www.army.mod.uk

Army Museum Ogilby Trust
58 The Close
Salisbury
Wiltshire SP1 2EX
01722 332811
www.armymuseums.org.uk

Army Records Centre
Ministry of Defence
Historical Disclosure
Mail Point 400
Kentigern House
65 Brown Street
Glasgow G2 8EX
0141 224 3030
www.army.mod.uk/contacts/
divisions/records.htm

Bank of England Archive Section
Threadneedle Street
London EC2R 8AH
0207 601 5096
www.bankofengland.co.uk/
archive.htm

Borthwick Institute for Archives
University of York
Heslington
York YO10 5DD
01904 321166
www.york.ac.uk/inst.bihr

British Library
Oriental and India Office Collections
96 Euston Road
London NW1 2DB
0207 412 7873
www.bl.uk/collections/
orientalandindian.htm

British Library Newspaper Library
Colindale Avenue
Colindale
London NW9 5HE
0207 412 7353
www.bl.uk/collections/
newspapers.html

Catholic Family History Society
The Secretaries
45 Gates Green Road
West Wickham
Bromley Kent BR4 9DE
www.catholic-genealogy.com

Catholic Record Society
c/o 12 Melbourne Place
Wolsingham
Durham DL13 3EH
01388 527747
www.catholichistory.org.uk/crs/
index.htm

Family History Monthly
Diamond Publishing Ltd.
Unit 101, 140 Wales Farm Road
London W3 6UG
0870 732 8080
www.familyhistorymonthly.com

Family Records Centre
1 Myddleton Street
London EC1R 1UW
020 8392 5300
www.familyrecords.gov.uk/frc

Federation of Family History Societies (FFHS)
PO Box 2425
Coventry CV5 6YX
07041 492032
www.ffhs.org.uk

Michael Gandy
140 Hampden Way
Southgate
London N14 5AX
Mgandy@clara.co.uk

Guildhall Library
Aldermanbury
London EC2P 2EJ
0207 332 1868
http://cityoflondon.gov.uk

Hyde Park Family History Centre (Mormons)
64/68 Exhibition Road
South Kensington
London SW7 2PA
020 7589 8561
www.familysearch.org

Imperial War Museum
Lambeth Road
London SE1 6HZ
020 7416 5320
www.iwm.org.uk

Irish Genealogical Research Society (IGRS)
Church of St.. Magnus the Martyr
Lower Thames Street
London EC3 6DN
(open on Saturdays 2-6)
www.igrsoc.org

Irish Origins
12 Greenhill Rents
Farringdon
London EC1M 6BN
020 7251 6117
www.irishorigins.com

John Rylands Library
The University of Manchester
Oxford Road
Manchester M13 9PL
0161 306 6000
www.library.manchester.ac.uk/

National Archives (TNA)
Ruskin Avenue
Kew, Richmond
Surrey TW9 4DU
020 8876 3444
www.nationalarchives.gov.uk

National Library of Wales
(Llyfrgell Genedlaethol Cymru)
Aberystwyth
Ceredigion SY23 3BU
01970 632800
www.llgc.org.uk

National Maritime Museum
Park Row
Greenwich
London SE10 9NF
020 8858 4422
www.nmm.ac.uk/

Parish Register Transcription Society
50 Silvester Road
Cowplain Waterlooville
Hampshire PO8 8TL
www.prtsoc.org.uk

Post Office Archives
Freeling House
Phoenix Place
London WC1X 0DL
0207 239 2570
www.postalheritage.org.uk

Practical Family History and **Family Tree Magazine**
61 Great Whyte
Ramsey
Huntingdonshire PE26 1HJ
08707 662272
www.family-tree.co.uk/

Principal Probate Registry (PPR)
Principal Registry of the Family Division
First Avenue House
42-49 High Holborn
London WC1V 6NP
020 7947 7017
www.courtservice.gov.uk

Royal Air Force Museum
Grahame Park Way
Hendon
London NW9 5LL
0208 205 2266
www.rafmuseum.org.uk/

Royal Air Force Personnel and Training Command
Branch PG 5a(2) (for officers) and P Man 2b(1) (for non-officers)
RAF Innsworth
Gloucestershire GL3 1EZ
www.raf.mod.uk/ptc/
ptchome.html

Royal Marines Museum
Eastney Barracks
Southsea PO4 9PX
0239 281 9385
www.royalmarinesmuseum.co.uk

Royal Naval Career Management
Disclosure Cell
Room 109 Victory Building
HM Naval Base
Portsmouth PO1 3LS
023 92 7 27531
www.royalmarinesregimental.co
.uk/histrecords.html

Royal Naval Personnel website
www.royal-navy.mod.uk/
server/show/nav.00h007001

Society of Genealogists (SoG)
14 Charterhouse Buildings
Goswell Road
London EC1M 7BA
020 7251 8799
www.sog.org.uk

Mrs E.R. Stage (Coastguard records)
150 Fulwell Park Avenue
Twickenham
Middlesex TW2 5HB

United Reformed Church Archives
86 Tavistock Place
London WC1H 9RT
020 7916 2020
urc@urc.org.uk

Your Family Tree
30 Monmouth Street
Bath BA1 2BW
01225 442244
www.yourfamilytreemag. co.uk/

Scotland

General Register Office
New Register House
Charlotte Square
Edinburgh EH1 3YT
0131 334 0380
www.gro-scotland.gov.uk

Mitchell Library
North Street
Glasgow G3 7DN
0141 287 2999
www.mitchelllibrary.org

National Archives of Scotland (NAS)
HM General Register House
2 Princess Street
Edinburgh EH1 3YY
0131 535 1334
www.nas.gov.uk

National Library of Scotland
George IV Bridge
Edinburgh EH1 1EW
0131 623 3700
www.nls.uk

United States

Daughters of the American Revolution
1776 D Street, NW
Washington DC 20006-5303
(202) 628-1776
www.dar.org/

Family History Library
(Genealogical Society of Utah)
35 North West Temple Street
Salt Lake City
Utah 84150-3400
801-240-2584 or 866-406-1830
www.familysearch.org

Irish Ancestral Research Association (TIARA)
Dept. W 2120
Commonwealth Avenue
Auburndale
Massachusetts 02466-1909
www.tiara.ie

Irish Genealogical Society Intl
5768 Olson Memorial Highway
Golden Valley
MN 55422
(not by telephone)
www.irishgenealogical.org

Library of Congress
101 Independence Ave, SE
Washington, DC 20540
202 707-5000
www.loc.gov

National Archives and Records Administration
8601 Adelphi Road
College Park
MD 20740-6001
1-866-272-6272
www.archives.gov

National Archives and Records Administration
Pennsylvania Avenue
Washington D.C. 20408
202-501-5404
www.archives.gov

National Genealogical Society
4527 17th Street North
Arlington
Virginia 22207-2399
www.ngsgenealogy.org

New England Historic and Genealogical Society
101 Newbury Street
Boston
Massachusetts 02116
(617) 536-5740
www.newenglandancestors.org

Canada

Maritime History Archive
Memorial University of
Newfoundland
St.. John's NF, A1C 5S7
00 1 709 737 8428
www.mun.ca/mha/archive.php

National Archives of Canada
395 Wellington Street
Ottawa
Ontario K1A ON3
613-995-5138
www.collectionscanada.ca

For provincial archives see
www.collectionscanada.ca/
genealogy/022-802-e.html

United Empire Loyalists' Library
50 Baldwin St.., Suite 202
Toronto, Ontario, Canada
M5T 1L4
(416) 591-1783
www.uelac.org

Argentina

Archivo General de la Nacion
Leandro N. Alem 246
C1003AAP
Buenos Aires
(5411) 4331-5531/33
www.mininterior.gov.ar/agn/

Bibliotheca Nacional
Agüero 2502 – (C1425EID)
Ciudad Autónoma de Buenos Aires
República Argentina
(011) 4808-6000
www.bibnal.edu.ar/PAGINAS/co
ntactenos.htm

Centro de Estudios Migratorios Latinoamericanos
Avenida Independencia 20
1099 Capital Federal
(5411) 4342-6749
www.guiasolidaria.pccp.net.
ar/migrantes/04-cemla.htm

Dirección General de Registro Civil
(Civil registration for Buenos Aires City)
Uruguay 753
4373-8441/45
www.buenosaires.gov.ar/
registrocivil/Tramites/partidas/
?menu_id=15753

Instituto Argentino de Ciencias Genealógicas
Calle Balcarce 1064
1064 Buenos Aires
www.genealogia.org.ar/

Registro Provincial de la Personas Oficina Expedición de Partidas
(Civil registration for Buenos Aires province)
Calle 1 Y 60
CP 1900
La Planta
Provincia de Buenos Aires,
0221-4296226
www.gob.gba.gov.ar/html/
gobierno/rpp/partidas.htm

Australia

For state archives and other useful institutions, see the
National Archives' Factsheet 2,
'Addresses of other Australian
archival institutions'
www.naa.gov.au/publications/
fact_sheets/fso1.html

Dixson Library
State Library of New South Wales
Macquarie Street
Sydney NSW 2000
(02) 9273 1414
www.sl.nsw.gov.au

National Archives of Australia
PO Box 7425
Canberra BCE
ACT 2610
1300 886 881
(Overseas callers: 61 2 6212 3900)
www.naa.gov.au

National Library of Australia
Parkes Place
Canberra, ACT 2600
+ 61 2 6262 1111
www.nla.gov.au

Society of Australian Genealogists
379 Kent Street
Sydney NSW 2000
(02) 9247 3953
www.sag.org.au/indexo.htm

New Zealand

A directory of New Zealand archives
is at www.archives.govt.nz/
doingresearch.php#directory

National Archives of New Zealand
Head Office
10 Mulgrave Street
Thorndon
Wellington
(64-4) 499 5595
www.archives.govt.nz

**National Library of New Zealand
(Te Puna MÇtauranga o Aotearoa)**
Corner of Molesworth and Aitken
Streets, Wellington: postal address:
PO Box 1467
Wellington 6140
+64-4-474 3000
www.natlib.govt.nz

New Zealand Society of Genealogists Inc.
P O Box 14036
Panmure
Auckland 1741
+64 9 570 4248
www.genealogy.org.nz

Registrar General of Births, Deaths & Marriages
PO Box 10-526
Wellington
Level 3, Boulcott House
47 Boulcott Street
Wellington
0800 22 52 52 (New Zealand only)
(+64 4) 474-8150
www.bmd.govt.nz
Provides links to the other registrars

Éire

Add 01 if dialling within Éire or 00
353 1 if outside Éire

Adoption Board
Hawkins House
Hawkins Street
Dublin 2
635 4000
www.midlands.ie/content/
5gov/5_10.htm

Association of Professional Genealogists in Ireland
c/o The Genealogical Office
2 Kildare Street
Dublin 2
603 0200
www.apgi.ie

Church of Ireland College of Education
Upper Rathmines Road
Dublin 6
497 0033
www.cice.ie

Church of Jesus Christ of Latter-Day Saints (Mormons) Family History Centre (FHC)
The Willows
Finglas Road
Glasnevin
Dublin 11
8306684
www.familysearch.org

Defence Force Headquarters
Enlistment Personal Section
Park Gate
Infirmary Road
Dublin 7
(for officers: Military Archives,
Cathal Brugha Barracks,
Dublin 6)
8042000
www.defence.ie

Department of Folklore
University College
Belfield
Dublin
7167777
www.ucd.ie/irishfolklore

Department of Public Enterprise
Personnel Unit
25 Clare Street
Dublin 2
6041520

Dublin City Library and Archive
138-142 Pearse St.
Dublin 2
6744999
www.dublincity.ie

Eneclann/Archive CD Books (Ireland)
Unit 1
Trinity Enterprise Centre
Pearse Street
Dublin 2
6710 338
www.eneclann.ie and
www.archivecdbooks.ie

Federation of Services for Unmarried Parents and their Children
36 Rathmines Road
Dublin 6
868 3020
www.adoptionireland.com

Flyleaf Press
4 Spencer Villas
Glengeary
Co. Dublin
2845906
www.flyleaf.ie/

Garda Archives
Dublin Castle
Dublin 2
6669998
www.garda.ie/angarda/
museum.html

Genealogical Office (GO)
Genealogical Office
2 Kildare St.
Dublin 2
6618811
www.nli.ie/new_office.htm

Genealogical Society of Ireland
11 Desmond Avenue
Dún Laoghaire
Co. Dublin
(no telephone number)
www.familyhistory.ie

Grand Lodge of Freemasons of Ireland
Freemason's Hall
17 Molesworth Street
Dublin 2
www.irish-freemasons.org/

Huguenot Society of Great Britain and Ireland
Sunhaven
Dublin Road
Celbridge
Co. Kildare
www.huguenotsociety.org.uk

Irish Family History Society
P.O. Box 36
Naas
Co. Kildare
http://homepage.eircom.net/~ifhs/

Irish Genealogy Ltd
ESB Complex
Parnell Avenue
Harold's Cross
Dublin 12
6042134
www.irishgenealogy.ie

Irish Jewish Museum
3-4 Walworth Road
S. Circular Road
Dublin 8
453 1797
www.jewishireland.org/
museum.html

Irish Roots Magazine
Belgrave Publications
Belgrave Avenue
Cork
www.irishrootsmagazine.com

Law Society of Ireland
Blackhall Place
Dublin 7
672 4800
www.lawsociety.ie/

National Archives of Ireland (NAI)
Bishop Street
Dublin 8
4072300
www.nationalarchives.ie

National Library of Ireland (NLI)
Kildare St.
Dublin 2
6618811
www.nli.ie

National Museum of Ireland – Archaeology & History
Kildare Street
Dublin 2
Ireland
6777444
www.museum.ie

National Museum of Ireland – Country Life
Turlough Park
Castlebar
Co. Mayo
6486 392
www.museum.ie

Ordnance Survey Office
Phoenix Park
Dublin 8
8206100
http://slarti.ucd.ie/ospage.html

Registrar General of Ireland (GRO)
First Floor
Joyce House
8-11 Lombard Street
Dublin 2
635 40000
www.groireland.ie

Registrar General of Ireland
administrative and corresponding headquarters:
Convent Road
Roscommon
90 6632900
www.groireland.ie

Registry of Deeds
Henrietta St.
Dublin 1
6707500
www.landregistry.ie

Representative Church Body Library (RCBL)
Braemor Park
Rathgar
Dublin 14
4923979
www.ireland.anglican.org/library

Royal College of Physicians of Ireland
Frederick House
19 South Frederick Street
Dublin 2
8639700
www.rcpi.ie/

Royal College of Surgeons in Ireland
123 St. Stephen's Green
Dublin 2
402 2100
www.rcsi.ie

Royal Irish Academy
19 Dawson Street, Dublin 2
6762570
www.ria.ie/

Society of Friends Library
Quaker House
Stocking Lane
Rathfarnham
Dublin 16
4956890
www.quakers-in-ireland.org

South Dublin County Library
Unit 1, The Square Industrial Complex
Tallaght
Dublin 24
459 7834
www.library.ie/public/
southdub.shtml

Trinity College Dublin
College Green, Dublin 2
896 1000
www.tcd.ie/

Valuation Office
Irish Life Centre
Abbey Street
Dublin 1
817 1000
www.valoff.ie/
(but due to move to Youghal, Co. Cork)

Northern Ireland

Association of Ulster Genealogists and Record Agents
The Secretary
Glen Cottage
Glenmachan Road
Belfast BT4 2NP
www.augra.com

Baptist Union of Ireland Offices
117 Lisburn Road
Belfast BT9 7AF
028 9066 3108
www.baptisthistory.org.uk/

Linen Hall Library
17 Donegall Square North
Belfast BT1 5GB
028 9032 1707
www.linenhall.com

North of Ireland Family History Society
c/o Graduate School of Education
69 University Street
Belfast, BT7 1HL
www.nifhs.org

Presbyterian Historical Society
Church House
Fisherwick Place
Belfast BT1 6D
028 9032 2284
www.presbyterianireland.org/
phsi

Public Record Office of Northern Ireland (PRONI)
66 Balmoral Avenue
Belfast BT9 6NY
0232 661621
www.proni.gov.uk

Registrar General of Northern Ireland (RGNI)
Oxford House
49-55 Chichester Street
Belfast BT1 4HL
028 90 252000
www.groni.gov.uk

RUC Personnel Branch
RUC Headquarters
Lisnasharragh
42 Montgomery Road
Belfast BT6 9LD
028 9065 0222
www.psni.police.uk/

Society of Friends Library (Quakers)
Meeting House
Railway Street
Lisburn
Co., Antrim BT28 1EP
(postal enquiries only)
(no telephone number)

Somme Heritage Centre
233 Bangor Road
Newtownards
Co. Down BT23 7PH
028 91823202
www.irishsoldier.org

Ulster Historical Foundation
12 College Square East
Belfast BT1 6DD
028 90 332288
www.ancestryireland.com

Wesley Historical Society (Irish Branch)
Edgehill College
9 Lennoxvale
Belfast BT9 5BY
028 9066 5870

Index

Acknowledgments

My thanks go to Denise Bates and Louise Stanley for conceiving the idea for this book and commissioning it — and thus sending me on a wonderful journey through Ireland's past — and my agent Anna Power for her care of the project. Nicola Chalton of Basement Press edited the manuscript with meticulous care. She, Pascal Thivillon and Justin Martin were miraculously successful in fulfilling even my most impossible ideas for illustrations.

Many people have helped me create this work or allowed me use of parts of their family histories, particularly: Roland and Caroline Back (for their hospitality in Galway); Ann Black; Mark Bonthrone; Bryn Carr (Family Genetics Ltd); Phillip Chapman; Ashley Coursey (Family Tree DNA); Dr. Anabel Smart; John Crowley; Scott Crowley; Tom Crowley and all the members of the Crowley DNA project; Brian Donovan (Eneclann Ltd); Maryan Egan-Baker (Family Sleuths); Michael Gandy; Fergus Gillespie (Chief Herald of Ireland); Peter Goble; Patrick Hawe (Chief Herald's Office); Ann Horan (Irish Midlands Ancestry); Catherine Keane (G.R.O., Éire); Marie Kilduff; Anne Lee-French; Dr. Rodolfo Martin MacAllister; The MacDermot, Prince of Coolavin; Justin Martin (one of Irish genealogy's finest); Rosamond Minton; Edmundo Murray (for his unpublished thesis *How the Irish Became Guachos Ingleses: Diasporic Models in Irish-Argentinean Literature*); Gwen O'Callaghan; Gregory O'Connor (Principal archivist, NAI); Colm O'Dalaigh (GRO, Éire); Ursula Odendahl; Joseph O'Gara; Jeremy Palmer and Jacqui Kelly of www.anzestry.com; Margaret Pantall; Ann Rietchel; Mary Skelly (Roscommon Heritage Centre); Mary Sullivan (Cavan Genealogy); Susan Thompson, Michael Watts and Valerie Weeks.

I used to sit at the back of physics and chemistry lessons with my old school friend Andrew Prendergast, whose mother was a Mac Tiernan, and he would wile away the interminable hours telling me about his fascination with ancient Irish myth and genealogy. His enthusiasm proved infectious: thank you so much, wherever you are.

Picture credits